3

D1221640

Wittgensteinian
Themes

TOWNSEND MEMORIAL LIBRARY
UNIVERSITY OF MARY HARDIN-BAYLOR
BELTON, TX 76513

193
W831m

193 W831m
Malcolm, Norman.
Wittgensteinian themes

BOOKS BY NORMAN MALCOLM

Ludwig Wittgenstein: A Memoir (1958)

Dreaming (1959)

Knowledge and Certainty (1968)

Problems of Mind: Descartes to Wittgenstein (1971)

Memory and Mind (1977)

Thought and Knowledge (1977)

Consciousness and Causality: A Debate on the Nature of Mind,
with D. M. Armstrong (1984)

Nothing Is Hidden: Wittgenstein's Criticism of His Early Thoughts (1986)

Wittgenstein: A Religious Point of View? (1993)

Wittgensteinian Themes

ESSAYS 1978–1989

Norman Malcolm

EDITED BY

Georg Henrik von Wright

TOWNSEND MEMORIAL LIBRARY
UNIVERSITY OF MARY HARDIN-BAYLOR
BELTON, TX 76513

CORNELL UNIVERSITY PRESS

Ithaca and London

Copyright © 1995 by Cornell University

All rights reserved. Except for brief quotations in a review,
this book, or parts thereof, must not be reproduced in any
form without permission in writing from the publisher. For
information address Cornell University Press, Sage House,
512 East State Street, Ithaca, New York 14850.

First published 1995 by Cornell University Press.
First printing, Cornell Paperbacks, 1996.

Printed in the United States of America

Library of Congress Cataloging-in-Publication Data

Malcolm, Norman, 1911-1990
    Wittgensteinian themes : essays, 1978-1989 / Norman Malcolm :
edited by Georg Henrik von Wright.
        p.   cm.
    Includes bibliographical references and index.
    ISBN 0-8014-3042-9 (alk. paper).—ISBN 0-8014-8381-6 (pbk. : alk. paper)
    1. Wittgenstein, Ludwig, 1889–1951.   2. Philosophy, English—20th
century.   I. Wright, G. H. von (Georg Henrik), 1916– .
II. Title.
B3376.W564M25   1995
192—dc20   94-47014

    ⊗ The paper in this book meets the minimum requirements
of the American National Standard for Information Sciences—
Permanence of Paper for Printed Library Materials, ANSI Z39.48-1984.

                cloth: 10 9 8 7 6 5 4 3 2 1
                paper: 10 9 8 7 6 5 4 3 2 1

Contents

TOWNSEND MEMORIAL LIBRARY
UNIVERSITY OF MARY HARDIN-BAYLOR
BELTON TX 76513

Editor's Preface

Essays and lectures by Norman Malcolm have been collected earlier in two volumes. The first, *Knowledge and Certainty*, published by Prentice-Hall, contains writings from 1950 to 1963. The second, *Thought and Knowledge*, appeared from Cornell University Press, and its contents range over the period 1964–76. Both volumes are long out of print.

The present collection includes Malcolm's most important philosophical essays from the year 1978 to his death twelve years later. Omitted are a few reviews and polemical pieces; two posthumously published contributions to Festschrifts in honor of Professor Peter Geach and Professor Peter Winch, respectively; and two essays dealing with aspects of my own philosophy. A reason for omitting the last two is that they are best read together with my replies to them in the publications where the essays originally appeared. One, called 'Mind and Action', was published in *Perspectives on Human Conduct*, edited by Lars Hertzberg and Juhani Pietarinen (Leiden: E. J. Brill, 1988). The other, 'Intention and Behavior', was written for the volume of the Library of Living Philosophers devoted to my philosophy.

Wittgenstein is the philosopher who most deeply influenced Malcolm. Malcolm's whole literary output testifies to this. Both when he is propounding views of his own and when he is criticizing those of somebody else, he nearly always supports his position with references to and quotations from Wittgenstein. But in his earlier works and also those of his maturity—culminating, I should say, in *Memory and Mind* (1977)— he seldom deals *directly* with the views of Wittgenstein. Later there is a noticeable change. The last book he published in his lifetime, *Nothing Is Hidden* (1986), is also his first major contribution to Wittgenstein scholarship. Its theme is 'Wittgenstein's criticism of his early thoughts'. In the vast secondary literature on Wittgenstein it is one of the few works that take seriously Wittgenstein's word in the preface to *Philosophical Investigations* that his later thoughts could be seen in the right light only by contrast with and against the background of the *Tractatus* way of thinking. Between the 'two Wittgensteins' there is a profound divide but also a deep continuity. Malcolm, better than perhaps anybody else, was able to appreciate both these features of Wittgenstein's lifework.

In the last year of his life, Malcolm finished yet another Wittgensteinian study, which he intended to publish as a book. It comments on a remark Wittgenstein once made to his friend M. O'C. Drury to the effect that, although not being himself a religious man, he could not help seeing every problem from a religious point of view. The manuscript was published in 1993 under the title *Wittgenstein: A Religious Point of View?* with a critical discussion by the editor, Peter Winch, of Malcolm's treatment of the subject.

Several of the papers in this volume likewise deal directly with specific aspects of Wittgenstein's philosophy, even in cases when Wittgenstein's name does not appear in the title. (The last essay, 'Disentangling Moore's Paradox', is a case in point.) The title *Wittgensteinian Themes* therefore seems appropriate for the collection.

Some topics in Wittgenstein's philosophy are notorious for causing Wittgenstein scholars difficulties. Opinions are often violently opposed. One such topic is rule-following. According to some interpreters, among them Malcolm, Wittgenstein thought that following a rule presupposes a community in which there is agreement as to whether a particular action is, or is not, in conformity with a given rule. According to another opinion, Wittgenstein did not think that the practice of rule-following presupposes a social community; even when restricted to a single individual, the adoption and following of a rule can make good sense. Proponents of this second position have been, among others, two well-known Wittgenstein scholars, Gordon Baker and Peter Hacker. Malcolm's essay 'Wittgenstein on Language and Rules' is a forceful defense of his position against theirs. Malcolm's paper was published in the journal *Philosophy* the year before he died. The polemics, however, did not end with it. The two authors answered with a paper titled 'Malcolm on Language and Rules'. Malcolm's papers and theirs, in my opinion, together constitute a nice specimen of philosophical polemics, *fortiter in re* and yet *suaviter in modo*, and I would have favored the inclusion of Baker and Hacker's joint paper in the present collection.

Another controversial theme concerns the relation of Wittgenstein's philosophy to idealism. The topic has many different ramifications. Some relate to Wittgenstein's thoughts on solipsism in the *Tractatus* and to his early leanings toward some form of phenomenalism and his reactions to them in the writings after his return to Cambridge in 1929. Malcolm has made insightful comments on these early forms of Wittgensteinian 'idealism'. Several students of Wittgenstein, however, have discerned a differently styled idealistic slant in his later writings. Thus, among others, Bernard Williams in an influential essay, entitled 'Wittgenstein and Idealism', of the early 1970s attributes to Wittgenstein a peculiar form of 'non-individualistic solipsism' or 'transcendental idealism'. Malcolm's paper of the same title, published ten years after Williams's, is a criticism of this interpretation. Malcolm's aim is to show, against Williams, that no tendency whatsoever 'towards any form of idealism is to be found in Wittgenstein's later philosophy'. In my opinion this is one of the most forceful and best argued of Malcolm's polemical writings. But it also illustrates some bias in Malcolm's understanding of Wittgenstein which, quite apart from controversies on idealism, not all Wittgenstein scholars are willing to share. The bias in question can be characterized by such adjectives as 'behaviorist', 'anti-mentalist', 'anti-theoretic', and, in a wider setting of cultural values, 'anti-scientistic'.

Characteristic samples of the behavioristic slant of Malcolm's thinking are the first of the two papers, here printed, on the concept of thinking and the essay called 'Wittgenstein: The Relation of Language to Instinctive Behavior'. Both also deal with one of the main targets of Malcolm's later philosophical polemics, namely the 'rationalist' ('cognitivist') tendency of contemporary philosophers of language (Noam Chomsky, Jerry A. Fodor, and others) to postulate an innate system of representations. Malcolm regards this as a speculative construction, the existence and nature of which are beyond the reach of empirical testing. The linguistic ability that this new form of conceptual 'nativism' is supposed to explain is, as Malcolm says, 'grafted on instinctive behavior' open to inspection to anybody who reflects on the foundations of language learning.

In 'Language Game (2)' Malcolm applies his idea of the importance of expressive behavior to the 'possibility' of thought and language for defending, against criticism propounded by Rush Rhees, Wittgenstein's contention that the language game in question could be 'the whole language of a tribe'. Rhees doubted that the primitive play with words envisaged in Wittgenstein's description was sufficient to establish the language-character of the communicative interaction between the builders. Malcolm's point against Rhees is that we can imagine forms of behavior on the part of the participants in the game which are sufficiently 'human-like' to make the concept of language applicable to the case. I find Malcolm's point well taken. In a posthumously published short essay called 'Language without Conversation', not included in this volume, he defends his view also against criticism in support of Rhees's position by Raymond Gaita (*Philosophical Investigations* 15 [1992]).

Two younger contemporaries whose thoughts Malcolm much appreciated, though, I think, for rather different reasons, are Elizabeth Anscombe and Saul Kripke. With Anscombe he has in common the inspiration from Wittgenstein and a similarity of approach to the questions that torment philosophers. Like some other former pupils of Wittgenstein's he had learned much from the way Anscombe had brought to focus the concept of intention and intentional acting. Two essays in the collection take their point of departure in two 'powerful papers' by Anscombe. In the first Malcolm endorses and argues for Anscombe's view that the first-person pronoun 'I' is not a referring term. The second paper discusses her already famous example of the man who was aiming at what he took to be a stag but which in fact was his father. If I understand him right, Malcolm does not dispute the way in which Anscombe deals with the case under discussion. But he disputes her view that every perception necessarily has an intentional object, some thing that we 'see as' or 'take to be' the material object of the perception.

I find the two essays on Kripke extremely enjoyable reading. I see them as fragments of a dialogue between two powerful but also very different types of philosophic mind. Kripke's thoughts, I should say, fascinated Malcolm because they seemed to him at the same time ingenious and wrongheaded. This holds not only for Kripke's views of natural kinds and of the standard meter, which are the topics of the essays in the present collection. As can be expected, Malcolm also disagreed with Kripke's contention that Wittgenstein had discovered a new type of argument for skepticism. Kripke's views of the matter have stirred a lively debate. Malcolm makes a contribution to it in the chapter on rule-following in *Nothing Is Hidden*. It is to be regretted that he did not deal with it at greater length in a separate publication.

———

In selecting and editing this collection of essays from the last twelve years of Norman Malcolm's long and distinguished career as a philosopher, I have profited from the help and good advice of people who were close to him—in England and the United States. I am grateful to Mrs. Ruth Malcolm for encouragement and unfailing assistance to help me ascertain details about the provenance of the various essays. Finally, I wish to thank the director of Cornell University Press, John Ackerman, for editorial advice and for his willingness to publish the philosopher who did more than anybody else to make the Sage School one of the major places for the study and teaching of philosophy in the English-speaking world.

The papers published in this book originally appeared as follows:

'Thinking'. In *Wittgenstein and His Impact on Contemporary Thought.* Proceedings of the 2d International Wittgenstein Symposium, Kirchberg, Austria, 29 August to 4 September 1977. Vienna: Hölder-Pichler-Tempsky, 1978. Pp. 411–18. Reprinted by permission of the publisher.

'Whether "I" Is a Referring Expression'. In *Intention and Intentionality: Essays in Honour of G. E. M. Anscombe,* ed. Cora Diamond and Jenny Teichman. Brighton: Harvester Press, 1979. Pp. 15–24.

'"Functionalism" in Philosophical Psychology'. Paper given at a meeting of the Aristotelian Society, London, 2 June 1980. In *Proceedings of the Aristotelian Society,* New Series 80 (1979–80), 211–29. Reprinted by courtesy of the Editor of the Aristotelian Society: © 1979–80.

'Kripke on Heat and Sensations of Heat'. *Philosophical Investigations* 3 (1980), 12–20. Blackwell Publishers, copyright holder.

'Kripke and the Standard Meter'. *Philosophical Investigations* 4 (1981), 19–24. Blackwell Publishers, copyright holder.

'Wittgenstein: The Relation of Language to Instinctive Behaviour'. *Philosophical Investigations* 5 (1982), 3–22. The J. R. Jones Memorial Lecture, University College, Swansea, May 1981. Blackwell Publishers, copyright holder.

'Wittgenstein and Idealism'. In *Idealism Past and Present*, ed. G. Vesey. Royal Institute of Philosophy Lecture Series 13, Supplement to *Philosophy* (1982). Cambridge: Cambridge University Press, 1982. Pp. 249–67. © 1982 Cambridge University Press. Reprinted with permission of Cambridge University Press.

'The "Intentionality" of Sense-Perception'. *Philosophical Investigations* 6 (1983), 175–83. Blackwell Publishers, copyright holder.

'Subjectivity'. *Philosophy* 63 (1988), 147–60. © 1988 Cambridge University Press. Reprinted with the permission of Cambridge University Press.

'Turning to Stone'. *Philosophical Investigations* 12 (1989), 101–11. Blackwell Publishers, copyright holder.

'Wittgenstein on Language and Rules'. *Philosophy* 64 (1989), 5–28. © 1989 Cambridge University Press. Reprinted with the permission of Cambridge University Press.

'Language Game (2)'. In *Wittgenstein: Attention to Particulars: Essays in Honour of Rush Rhees*, ed. D. Z. Phillips and P. Winch. London: Macmillan; and New York: St. Martin's, 1989. Pp. 35–44. Reprinted by permission of the publishers.

'The Mystery of Thought'. In *A Wittgenstein Symposium, Gerona, 1989*, ed. J. M. Terricabras (Amsterdam: Editions Rodopi, 1993). Pp. 53–66. Reprinted by permission of the publisher.

'Disentangling Moore's Paradox'. In *Wittgenstein: Mind and Language*, ed. Rosaria Egidi (Dordrecht: Kluwer Academic Publishers, 1994). Pp. 195–205. Copyright © 1994 by Kluwer Academic Publishers. Reprinted by permission of Kluwer Academic Publishers.

'Norman Malcolm', memorial talk by G. H. von Wright, *Philosophical Investigations* 15 (1992), 215–22. Blackwell Publishers, copyright holder.

Wittgensteinian
Themes

1

Thinking

1

Suppose that in conversation with a group of people I make a certain remark. Later, one of those present says to me: 'Were you thinking when you made that remark?'. I ask: 'What do you mean?'. He says: 'Well, what you said was rather disparaging of Italians. Had you forgotten that Mr. A., who was present in the group, is Italian?'. I exclaim: 'Oh, I had forgotten! I wasn't thinking when I said that. I certainly did not want to offend Mr. A.'.

There are other sorts of cases in which it could be said, in ordinary language, that a person spoke without thinking, or was speaking without thinking. For example, a friend asks me on the phone for directions to the Royal Opera House, and I respond with directions from *my* house instead of from *his* house, which is where he would be starting from. This would be speaking without thinking. A third sort of case is the following: You are working in a theater box office. Each time the phone rings you pick up the receiver and say: 'I regret to inform you that the performance is completely sold out'. You repeat this message automatically each time you answer the phone, not even listening to what the person at the other end of the line is saying. A fourth case: An army sergeant addresses a new group of recruits each day. He informs them of their daily schedule, how to make up their bunks, when they can receive weekend leaves, and warns them to keep their shoes shined. Later he confides to us that he has given this talk so many times that when he delivers it he is usually thinking about something else: he just 'rattles it off'. This example is unlike the first and second cases. It is similar to the third, yet different, since the sergeant is looking at the recruits as he speaks, and they are looking at him; whereas in the box office example you repeated the message over and over into the telephone. A fifth case is the following: Some first-year college students are telling me about the nature of sensation. They say, for example, that if one's foot is injured a sensation travels from the foot to the brain; that the brain interprets the sensation as pain, and transmits to the foot the order to take some protective action. I say to the students that they are speaking without thinking: I mean that they are talking nonsense. Finally, this sixth case: A friend is seriously ill. He is conscious and occasionally talks, but his speech is incoherent; his sentences are unrelated to one another. Now in this case we would hardly say of him that 'He isn't thinking of what he is saying' or that 'He is speaking without thinking'; but that 'He is very ill and his speech is delirious'. Since this is *not* an example of 'speaking without thinking', it does not belong on my list. Yet I am putting it there for the sake of contrast with the other cases. It might be that occasionally a seemingly intelligible sentence occurs in the sequence of his utterances. The question might then arise whether when he said *that* he was thinking, or was it too a part of his delirium?

2

In *Zettel*[1] Wittgenstein says: 'Nur unter ganz speziellen Umständen tritt die Frage auf, ob *denkend* geredet wurde oder nicht'. I would favor the following cumbersome English translation: 'When a person is speaking, only in very special circumstances does the question arise whether he is or is not speaking without thinking'. Wittgenstein remarks:

> If a normal human being is holding a normal conversation under normal circumstances, and I were to be asked what distinguishes thinking from not-thinking in such a case—I should not know what

1. Ludwig Wittgenstein, *Zettel*, ed. G. E. M. Anscombe and G. H. von Wright, trans. G. E. M. Anscombe (Oxford: Blackwell, 1967), 95. I have sometimes departed from Anscombe's translation. Hereafter citations of this work will appear in my text, marked as 'Z' followed by paragraph number.

answer to give. And I could *certainly not* say that the difference lay in
something that went on or failed to go on during the speaking. (*Z* 93)

I have been trying to illustrate Wittgenstein's point by describing cases
in which the question whether a person was speaking without thinking
would arise. In each case the circumstances were special, and furthermore in different ways, thereby giving different *senses* to the phrase,
'speaking without thinking'. In the first case it meant that an offensive
remark was made unintentionally; in the second that the answer was irrelevant to the inquirer's need; in the third that a sentence was repeated automatically; in the fourth that a memorized talk was delivered
with the speaker's thoughts elsewhere; in the fifth that remarks about
'the nature of sensation', which are believed by the speaker to be significant, are actually nonsensical; in the sixth that the speaker's talk is
delirious. In this last case when an occasional rational-seeming utterance occurs, the question does arise whether the speaker was thinking
of what he was saying, or perhaps better, whether he understood, or
knew, what he was saying.

3

In the absence of special circumstances one does not *understand* the
question, 'Was he thinking when he said those things?'. For example,
a friend is telling me of his recent trip to Crete: of the thrilling beauty
of the mountainous terrain; of the friendliness and honesty of the inhabitants; of the great architectural remains; and so on. If someone
asked, 'Was he thinking while he was talking?', I would not know what
was *meant*. (Certainly I would not reply, 'Of course he was!'.) The question is unlike the question, 'Was he chewing gum while he was talking?'. 'Was he thinking while he was talking?' bears a superficial
resemblance to this other question, yet is misleading. For chewing
gum is a clearly understood activity that might or might not accompany speech. With thinking it is not clear what the accompanying activity is supposed to be. We understood the statement that a person
was speaking without thinking, when this meant that he said something offensive unintentionally, or that his answer was irrelevant, or
that his remarks were conceptual nonsense, and so on. But being relevant or irrelevant, intentionally or unintentionally offensive, making

conceptual sense or not, are not activities or happenings that might or might not accompany speech.

4

In philosophy we have an overwhelming inclination to ask, 'What *is* thinking?', and to assume that it is a process or activity that is there when we speak, at least when our speech is rational, coherent, to the point. We are inclined to suppose that of course the question of what thinking is has an answer, although we don't know yet what it is. The classical empiricists assumed that thinking consists of a sequence of 'ideas' that were conceived to be image-like entities. William James believed that thinking consists in a continuous flow of feelings of tendency. In the *Tractatus* Wittgenstein held that thinking consists in part of creating representations that are isomorphic with possible or actual states of affairs. Some philosophers, psychologists, and neurophysiologists believe that thinking is a physical process in the brain.

Our predominant inclination is to assume that thinking ought to be something introspectible. In the *Investigations*,[2] Wittgenstein is sarcastic about this assumption:

> 'Can one think without speaking?'—And what is *thinking*?—Well, don't you ever think? Can you observe yourself and see what is going on? It should be quite simple. You do not have to wait for it as for an astronomical event and then perhaps make your observation in a hurry.

The following quotation from an article by Jaegwon Kim and Richard Brandt provides a nice illustration of the assumption that thinking is an introspectible process, and that a thought is an introspectible event:

> We assume that a thought can be characterized as a purely psychical event, as a kind of occurrence which is introspectible, and that such characterization is distinct from a semantic description of it—an account of what it is about, what role the symbols that occur in the

2. Wittgenstein, *Philosophical Investigations*, ed. G. E. M. Anscombe and Rush Rhees, trans. G. E. M. Anscombe (Oxford: Blackwell, 1967), 327. I have made some departures from Anscombe's translations. Hereafter citations of this work will appear in the text, marked as '*PI*' followed by paragraph number.

thought have in the speaker's language system, the connection of these with expectations, and so on. We are concerned here only with thoughts as purely psychical events.[3]

They regard thoughts as 'phenomenal occurrences', along with itches, tickles, daydreams, and afterimages, in contrast with quasi-dispositional states such as desiring or believing.

The trouble is that we don't know what could be meant by the introspectible content of a thought. I might have the thought that Washington, D.C., would be a good place to hold the next philosophical convention, and when I have that thought I may have a mental image of the Washington Monument. But I could have had that thought without that image, or the image without the thought. The image is not the thought nor essential to it; and yet the image might be the only introspectible item that occurred. If I were a member of a committee that had to decide where the next convention will be located, the others on the committee might be interested in my suggestion of Washington, D.C. But that I had an image of the Washington Monument?—they couldn't care less. As Wittgenstein says: 'It is very noteworthy that *what goes on* in thinking almost never interests us. It is noteworthy, but not queer' (*Z* 88). What makes a thought challenging, boring, superficial, irrelevant, or profound has nothing to do with anything introspectible that occurred when the thought occurred.

5

If we cannot find out what thinking is by observing ourselves when we are thinking, where shall we turn? Well, it might provide some illumination if we took note of the *variety* that comes under the heading of thinking. I don't mean the variety in topics of thought, but rather in *forms* of thinking—what Wittgenstein calls 'Lebensäußerungen' ('expressions of life'); as when he says that the concept of thinking is 'a concept that joins together many expressions of life' (*Z* 110).

One such form of thinking, described by Wittgenstein (*Z* 100), is the following: A person is constructing something out of pieces of material. He rejects some pieces, selects others, measures, and compares pieces.

3. Jaegwon Kim and Richard Brandt, 'The Logic of the Identity Theory', *Journal of Philosophy* 64 (Sept. 7, 1967), 516n.

His facial expressions and gestures sometimes show irritation, satisfaction, puzzlement, indecision, triumph. Also he makes natural sounds of annoyance, surprise, satisfaction. 'But he does not utter a single word'.

Wittgenstein imagines that the whole activity is filmed, including the sounds. We can suppose that this worker is shown the film. As he watches it he makes remarks of this sort: 'Then I thought: No, that won't do, I must try it another way', and so on.

Wittgenstein now challenges us with the question: Would this be a *false* account of what actually went on? For the worker 'had neither spoken during the work nor imagined these words'.

Surely, we are strongly inclined to say that the worker did *not* have those thoughts; or at least, if he did have them their occurrence was not revealed in the film. Both example and question are brilliant; for they catch hold of and draw out our temptation to believe that if the worker had not spoken any words, either aloud or silently, nor imagined any, then if at a certain point in his work he actually did think, 'This piece is too short', this thinking was an action or process *in addition to* the occurrences recorded in the film. We want to say that nothing in the film discloses such a thought as 'This piece is too short'.

Our inclination here is tremendously interesting. It seems to be the same as Descartes's notion that thinking is disclosed *only* in language.

6

The fact is, however, that thinking can be displayed in wordless behavior, just as fright can be. There is work that displays no thinking, as when a laborer in an assembly line repetitiously turns one bolt after another. But the worker in *Zettel* 100 is testing, comparing, measuring; he shows hesitation, disappointment, satisfaction. He is not working 'mechanically'. There is thinking in his work. But as Wittgenstein says: 'Of course we cannot separate his "thinking" from the activity. The thinking is not an accompaniment of the work, any more than in thoughtful speech' (*Z* 101). Our reluctance to admit that the wordless activity exhibits thinking should also make us reluctant to say that even speech exhibits thinking. In both cases we should say that thinking is something different, that might or might not be present. We feel that we ought to be able to focus on the thinking itself, apart from the speaking or working—but we don't know how to do it. All we can do is to offer this sort of defense: 'Surely speech or work can occur without there being any think-ing; and thinking can occur in the absence of speech or work'. Although this remark is true, it fosters an illusion—namely, the illusion that think-ing is something *essentially* 'mental', a process or activity 'in the mind'.

7

Perhaps the best way of trying to undermine this illusion is to survey some of the various cases of thinking. Wittgenstein says:

> Bear in mind that our language might possess a variety of different words: one for 'thinking out loud'; one for thinking as one talks to oneself in the imagination; one for a pause during which something or other floats before the mind, after which, however, we are able to give a confident answer.
>
> One word for a thought expressed in a sentence; one for the light-ning thought which I may later 'clothe in words'; one for wordless thinking as one works. (*Z* 122)

In the *Investigations* a similar thing is said about expecting:

> We say "I am expecting him", when we believe that he will come, though his coming does not *occupy our thoughts*. (Here "I am expect-ing him" would mean "I should be surprised if he didn't come"—and that will not be called a description of a state of mind.) But we also say "I am expecting him" when it is supposed to mean: I am eagerly awaiting him. We would imagine a language in which different verbs were consistently used in these cases. And similarly more than one verb where we speak of 'believing', 'hoping' and so on. Perhaps the concepts of such a language would be more suitable for understand-ing psychology than the concepts of our language. (*PI* 577; see *Z* 49 for similar remarks about *intending*)

Following Wittgenstein's suggestion let us consider some of the differ-ent cases of thinking: (1) 'Thinking aloud': For example, you are plan-ning a long trip; you are consulting a map, calculating distances, deciding where to stop each night—all of this is done aloud. Or you re-mind yourself aloud of the various errands you have to do today, think-ing aloud of the best order in which to do them. (2) 'Pausing to think':

You have been asked what the word 'sybarite' means. At first nothing occurs to you. You repeat the word. You close your eyes and remain silent, perhaps seeing an image of the word. Suddenly the word 'pleasure' occurs to you. Then, with a feeling of confidence, you say: 'A sybarite is one who cultivates the pleasures of the senses'. It would be right to say that during the silent interval you were thinking about the question and thought out the answer. But notice how *fragmentary* was what went on. (3) 'Thinking in conversation': A friend has proposed a course of action for himself. You criticize the prudence of it, pointing out some probable consequences that would be unwelcome to him. All of this thinking is done in speech. As Wittgenstein says: 'When I think in language, there aren't "meanings" going through my mind in addition to the verbal expressions: but the language itself is the vehicle of thinking' (*PI* 329). (4) 'Silent thinking': Before going to sleep at night you recall a brief conversation you had with an acquaintance during the day. You see his face. You have the impression that something was troubling him, and you are speculating as to what it might be. This thinking is done without words. Or: You are playing chess and it is your move. With a feeling of tension you consider several possible moves and anticipate your opponent's countermoves. Finally, you make a decision. This thinking, too, is done without words. (5) 'Putting thought into one's word': This is the case of *Zettel* 100 over again. You are constructing something. You select, reject; compare, measure, test. During this activity you might even be carrying on a conversation about some unrelated matter. You are putting thought into your work—which is not the same as working thoughtfully. As Wittgenstein says: You might act in such a way, while taking measurements, that an onlooker would say that you had—without words—thought: If two magnitudes are equal to a third, they are equal to one another. 'But what constitutes the thinking here is not a process which has to accompany the words if they are not to be spoken without thought' (*PI* 330).

8

Our inclination to suppose that thinking is essentially a 'mental activity', something that one does 'in one's mind', is not confirmed by a survey of this small group of cases of thinking. Quite the contrary. Only the second and fourth cases ('Pausing to think' and 'Silent thinking') would be called thinking in one's mind. Certainly not 'Thinking aloud', or 'Thinking in conversation' or 'Putting thought into one's work'. Thinking in one's mind is only *one* form of thinking.

We may, however, hold fast to our inclination to believe that thinking is always 'mental'. Accordingly, we will say that thinking aloud, thinking in conversation, and putting thought into one's work are cases of thinking only because mental thinking underlies them. Thinking in one's mind is primary, fundamental.

I believe that exactly the reverse is true. There *could* be people who did all of their thinking aloud, or in conversation, or in work. As Wittgenstein says: 'Imagine people who could only think aloud! (As there are people who can only read aloud)' (*PI* 331). Whereas there could not be people who always did their thinking only in their minds.

9

Consider the analogy of calculating (adding, multiplying, dividing). One can multiply aloud, on paper, or in one's head. If you multiply aloud that is not *called* multiplying 'in your head'. Suppose it were said: 'Whenever people multiply they multiply in their heads'. A strange contention! The words, 'multiplying in one's head', could not have their ordinary meaning here. For *that* implies that the multiplying was *not* aloud or in writing. Furthermore, the ability to multiply in one's head logically presupposes the ability to multiply aloud or in writing. And that is *necessarily* so. For a person who was *not able* to execute any processes of multiplication, aloud, in writing, or in other outward signs, could not be said to be multiplying in his head, even if he was usually able to produce the right answer to multiplication problems! The ability to multiply in one's head is necessarily secondary to, derivative of, the ability to display multiplying in physically perceptible signs and actions.

Isn't there a similarity here between calculating and thinking? A child who had never manifested in words, gestures, or play the working out of simple problems could not be said to work them out 'in his mind', any more than he could be said to know 'in his mind' the names of colors, if he was unable to say their names, or to point to or fetch the right colors when their names were called out. Thinking in one's mind (silent thinking, pausing to think) is not the most fundamental form of thinking, but instead presupposes thinking in play, work, or words.

Since thinking in one's mind is only one of the phenomena of thinking (just as calculating in one's head is only one of the phenomena of calculating), and since it is necessarily a secondary form of thinking, then of course thinking is not essentially a 'mental' process. Silent thought, inward reflection, thinking something over in one's mind, often occur in the course of conversation. But often they do not, especially when the verbal exchanges are rapid or excited.

10

Nevertheless, the notion that there is a mental process of thinking present in all adaptive behavior attracts us powerfully. We are inclined to imagine this thinking 'as the stream which must be flowing under the surface' of talking, writing, working, playing, whenever these are not merely 'mechanical' (Z 107). A philosopher may say that he acknowledges the ordinary distinctions between thinking aloud, thinking in conversation, putting thought into one's work, on the one hand, and silent thinking, inward reflection, thinking out something in one's mind, on the other. He will admit that the ordinary criteria for 'pausing to think' or 'thinking out something in one's mind' are only sometimes satisfied in normal purposive behavior and intelligent conversation. What he postulates is a mental process of thinking that *underlies* the ordinary distinction between silent inner reflection, on the one hand, and, on the other hand, thinking in conversation or putting thought into one's work (as evidenced in the carpenter's wordless comparing, testing, measuring).

According to this view (espoused, for example, by Jerry A. Fodor in his recent book, *The Language of Thought*), all concept learning, all perceptual recognition, all purposeful behavior *requires* the forming, testing, and confirming of generalizations. For example, no one has mastered the English predicate 'is a building' unless he has learned that it falls under a generalization of this form: 'y is a building' is true if and only if Gx.[4] No one has learned to pick out buildings from nonbuildings and to recognize them as 'buildings' unless he has learned a generalization that determines the extension of 'is a building'. Such a

---

4. Jerry A. Fodor, *The Language of Thought* (Hassocks, Sussex: Harvester Press, 1976), p. 62.

generalization is called 'a truth rule'.[5] A necessary part of learning a language, according to Fodor, consists in developing the ability to hypothesize and confirm truth rules for the predicates of the language.

This view admits that probably no English speaker has *conscious* knowledge of the generalization that determines the extension of 'is a building'. It is even possible that the generalizations governing this and other natural language predicates should *never* be consciously accessible.[6] Nevertheless, the processes of forming generalizations and of confirming or disconfirming their application to sensory input, even though unconscious, are plainly processes of *thinking*.

It is worth noting that in Wittgenstein's *Tractatus* there is a remark suggestive of the view that a large part of the thinking involved in the daily employment of language is unconscious: 'Human beings possess the ability to construct languages capable of expressing every sense, without having any idea how each word has meaning or what its meaning is—just as people speak without knowing how the individual sounds are produced'.[7] Previously we were dealing with the assumption that the nature of thinking ought to be open to introspection. The present view does not make this assumption.

11

I will comment here on only two of the questions raised by Fodor's view. First, what is the nature of the claim that concept learning, perception, and 'considered action' *require* unconscious mental processes, called by Fodor 'computation'? Fodor gives three different answers: (1) The postulate that considered action, perception, and learning are based upon computational processes is 'a precondition for any sort of serious theory construction in cognitive psychology'.[8] (2) It is 'an empirical question whether psychological processes are computational processes'.[9] (3) 'We cannot begin to make sense of the phenomena' (namely, learning, perception, action) 'unless we are willing to view

5. *Ibid.*, p. 59.
6. *Ibid.*, p. 49.
7. Wittgenstein, *Tractatus Logico-Philosophicus*, trans. D. F. Pears and B. F. McGuinness (New York: Humanities Press, 1961), 4.002.
8. Fodor, *Language of Thought*, p. 34.
9. *Ibid.*, p. 47.

them as computational'. Indeed the theory that they are computational 'would seem to be' the *only* kind of theory 'that is conceivable'.[10]

My comments are, first, that the fact, if it is a fact, that the realm of theorizing known as cognitive psychology presupposes that the phenomena are computational, does not provide much support for this postulation; second, the claim that the question is 'empirical' is dubious, since the postulated computational processes are presumed to be unconscious; third, Fodor's belief that the computational theory appears to be the only 'conceivable' theory indicates that for Fodor this postulation tends to be *a priori* rather than empirical, and also indicates that for him it is an *a priori* requirement that there must be a true *theory* of the phenomena.

12

Next, let us consider Fodor's assumption that one has not mastered a predicate unless one has learned a generalization that determines the extension of the predicate. This assumption is in conflict with Wittgenstein's insight into the notion of 'family resemblance'. Fodor has read Wittgenstein but has failed to grasp this point. Apparently he has confused it with the fact that many predicates of ordinary language are 'fuzzy-edged', that is, in some cases have no determinate truth value.[11] This is an important point but is not what 'family resemblance' means. To say that the word 'game' ranges over a 'family of cases' means that there is *nothing* common to all games on account of which we call all of them games.[12] It does *not* mean that there is something common to all games, namely, a family resemblance. What holds for 'game' holds for such disparate words as 'number', 'deriving', 'reading', 'being guided'; and also for 'learning', 'perception', 'action'.

Whenever a word is a family resemblance word *there is no true generalization* that determines its extension—unless one allows as a 'generalization' the triviality that '*x* is a building' is true if and only if *x* is a building.[13] If there is no generalization determining the extension of

10. *Ibid.*, p. 36.

11. *Ibid.*, pp. 62–63.

12. See *PI* 65–68.

13. Fodor seems to countenance such trivialization. See his *Language of Thought*, p. 59, n. 5.

a predicate there is no 'truth rule' for that predicate. Since a host of predicates in any natural language are family resemblance predicates, learning truth rules cannot be an overwhelmingly important requirement for learning a language.

It is far from clear to me why it should seem *obvious* to a philosopher that if one knows the extension of a predicate one knows a generalization that determines its extension—but I cannot fully probe that temptation here. I will limit myself to the surmise that at least one source of the temptation to make this assumption is the belief that unless a person knew, either consciously or unconsciously, an appropriate generalization he would not be *guided* in his application of the predicate and therefore would have no mastery of its application. In his later philosophy Wittgenstein shows again and again the fallacy of this reasoning. His point, put briefly, is this: If I had a generalization in my possession I should still have to know how to *apply* the generalization. If this required that I had to be guided by a rule (a rule that told me how to apply the generalization) then I should need a further rule to tell me how to apply *that* rule. And so on. Thus the claim that my mastery of a predicate requires that I know a generalization leads to an infinite regress. Since this is absurd it cannot be a legitimate demand of reason that my mastery of a predicate requires that I be *guided* by a generalization. As Wittgenstein says in the *Investigations*: 'Don't always think that you read off your words from the facts; that you portray these facts in words according to rules. *For you would still have to apply the rule in the particular case without guidance*' (*PI* 292; my emphasis).

One thing that Wittgenstein is doing in his remarks about the concept of a *game* is rejecting the assumption that one's mastery of the predicate 'game' presupposes the knowledge of a generalization. He says that his knowledge of what a game is does not consist in any definition of 'game', either formulated or unformulated, or in any truth rule (*PI* 75, 76). Instead, 'my concept of a game' is *completely* expressed in things of this sort: 'my describing examples of various kinds of games; showing how all sorts of other games can be constructed on the analogy of these; saying that I would hardly call this and this games; and so on' (*PI* 75). Not only does that list contain no mention of a generalization that determines the extension of the predicate, or of necessary and sufficient truth-conditions, but in the next remark Wittgenstein explicitly excludes such things, when he says that if any 'sharp boundary' were proposed, he 'could not acknowledge it' as a

boundary that he had always wanted to draw, or had already drawn in
his mind.

13

This question of truth-conditions or truth rules is closely connected
with our problem about *thinking*. The *Tractatus* says that 'to understand
a proposition means to know what is the case if it is true' (4.024), and
that 'a proposition is the expression of its truth-conditions' (4.431). Lying behind this is the notion that every proposition is a truth-function
of elementary propositions and has one and only one complete analysis into elementary propositions. It is conceded, as we saw, at *Tractatus*
4.002, that we have no *conscious* knowledge of the analysis of many, if
any, propositions of ordinary language. This implies that in our employment of those propositions in daily life we are engaged in complicated, *subterranean* processes of thinking.

The idea that to understand a proposition is to know its truth-conditions is widely accepted in philosophy. John Searle, for example, says:

> To know the meaning of a general term and hence a predicate ex-
> pression is to know under what conditions it is true or false. . . . The
> older philosophers were not wrong when they said: to know the
> meaning of a proposition is to know under what conditions it is true
> or false.[14]

Fodor remarks that 'many philosophers have found it plausible that
one understands a predicate only if one knows the conditions under
which sentences that contain it would be true'.[15] He accepts this assumption and draws from it the consequence that learning a predicate
involves learning some generalization determining its extension; and
the further consequence that employing the predicate involves hy-
pothesizing and confirming the generalization.[16] This mental activity is
not presumed to be consciously accessible. Fodor's view, like that of the
Tractatus, envisages that all of us, most of the time, are doing a tremen-
dous lot of thinking ('Computation') that is hidden from ourselves as

14. John R. Searle, *Speech Acts* (Cambridge: Cambridge University Press, 1969), p. 125.
15. Fodor, *Language of Thought*, p. 59.
16. *Ibid.*

well as from others. This thinking is not *displayed* in speaking and acting, but is supposed to underlie them.

The claim that a person 'understands' a predicate only if he knows the truth-conditions for sentences containing the predicate ignores many distinctions. One person might be said to understand the expression *viola da gamba*, meaning that he knows it is the name of some musical instrument or other, although he doesn't know which one—in contrast with a person who has no idea to what the term refers; but also not to understand it in comparison with a person who knows that it is the name of some string instrument and not of a horn; but the latter does not understand the term in comparison with a person who can point out which string instrument it is; but again the latter does not understand it in contrast with someone who can give an account of the differences between the *viola da gamba* and the *violin*.

The notion that understanding a predicate requires the knowledge of truth-conditions is not supported by examples. Is your friend 'perplexed', or 'anxious', or 'concerned' about a certain matter? These predicates do not mean exactly the same. Circumstances and evidences may make one more appropriate than the others, without its being implied that there is a general rule for each predicate. On receiving some information a person may be 'surprised', 'mildly surprised', 'greatly surprised', 'astounded', or 'overwhelmed'. Facial expressions, exclamations, other reactions, subsequent behavior, may indicate one of those predicates to be the more suitable. But do we have any conception of a general truth rule for each predicate, and a different one for each? Of course not. Language is a finer instrument than that.

The assumption that every predicate is governed by a truth rule distorts our philosophical understanding of the concept of thinking. It supports the illusion that thinking is a hidden mental process. It prevents us from realizing that thinking is often *exhibited* in work, play, writing, conversation, and is not something that can only be inferred or postulated to explain those activities.

To suppose that thinking is, by its very nature, a 'mental activity' is a mistake produced by a failure to realize that there are different life-expressions of thinking, and also by the temptation to imagine that underlying these different forms or expressions of thinking there is the *real* thinking. Thinking is indeed often a mental activity; but equally often it is not.

2

Whether 'I' Is a
Referring Expression

I wish to discuss Professor Elizabeth Anscombe's powerful paper, 'The First Person'.[1] Her principal theme is that the first person pronoun 'I' is not a referring expression. To be sure, there is an overwhelming inclination to suppose that when a speaker utters a sentence in which 'I' occurs as grammatical subject, then *of course* the speaker uses 'I' to refer to, to stand for, to designate, one particular individual thing; one is tempted to suppose that the very function of the first person pronoun in any language that has it is to enable a speaker to make a unique reference, to select out one and only one thing, from all the beings, things, or objects that there are in the world. Descartes certainly believed that 'je', 'moi', 'ego', were used by him to refer to a certain thing. Having apparently discovered that *je pense, donc je suis* is a truth that cannot be shaken by even the most extravagant skepticism, Descartes then proceeded, as he reports in Part IV of the *Discourse*, to examine with attention 'ce que j'étais'—in other words, to try to find out what is the nature of that thing to which he refers by 'je' or 'moi'. His conclusion was that 'j'étais une substance dont toute l'essence ou la nature n'est que de penser'. He is supposing that he uses 'je' to refer to a 'substance'; and by a 'substance' he certainly means a *thing*, that has a nature and properties. He draws the further conclusion that 'ce moi' is entirely distinct from the body, and easier to know than the body, and

---

1. G. E. M. Anscombe, 'The First Person', in *Mind and Language*, ed. S. Guttenplan (Oxford: Clarendon Press, 1975).

that even if there was no body 'ce moi' would still be just what it is. Similarly, in the *Second Meditation*, when he asks 'But what then am I:' (*Sed quid igitur sum?*), he surely seems to be asking 'What sort of thing is this 'I'-thing?'. His answer is 'A thinking thing' (*Res cogitans*).

Hume speaks rather scornfully of those philosophers

> who imagine that we are every moment intimately conscious of what we call our SELF; that we feel its existence and its continuance in existence; and are certain, beyond the evidence of a demonstration, both of its perfect identity and simplicity.[2]

Hume declares that he is not aware of any such thing:

> For my part, when I enter most intimately into what I call *myself*, I always stumble on some particular perception or other, of heat or cold, light or shade, love or hatred, pain or pleasure. I never can catch *myself* at any time without a perception, and never can observe any thing but the perception.

Hume still assumes, however, that 'I' and 'myself' are referring expressions; they refer, however, not to an enduring thing of 'perfect identity and simplicity', but to a collection or 'bundle' of perceptions. In an appendix to the *Treatise* he says:

> When I turn my reflexion on *myself*, I never can perceive this *self* without some one or more perceptions; nor can I ever perceive any thing but the perceptions. 'Tis the composition of these, therefore, which forms the self.

Yet Hume confesses himself to be baffled by this view, because he cannot 'explain the principle of connection' that unites the successive perceptions.

Thomas Reid rejects Hume's proposal that the *I* or *self* is a collection of successive thoughts, feelings, sensations, and reaffirms the Cartesian view:

> I see evidently that identity supposes an uninterrupted continuance of existence. That which hath ceased to exist, cannot be the same with that which afterwards begins to exist; for this would be to sup-

2. David Hume, *Treatise*, Book I, Section VI.

pose a being to exist after it ceased to exist, and have had existence before it was produced, which are manifest contradictions. Continued uninterrupted existence is therefore implied in identity.[3]

Reid goes on to say:

> My personal identity, therefore, implies the continued existence of that indivisible thing which I call myself. Whatever this self may be, it is something which thinks, and deliberates, and resolves, and acts, and suffers. I am not thought, I am not action, I am not feeling; I am something that thinks, and acts, and suffers. My thoughts and actions, and feelings, change every moment—they have no continued, but a successive existence; but that *self* or *I*, to which they belong, is permanent, and has the same relation to all the succeeding thoughts, actions, and feelings, which I call mine.

Reid seems to suppose that there is an individual thing which *he* designates by the words 'I' and 'myself'. In his remark that his personal identity 'implies the continued existence of that indivisible thing *which I call myself*' (emphasis added), there is a strong hint that 'I' and 'myself' are used by him as *names* of an entity that endures continuously throughout Reid's life. Reid implies of course that every English speaker uses 'I' and 'myself' as Reid does; that is to say, each speaker uses those pronouns to designate an entity that exists continuously throughout the life of the speaker. But of course each speaker uses those pronouns to refer to an entity that is numerically different from the entity that any other speaker refers to when he employs those pronouns.

Thus Reid appears to have held the view which Anscombe characterizes as the view that not only is 'I' a name, but that it is 'logically a proper name'.[4] One feature of the philosophical notion of that which is 'logically a proper name' is that it has, as Anscombe puts it, a 'guaranteed reference'. Russell said of the name 'Romulus' that it is not really a name, but a truncated or telescoped description: 'If it were really a name, the question of existence could not arise, because a name has got to name something or it is not a name'.[5] The 'names' of the *Tractatus*

---

3. Thomas Reid, *Essays on the Intellectual Powers*, Essay III, Chap. IV.

4. Anscombe, 'The First Person', p. 49. Hereafter I will put page references to Anscombe's essay into the text.

5. Bertrand Russell, 'The Philosophy of Logical Atomism', in *Logic and Knowledge*, ed. R. C. Marsh (London: Allen and Unwin, 1956), p. 243.

had this feature of guaranteed reference because the object that a *Tractatus* name meant or stood for was *the meaning* of the name.[6] Anscombe remarks that *if* 'I' is a name, that is, if its job is to refer to or designate something, then it has this feature of guaranteed reference:

> "I"—if it makes a reference, if that is, its mode of meaning is that it is supposed to make a reference—is secure against reference-failure. Just thinking "I . . ." guarantees not only the existence but the presence of its referent. It guarantees the existence *because* it guarantees the presence, which is presence to consciousness. But N.B. here "presence to consciousness" means physical or real presence. For if the thinking did not guarantee the presence, the existence of the referent could be doubted. For the same reason, if "I" is a name it cannot be an empty name. I's existence is existence in the thinking of the thought expressed by "I . . ." This of course is the point of the *cogito*. (Pp. 54–55)

But if 'I' is a name, or if not a name then perhaps a demonstrative, what is the nature of the object to which it refers? There have been several different ideas about this. First, there is the notion of Descartes and Reid that the object to which 'I' refers is something that is indivisible, immaterial, containing no parts; is that which thinks, acts, suffers; and is permanent throughout the life of a human being. In short, it is a Self or Soul. A second idea is that the object to which 'I' refers is a living, walking, speaking, human being, such as N.M. or E.A. Obviously these are different ideas about the reference of 'I'. The living, walking, speaking N.M. is not indivisible; for N.M. could be drawn and quartered. A third notion is that 'I' refers to a sequence or 'bundle' of thoughts, sensations, feelings. Anscombe proposes a fourth candidate, namely, that what 'I' refers to is *this body* (pp. 57–58).

Let us consider these candidates in reverse order. Anscombe calls attention to the possibility of one's getting into a state of 'sensory deprivation', in which one could not see, hear, talk, or feel anything by touch, or have any sensations in or on one's body, because all of it is anesthetized. If I were in a condition of sensory deprivation, *this body* would not be present to my senses; moreover, there is no way at all in

6. Ludwig Wittgenstein, *Tractatus Logico-Philosophicus*, trans. D. F. Pears and B. F. McGuinness (London: Routledge and Kegan Paul, 1962) 3.2–3. See Wittgenstein's *Philosophical Investigations*, ed. G. E. M. Anscombe and Rush Rhees, trans. G. E. M. Anscombe (Oxford: Blackwell, 1973), para. 46 (hereafter cited *PI*).

which it would be *present to me* (p. 58). The postulated condition of sensory deprivation need not, however, be a condition of unconsciousness. I could think to myself: 'I am in a strange condition'. I might even wonder whether I had become disembodied. I could have many other 'I'-thoughts. But as long as I was in the state of sensory deprivation, the 'I' in those 'I'-thoughts would not designate or denote *this body*. Thus if 'I' is supposed to be a referring expression with a guaranteed reference to some one and the same thing, then *this body* does not fill the bill.

The proposal that 'I' refers to a course, flow, sequence, stream, collection, group, bundle, or totality, of sensations, thoughts, and feelings, seems quite worthless. If 'I' is supposed to refer to each thought or sensation as it occurs, then the reference of 'I' would be continually shifting, often with great rapidity. It would be hard to see the difference between the word 'I' having that sort of reference and its not being a referring expression at all. On the other hand, if 'I' is not supposed to refer to the various particular thoughts, sensations, feelings, but instead to that by virtue of which they are the thoughts, etc., of some one and the same person, then it is impossible to understand, as Hume realized, what the connecting principle might be; and also impossible to see what role there would be for 'I' as a referring expression. If we say that the object that 'I' designates is a thing that *has* those thoughts then, of course, we have moved entirely away from Hume, and toward one or the other of the first two theories.

Let us turn to the second view mentioned in our list, namely, the view that 'I' is used by each speaker to refer to a living, corporeal, human being, with a particular history, such as N.M. or E.A. It is true that on this view there will be, in a sense, a guaranteed reference for 'I'. If *I* say, 'I broke the vase', this is true if and only if N.M. broke the vase; and if *I* say 'I am confused' this is true if and only if N.M. is confused. Every speaker or thinker is a real person, X, and every 'I'-thought will be a thought of the person, X, who is the thinker. But, as Anscombe points out, if someone

> . . . takes this as an adequate account of the guaranteed reference of "I", then he will have to grant that there is a further sort of 'guaranteed reference', which "I" does *not* have. Guaranteed reference for that name "X" in this further sense . . . would entail a guarantee, not just that there is such a thing as X, but also that what I take to be X *is* X. (P. 57)

It is not true, however, that when I use 'I' it has guaranteed reference in this further sense. Through being misinformed or duped, or from some mental aberration, I might believe I was John Smith, not merely bearing the name 'John Smith' but also having the origin and history of John Smith. Yet if I said 'I am writing a letter', this could be true even though I mistakenly believed that I was John Smith. My mistaken identification of myself as John Smith would have no bearing at all on the truth or falsity of my statement, 'I am writing a letter'. This proves that the 'I' in that statement cannot *mean* or *stand for* John Smith, since if it did the statement would be false. Anscombe says:

> It seems clear that if "I" is a 'referring expression' at all, it has both kinds of guaranteed reference. The object an "I"-user means by it must exist so long as he is using "I", nor can he take the wrong object to be the object he means by "I". (P. 57)

This is an oblique way of arguing that there is *no* object the 'I'-user means by 'I'. If he mistakenly believed himself to be such-and-such a person, and if he did use 'I' to mean that person, then he would be taking the wrong object to be the object he means by 'I'.

It is obvious, however, that if I had false beliefs about my origin and course of life, this would be irrelevant to the truth and the meaning of such statements of mine as that 'I am tired', 'I am seated in a chair', 'I intend to go to the movies'. This would also be the case if, suffering from amnesia, I was totally bewildered about my identity—had no idea at all as to who I was.

Wittgenstein remarks that when I say 'I'm in pain', I am *not* saying that such-and-such a person is in pain.[7] And in *The Blue Book* he makes the seemingly paradoxical remark that 'In "I have pain", "I" is not a demonstrative pronoun'.[8] The impression of paradox will disappear if we ask ourselves, 'What job does a demonstrative do?'. The answer is that the words 'this', 'that', 'he', 'she', 'it', are used to pick one thing out from others. Which person or thing the demonstrative word picks out is shown by a pointing gesture, or by a previously given name or description, or by the context of previous or subsequent remarks. Wittgenstein's point is that 'I' is not used like that. It does not mean

---

7. *PI* 404.
8. Wittgenstein, *The Blue and Brown Books* (Oxford: Blackwell, 1969), p. 68.

'such-and-such a person'. It does not designate 'a particular person'.[9] My saying, 'I'm in pain', may of course attract the attention of others to myself; but so also may my silent grimacing with pain. I do not, in the first case any more than in the second, mention, refer to, or mean one particular person among others.

Of course by 'I' I mean *myself.* But this is equivalent to: by 'I' I mean *I*; which says nothing, being a kind of tautology. If my 'I' meant a person of a particular identity, origin, and course of life, and I was not that person, then my statement, 'I am standing up', would be false, even if I was standing up—which is absurd.

This brings us to the first candidate on our list, namely, the notion that 'I' refers to the Cartesian Ego, Self, or Soul—the thinking thing. This seems to be the only possibility. 'Thus we discover that *if* "I" is a referring expression, then Descartes was right about what the referent was' (p. 58). But this view of Descartes, and of Reid, has nonsensical consequences. As Anscombe points out, not only is there 'the intolerable difficulty of requiring an identification of the same referent in different "I"-thoughts', but also there could be no guarantee that there was only *one* thinker of a single 'I' thought: 'How do I know that "I" is not ten thinkers thinking in unison?' (p. 58). Anscombe gives an accurate summary of the matter:

> Getting hold of the wrong object *is* excluded, and that makes us think that getting hold of the right object is guaranteed. But the reason is that there is no getting hold of an object at all. With names, or denoting expressions (in Russell's sense) there are two things to grasp: the kind of use, and what to apply them to from time to time. With "I" there is only the use. (P. 59)

The solution of the problems about the reference of 'I' is this: ' "I" is neither a name nor another kind of expression whose logical role is to make a reference, *at all*' (p. 60).

In reflecting on Anscombe's paper I have wondered whether 'I' might sometimes be a referring expression and sometimes not. In *The Blue Book* Wittgenstein seems to countenance such a view. He says:

> There are two different cases in the use of the word "I" (or "my") which I might call "the use as object" and "the use as subject". Ex-

9. See *PI* 405.

amples of the first kind of use are these: "My arm is broken", "I have grown six inches", "I have a bump on my forehead", "The wind blows my hair about". Examples of the second kind are: "*I* see so-and-so", "*I* hear so-and-so", "*I* try to lift my arm", "*I* think it will rain", "*I* have a toothache". One can point to the difference between these two categories by saying: The cases of the first category involve the recognition of a particular person, and there is in these areas the possibility of an error, or as I should put it: The possibility of an error has been provided for. . . . It is possible that, say in an accident, I should feel a pain in my arm, see a broken arm at my side, and think it is mine, when really it is my neighbour's. And I could, looking into a mirror, mistake a bump on his forehead for one on mine. On the other hand, there is no question of recognizing a person when I say I have a toothache. To ask "are you sure that it's *you* who have pains?" would be nonsensical.[10]

But does the fact that in regard to some 'I'-sentences the possibility of error has been provided for imply that in those sentences the role of 'I' is to refer to an object? I do not see that it does. Nor does it follow that in an 'I'-sentence where no possibility of error has been provided for, 'I' means a thing called 'the subject'.

A point made several times by Anscombe is that if 'I' is a name, or a demonstrative, or some other kind of referring expression the role of which is to make a 'singular reference' to an object or thing, then there must be some 'conception' that connects 'I' with the object.

> The use of a name for an object is connected with a conception of that object. And so we are driven to look for something that, for each "I"-user, will be the conception related to the supposed name "I", as the conception of a city is to the names "London" and "Chicago", that of a river to "Thames" and "Nile", that of a man to "John" and "Pat". Such a conception is requisite if "I" is a name. (Pp. 51–52)

The requirement of a 'conception' is not removed if 'I' is assumed to be a demonstrative instead of a name.

> Assimilation to a demonstrative will not—as would at one time have been thought—do away with the demand for a conception of the ob-

10. Wittgenstein, *The Blue and Brown Books*, pp. 66–67.

ject indicated. For, even though someone may say just "this" or
"that", we need to know the answer to the question "this *what*?" if we
are to understand him; and he needs to know the answer if he is to
be meaning anything. (P. 53)

Anscombe adds the following remarks in a footnote:

> This point was not grasped in the days when people believed in pure
> ostensive definition without the ground's being prepared for it. Thus
> also in those days it was possible not to be so much impressed as we
> ought to be, by the fact that *we can find no well-accounted-for term corre-*
> *sponding to "I" as* "city" does to "London". It was possible to see that
> there was no 'sense' (in Frege's sense) for "I" as a proper name, but
> still to think that for each one of us "I" was the proper name of an
> 'object of acquaintance', a *this*. What *this* was could then be called "a
> self", and the word "self" would be felt to need no further justifica-
> tion. (P. 53n.; my emphasis)

It seems right to say that we are unable to specify any conception or
well-understood general term that corresponds to 'I', such that in
saying 'I . . .' one means 'I' to refer to something falling under the conception or term. The conception 'human body' is well enough understood; but in a state of sensory deprivation, such as we previously
imagined, one might think, 'Perhaps I am bodiless'; and this thought
would be incoherent if the conception 'human body' corresponds to
'I'. The same objection would apply to the conceptions of 'human being' or 'person'; for in our usual employment and understanding of
these expressions, to be a human being or person includes having the
human physical form. Descartes's thought 'I have no body' actually entailed the thought 'I am not a human being'.

If we turn to 'self', 'soul', or 'mind', as conceptions corresponding
to 'I', the fact is that these expressions are not well understood. I
should hardly know what I was saying if I either asserted or denied that
I am a self, soul, or mind.

There are occasions on which I say to others, who want to know who
I am: 'I am N.M.', or 'I am the youngest son of Charles M.'. These are
true statements. But Anscombe makes the striking remark that although such statements are true they are not *identity* statements. She
says: 'If I am right in my general thesis, there is an important consequence—namely, that "I am E.A." is after all not an identity proposi-

tion' (p. 60). I think her point is that in a genuine identity proposition a distinctly conceived subject is connected with a distinctly conceived predicate. For example, 'Descartes was the author of *Meditationes de prima philosophia*'. Here the name 'Descartes' refers to a distinctly conceived subject—a human being, a Frenchman, who lived in the seventeenth century, did military service, invented analytical geometry, and so on. But when Descartes introduced himself to others by saying, 'I am René Descartes', he was not making an identity statement, although what he said was true.

If I were to lose my memory (perhaps from a concussion) so that I no longer knew who I was, it could be imagined that subsequently I became convinced by evidence and testimony presented by others, that my name is 'N.M.', that I was born in such-and-such a place of such-and-such parents, that the course of my life has been so-and-so. I should have found out who I am; I should have *learned my identity*. There might be a moment of sudden conviction at which I exclaimed: '*So*, *I* am N.M.; my parents were X and Y; the course of my life has been thus-and-so!'

I have found it tempting to think that this statement, made at the moment of my realization of my identity, would be a genuine identity proposition. But is this right? What reason is there for thinking that the use of 'I' in this statement is governed by a conception of an object, any more than it is in the utterance 'I am in pain', or in the thought that might occur in a condition of sensory deprivation, 'Perhaps I am bodiless'? I can see none.

Suppose that from extreme privation and suffering I no longer knew who I was. Lying on the ground amidst other enfeebled people, and feeling a savage thirst, I cry out, 'Water! Water!'. An attendant, looking around, says, 'Who wants water?'. I might call out 'I'; or might instead raise my hand. By uttering 'I', or by holding up my hand, I would equally be drawing attention to myself. But neither the hand gesture nor the utterance 'I' would imply a conception of myself that distinguished me from other persons. My utterance 'I' in response to the question would show that I still *retained a mastery of the use of* 'I', even though I had no conception of who I was.

My conclusion is that Anscombe is entirely right in her contention that 'I' is not a referring expression, despite our inclination to think it is. This is so, not only in respect to the first person, present tense *Äusserungen* ('I am in pain', 'I am thirsty'), to which Wittgenstein has drawn attention; but also in respect to statements such as 'I am sitting in a chair', where there is the possibility of error; and also in statements by which I intend to inform others of my identity ('I am N.M.', 'I am the youngest son of Charles M.'). *Nowhere* does 'I' have the role of designating or meaning a distinctly conceived object *or* subject.

3

'Functionalism' in Philosophy of Psychology

1

The expressions 'functionalism', 'functional analysis' and 'functional explanation' have been used to refer to several different ideas. The notion of a 'functional explanation' has been employed in anthropology, physiology, and psychology. One starts with the idea of 'a system'. A 'system' has parts or component elements, or exhibits certain processes or activities. According to Carl Hempel,[1] there is a notion of 'functional explanation' that is roughly the following: the 'function' of some part of a system is that it provides a necessary condition for the stability, health, or survival of the system. Hempel gives these examples: in anthropology the function of the rainmaking ceremonies of the Hopi Indians has been deemed to be the preservation of the tribe; in human physiology the function of the kidney has been taken to be the preservation of the health of the organism by discharging waste; in psychoanalysis the function of neurotic compulsive washing has been held to be the prevention of outbreaks of anxiety (307). A system is observed to have a certain part, or to exhibit some process or activity. The question is raised, what is the 'purpose' of this part, process, or activity? This is regarded as coming to the same as the question, what would be the effect on the survival, stability, or health of the system if this part, process, or

1. Carl G. Hempel, 'The Logic of Functional Analysis', in Hempel, *Aspects of Scientific Explanation* (New York: Free Press, 1965).

activity did not exist? As far as I can see, *this* notion of 'functional explanation' is *not* what I shall be concerned with in the present paper.

2

A second notion of 'functional analysis' or 'functional explanation' occurs in the writing of B. F. Skinner. The systems he is dealing with are animal or human 'organisms'. What is to be explained is the 'behavior' of a system. Skinner's mode of explanation does not appeal to 'inner' states, processes, or events, whether physical or mental, but to 'external variables'. He says:

> The objection to inner states is not that they do not exist, but that they are not relevant to a functional analysis. We cannot account for the behavior of any system while staying wholly inside it; eventually we must turn to forces operating upon the organism from without.[2]

Skinner's 'functional analysis' undertakes both to explain and to predict behavior in terms of 'external variables' or 'environmental variables'. The general slogan is: 'Behavior is a function of the environment'. Skinner says:

> The external variables of which behavior is a function provide for what may be called a causal or functional analysis. We undertake to predict and control the behavior of the individual organism. This is our 'dependent variable'—the effect for which we are to find the cause. Our 'independent variables'—the causes of behavior—are the external conditions of which behavior is a function. Relations between the two—the 'cause-and-effect relationships' in behavior—are the laws of a science. (*Ibid.*)

Skinner's brand of 'functional analysis' (sometimes called 'peripheralist' theory as contrasted with 'centralist' theory) has been heavily criticized by many writers. I do not wish to add anything here to that mass of writing.[3]

---

2. B. F. Skinner, *Science and Human Behavior* (New York: Macmillan, 1953), p. 35.

3. I addressed myself to Skinner's behaviorism in 'Behaviorism as a Philosophy of Psychology', in *Thought and Knowledge* (Ithaca: Cornell University Press, 1977).

3

A third viewpoint, also called 'functionalism', is currently put forward by various authors. My exposition of this version of 'functionalism'
is drawn largely from a work entitled *The Formal Mechanics of Mind* by
Stephen Thomas.[4] Here again we have the notion of a 'system'. A typewriter, a computer, a human being are examples of systems. A system receives 'inputs' and produces 'outputs'. Thomas introduces the notion
of a 'functional state' of a system. A functional state (F-state) is not defined as a physical part of a system. Instead it is defined as a relationship
between 'input' and 'output'. For example, a manual typewriter is so
constructed that when a key bearing the label 'a' is struck (input), the
machine prints the letter 'a' (output). An electric typewriter may exhibit the same input-output relationship, although the electric machine
operates on different physical principles and has a different internal
physical arrangement than does the manual machine. But since in both
machines there is this same input-output relationship, both machines
are said to exhibit the same F-state. F-states 'are defined in terms of external *functional* rather than internal structural distinctions' ('Mechanics of Mind', 124).
    We now come to the notion of 'a functional state table' (FST). An
FST is a list of the F-states of a system. It is a description of the 'operational properties of a system in abstraction from its internal concrete
structure' (*ibid.*, 125). If an FST for a certain system were both true and
complete, it would list all of the F-states, and only the F-states, that hold
for that system. It would be a complete description of the input-output
characteristics of that system.
    As applied to human beings, 'an FST of the postulated sort takes as
"inputs" different possible environmental situations and describes as
"outputs" various pieces of behavior' (*ibid.*, 135). An FST for a person
will list not only actual responses to actual environmental situations, but
also what the person's responses *would have been* in hypothetical situations.

> For an FST describes not only a person's actions in the situations that
> were actualized, but also what the person would have done in other

4. Stephen N. Thomas, *The Formal Mechanics of Mind* (Ithaca: Cornell University Press,
1978).

circumstances. The hypothesis, in other words, has a monopoly on all relevant behavior, actual or possible. (*Ibid.*, 150)

This thesis makes one wonder whether there is such a thing as a complete FST for a human being. But before going into this let us note the relationship that Thomas asserts to hold between the functional states and the mental states of a person. Thomas's functionalist hypothesis does not assert, and indeed, denies, that mental states are identical with F-states (*ibid.*, 139).

> The hypothesis is only that F-states *determine* mental states (that is, for each ordinary-language mental state, being in certain F-states is alleged to be a logically sufficient condition for being in that mental state). The postulated relationship between mental states and F-states is not one-to-one, but many-to-many. To each ordinary-language mental-state predicate . . . in general there will correspond (perhaps infinitely) many F-states that determine it, and each of these F-states, in general, simultaneously will determine (perhaps infinitely) many separate and distinct mental states. So the postulated relationship is a complex many-to-many correlation, and *not* identity between the states. (*Ibid.*, 139–40)

Mental states are logically determined by functional states. But since functional states are defined solely in terms of input-output characteristics and entail nothing whatever about the internal structures or mechanisms of a system, the same holds true for mental states: 'the applicability of mentalistic descriptions is logically independent of the nature of the particular mechanisms that enable subjects to realize these states' (*ibid.*, 145).

Thomas says that his functionalism is *compatible* with the assumption that a human being contains an immaterial soul or mind. His functionalism does require that the inputs to and outputs from a system are physical; but it does not require 'that realizations of FSTs determining mental descriptions are entirely constituted of physical parts' (*ibid.*, 160). The possibility that a system might contain nonphysical components is not, however, taken seriously. Thomas says that his functional state model

> may be transformed into a completely materialistic theory of mind simply by adding to it the very plausible assumption that in humans

the postulated FSTs are entirely realized by the nervous system and associated bodily mechanisms. (*Ibid.*, 161)

When Thomas adds to his functionalism this 'very plausible assumption' the resulting view is called 'physicalistic functionalism' or 'functional-state materialism'. This view is not, however, to be identified with the 'central-state materialism' of, for example, David Armstrong. Whereas central-state materialism holds that the mental states of a material system are identical with some of its internal physical states, functional-state materialism rejects this view (as we have already noted) and holds instead that the mental states of a material system are logically determined by its functional states; but the mental states are neither identical with the functional states, nor with the internal physical states of the system which 'realize' the functional states.

The relation of Thomas's 'physicalistic functionalism' to behaviorism is intriguing. The two forms of behaviorism that are of main philosophical interest, I think, are (1) Skinner's version of 'functional analysis', and (2) the view that is often called 'analytic' or 'logical' behaviorism. Both of these forms of behaviorism have declined in popularity in recent years. Some philosophers have, in the last few years, set forth views to which they have given the name 'functionalism', and which they have regarded as opposed to behaviorism. Not so with Thomas. Although Thomas rejects Skinner's position, for reasons that I won't go into, he does endorse 'analytic' behaviorism. Indeed, he considers analytic behaviorism to be *entailed* by his own version of 'functionalism'. Thomas says:

> My functionalist hypothesis entails that for each pure mental predicate, there exists some description of behavior whose satisfaction is a logically sufficient condition for that predicate's ascription. (*Ibid.*, 226)

The thesis that is said here to be entailed by Thomas's 'functionalism' is the thesis that Thomas labels 'analytic' behaviorism. Thomas is well aware that there has been considerable disagreement as to what exactly should be understood by the name 'analytic behaviorism'—whether, for example, it is supposed to mean that a behavioristic analysis of a mental predicate provides both necessary and sufficient conditions for its true application, or just necessary conditions, or just sufficient conditions (*ibid.*, 263–64). Thomas chooses the latter definition:

> Analytical behaviorism claims that for each mental predicate, 'M',
> there exists some description, 'Φ', expressed solely in terms of de-
> scriptions of behavior or dispositions to behavior, that specifies logi-
> cally sufficient conditions for the application of 'M'. (*Ibid.*, 270)

Now the 'functionalism' that Thomas espouses holds that 'for each
pure mental predicate, 'M', there exists an FST containing an F-state, S,
such that being in this F-state is a logically sufficient condition for the
true application of the mental description' (*ibid.*). Since an F-state just
is a particular grouping of input-output or stimulus-response characteristics, it would seem that Thomas's functionalism really does entail
analytic behaviorism, as this latter is defined by Thomas.

Previously I merely raised the question as to whether there is a complete FST for a human being. Let us return to this question. Remember
what an FST is: 'An FST is an abstract "input-output" characterization
that delineates or individuates "states" of a system exclusively in terms
of the system's input-output characteristics' (*ibid.*, 218). Presumably, a
'complete' FST for a particular human being, John Robinson, would in-
dividuate *all* of the functional states of Robinson. Now could anyone
discover by careful observation and experiments what Robinson's complete FST is? Apparently not. Thomas himself says that 'there is no procedure by which others can *conclusively* ascertain a subject's F-state (and
hence, his mental state) by any amount of behavioral or input-output
observation' (*ibid.*, 149n). If this is true of a single F-state then, a fortiori, it is true of a complete FST. And Thomas says this too: 'no series of
behavioral observations conclusively establishes someone's FST or functional state' (*ibid.*, 159). And again:

> Regardless of the extremes to which their behavioral experimenta-
> tion is carried, psychologists never will find it possible to ascertain
> with logical certitude the functional state table or functional state of
> any system they study. (*Ibid.*, 269)

The philosophical inclination to say that it is impossible to '*conclusively* establish', or to ascertain 'with logical certitude', any person's
'mental state', is something that is, or should be, familiar to all of us.
What usually lies behind this inclination is a temptation to impose upon
such phrases as 'conclusively establish' and 'with logical certitude' a
self-contradictory requirement. I think enough has been said elsewhere

about that confusion; so I won't try to add anything further to it here. But of course, in the everyday use of the word 'know' we often do know what some person's 'mental state' is, e.g. that the person is anxious, surprised, or irritable.

Now what about a person's 'functional state'? Do we ever know *that*, in the ordinary use of 'know'? I should think not. We may indeed know that when Robinson saw the bill for his automobile insurance, he turned pale and said 'Oh, no!'. But we must remember that, according to Thomas, Robinson's 'functional state', or at least his 'functional state table', includes not only his actual behavior when presented with an actual stimulus 'input', but also what Robinson's behavior *would have been* 'under various unrealized hypothetical conditions' (*ibid.*, 150). Would anyone know whether Robinson would have turned pale and said 'Oh, no!', *if* his bank account had contained twice as much money as it actually did; or *if* Mrs. Robinson had seen the bill first and had exclaimed in Robinson's hearing, 'This is dreadful! What shall we do?'? And so on, with an indefinite number of unrealized possibilities? A functional state table for a particular person is supposed to include 'all relevant behavior, actual or possible' (*ibid.*). We certainly do not ever have knowledge of that kind.

Do we have *any reason at all* for believing that functional states and functional state tables for human beings *do exist*? Thomas certainly would deny that any have been discovered. He speaks more than once of our not 'possessing' a 'complete' FST for a person (*ibid.*, e.g., 153, 154n). He even expresses some doubt as to whether there even *exists* a 'complete' FST for a person—that is, an FST that would show 'what that system would do for every possible "input"' (*ibid.*, 290). At the same time, Thomas frequently asserts *the existence* of FSTs. He says, as previously noted, that for each mental predicate 'there exists an FST containing an F-state' such that being in this F-state is a logically sufficient condition for the true application of the mental predicate (*ibid.*, 270). And Thomas declares that 'an FST describes not only a person's actions in the situations that were actualized, but also what the person would have done in other circumstances'. An FST 'has a monopoly on all relevant behavior, actual or possible' (*ibid.*, 150). Thus Thomas seems to be in an inconsistent position regarding the existence of a complete FST for any person. He both affirms it and doubts it.

Leaving this inconsistency aside, by far the main thrust of Thomas's book is to assert the existence of a complete FST for each human being.

Or rather, instead of flatly asserting that human FSTs exist, it would be more accurate to say that Thomas speaks of the existence of FSTs as being his 'hypothesis' or his 'postulation'. Now why should Thomas even *postulate* the existence of a human FST? He says: 'Although the hypothesis does not actually supply the FSTs it posits, the postulate of their existence is of fundamental importance to the scientific investigation of mind' (*ibid.*, 140). Why is the hypothesis of fundamental importance? For one thing, according to Thomas, 'it assures researchers that they can gain access to everything relevant to an organism's mental phenomena simply by attending to its functional characteristics' (*ibid.*, 141). For another thing, or perhaps it is the same thing, the hypothesis is supposed to solve a long-standing philosophical problem:

> If my functional hypothesis is true, it indeed solves the classical mind-body problem. For the hypothesis entails that a neural network (plus associated bodily mechanisms) can be in the mental or psychological states determined by the implemented FST. So the theory explains how a completely physical or material structure could undergo mental states, including any state of consciousness. The theory's ability to explain how a purely physical system could be the subject of any mental state shows that it indeed solves the 'mind-body problem' as traditionally conceived. (*Ibid.*, 164–65)

But since none of us knows of the existence of even a single human F-state, let alone of a complete human FST, how can the mere postulation of the existence of FSTs 'assure' those engaged in research on human psychology of anything at all? Furthermore, it is actually an *understatement* to say that 'we do not know' of the existence of any of the postulated human F-states or FSTs. Remember that the description of an F-state consists exclusively of a description of environmental physical 'inputs' and of physical behavioral 'outputs'. The claim is made that for any particular mental description, 'M', there is an F-state description which *entails* that mental description. When, however, we are presented with any description that merely enumerates physical 'inputs' and physical 'outputs' and which *does not include any mental terms*, we can, with a little reflection and imagination, think of various countervailing circumstances, such that 'M' would *not* be true even if the 'input-output' description were true. Thus no entailment holds. And we get no closer to an entailment by piling on more details of 'input-output'. Thomas could not remove this difficulty by stipulating that the complete F-state description would *include a denial* of each such countervailing circumstance (for example, that the person was pretending, spoofing, playacting, or engaged in some unsuspected enterprise, and so on). This device would not be available to Thomas because, first, it would bring mental terms, such as intentional descriptions, into the F-state description, which is not legitimate; and, second, because there is no finite number of possible countervailing circumstances: which means that the F-state description could not be completed.

We can see, therefore, that an F-state *description*, with the desired entailment property, cannot be produced! This being so, it is quite meaningless to postulate the existence of these imaginary functional states, or to declare that *if* the postulation of their existence is true then some classical philosophical problem is solved. The postulated functional states are merely a fantasy, indulged in by a number of philosophers.

4

I come now to the fourth and final version of 'functionalism' or of 'functional analysis' that I will consider. This version has been called, by K. V. Wilkes, 'structural-functional analysis'.[5] This functionalist view 'takes for granted the assumption that physicalism is in fact true' (*Physicalism*, 45). By 'physicalism' is understood the following: 'it is the attempt to correlate explanations of actions couched in psychological terms with descriptions and explanations of cerebral states, events, and processes couched in neurophysiological terms' (*ibid.*, 29). According to Wilkes, structural-functionalism is not 'reductionist' (*ibid.*, 66). This means that it does not try to find neurophysiological descriptions and explanations that are equivalent in meaning to, or paraphrases of, mental or psychological descriptions and explanations. Nor does it accept 'radical behaviorism', which is the view 'that behaviour can be described and explained with no reference whatever to non-physical terms' (*ibid.*, 10).

The method of structural-functionalism is divided into two stages. The first stage is to consider some characteristic activity of a system—for example, the memory-behavior of people and animals. At this stage the

5. K. V. Wilkes, *Physicalism* (London: Routledge and Kegan Paul, 1978), pp. 54–55.

activity under consideration is analyzed into functional parts, in terms of some theory of scientific psychology. Let us suppose that in the example of memory-behavior there is a theory that analyzes this phenomenon into the following functional parts: an input of information from learning or perception, encoding of the information, storage, decoding, retrieval, behavioral output. In other words, memory-behavior is divided, according to the theory, into a sequence of 'functions'. The second stage of the method is to try to locate, for each of these functions, a physical part of or physical process in the organism, which 'realizes' or carries out that function. In this method the sciences of psychology and neurophysiology work hand in hand. Psychology tries to identify functions; neurophysiology tries to find the physical states or processes that carry out those functions.

As J. A. Fodor puts it, stage one requires a psychological theory that provides functional characterizations of the mechanisms responsible for the production of behavior. For example, there might be a psychological hypothesis that not only does memory require the 'storage' of memory 'traces', but furthermore that *failures* of memory are due to the 'decay' of memory traces. The second stage of explanation will consist in 'the specification of those biochemical systems that do, in fact, exhibit functional characteristics enumerated by phase-one theories'.[6] When applied to the hypothesis about memory, stage two would involve a search for a subsystem of the organism that has the two properties of 'storage' and 'decay'.

According to Daniel Dennett in his book *Brainstorms*, structural-functionalism pictures a person 'as analogous to a large organization, with intercommunicating departments, executives, and a public relations unit to "speak for the organization" '.[7] This type of explanation of human behavior consists in 'analysing a person into an organization of sub-systems . . . and attempting to explain the behaviour of the whole person as the outcome of the interaction of these sub-systems' (*ibid.*, 153). This branch of functionalism is called 'centralist' (in contrast with a 'peripheralist' theory, such as Skinner's) and is also called 'cognitive' theory.

Although Dennett favors a functionalist theory of mind, he is acutely aware that it runs the risk of circularity. For example, it would be circular, and so nonexplanatory, to attempt to explain human memory by

---

6. J. A. Fodor, *Psychological Explanation* (New York: Random House, 1968), pp. 108–9.
7. Daniel C. Dennett, *Brainstorms* (Hassocks, Sussex: Harvester, 1979), p. 152.

· postulating a subsystem that is itself endowed with memory; or to explain how a person chooses between alternative courses of action by positing an internal state or process that does the choosing. Dennett formulates this difficulty in general terms:

> A non-question-begging psychology will be a psychology that makes no ultimate appeals to unexplained intelligence, and that condition can be reformulated as the condition that whatever functional parts a psychology breaks its subjects into, the smallest, or most fundamental, or least sophisticated parts must not be supposed to perform tasks or follow procedures requiring intelligence. (*Ibid.*, 83)

How can a psychology that is 'cognitive', 'centralist', or 'functional', avoid question-begging circularity? This is a serious problem. The Cambridge psychologist F. C. Bartlett was one of the earlier proponents of the notion of a 'cognitive structure', which he called a 'Schema'. He was concerned to understand how a tennis player, for example, is able to make the quick, efficient movements that are required for skill in tennis. This cannot be explained in terms of a series of learned reflexes, since the *novelty* of the situations and of the responsive bodily movements that occur in tennis play, cannot be accounted for in this way. Bartlett's theory was that all of the past training, actions, and reactions, in playing tennis, combine to form 'an active, organized setting' (a 'Schema'), which directs the bodily movements of subsequent play. Skill in driving a car would involve a different Schema; skill in playing the piano still another Schema; and so on. In tennis play each 'new sensory impulse' joins up with the already present tennis Schema. Bartlett says:

> What, precisely, does the 'schema' do? Together with the immediately preceding impulse it renders a specific adaptive reaction possible. It is, therefore, producing an orientation of the organism towards whatever it is directed to at the moment.[8]

Bartlett's solution gives rise to puzzling questions. In the first place, every normal person has a large number of skills, and therefore a large number of Schemata. Also, there will presumably be, at any moment, a large number of different 'sensory impulses'. Now how does an incoming sensory impulse manage to join up with the *right* Schema? Does the

8. F. C. Bartlett, *Remembering* (London: Cambridge University Press, 1932), pp. 207–8.

impulse *know* which Schema to attach to? Or does a Schema *know* which impulses belong to it? In the second place, how does a Schema succeed in producing an appropriate 'orientation of the organism'? How does the tennis Schema manage to produce the right postures and movements? Does the theory 'explain' skillful play by postulating a skillful Schema? Or are the skilled responses of a Schema to be accounted for by proposing a second-order Schema that directs the responses of the first one? Does the very ability or skill that was to be explained have to be invoked at another level? I offer this as an example of the threat of circularity, or of infinite regress, that confronts cognitive and functionalist theories.

The proponents of structural-functionalism are alert to this danger. They are aware that a large part of human behavior is described in ordinary life by what they call 'intentional' (or 'intensional') descriptions—that is, descriptions that imply something about what the behavior *meant*, or what the person's intention, goal, aim, or purpose was. At the beginning of their attempt to explain intentional behavior, the functionalists may postulate subsystems that are themselves characterized in intentional terms. Because of their commitment to physicalism, however, they realize that they cannot stop there. Their conception is that the functional analysis will continue downward. The operation of the subsystems that have been characterized in intentional language will in turn be subjected to functional analysis. The hope is that finally the course of explanation will terminate at 'the micro-level', where there are only chemical processes or the firings of neurons, and where (as Wilkes put it) 'we find no intentionality at all' (*Physicalism*, 65). The functionalist methodology does not seek to *translate* intentional descriptions into extensional descriptions. What it does hold is that at the end, when the functional analysis is completed, intentionality will have 'vanished' (*ibid.*, 66).

In his book *Content and Consciousness*, Dennett says:

There should be possible some scientific story about synapses, electrical potentials and so forth that would explain, describe and predict all that goes on in the nervous system. If we had such a story we would have in one sense an extensional theory of behaviour, for all the motions (extensionally characterized) of the animal caused by the activity of the nervous system would be explicable and predictable in these extensional terms, but one thing such a story would say nothing about was *what the animal was doing*. This latter story can only be told in Intentional terms, but it is not a story about features of the world *in addition to* the features of the extensional story; it just describes what happens in a different way.[9]

Dennett seems here to have the idea that the two modes of description, intentional and extensional, are describing *the same thing*. As he puts it, both are describing *what happens*; they only describe it 'in different ways'. A similar thought seems to be expressed in another of Dennett's comments. Having remarked that there is a 'lack of theoretically reliable *overt* behavioural clues for the ascription of Intentional expressions', Dennett goes on to say that

> this leaves room for *covert*, internal events serving as the conditions of ascription. We do not ordinarily have access to such data, so they could not serve as ordinary criteria for the use of ordinary Intentional expressions, but this is just a corollary of the thesis that our ordinary language accounts of behaviour are Intentional, and says nothing about the possibility in principle of producing a scientific reduction of internal states. Could there be a system of internal states or events, the extensional description of which could be upgraded into an Intentional description? (*Ibid.*, 39–40)

Dennett is inclined to think that the answer is, yes. In speaking of the 'reduction' of Intentional expressions to extensional expressions Dennett did not, I think, wish to say that correlated expressions in the two modes of description have the same meaning, but instead that they equally describe *what happens*, and further that the extensional description of internal physiological states and events is theoretically more reliable, and also more fundamental, than is the Intentional mode of description.

What are we to think of the program of structural-functionalism? How would it apply, for example, to human speech? People say things in conversation and sometimes their remarks are witty, ironic, sarcastic, boring, superficial, acute, angry, insensitive, rude, tender, and so on. Suppose that Mr. A had made an engagement to meet Mrs. A at a certain time in a downtown store. Mrs. A is on time but Mr. A is twenty minutes late. When he finally does arrive Mrs. A says, with irritation, 'Why have you

9. Dennett, *Content and Consciousness* (New York: Humanities Press, 1969), p. 78.

kept me waiting?'. Mr. A responds sarcastically, 'Are you always on time?'
Let us suppose that there is a structural-functional analysis of oral
speech-behavior. At the first stage there is a psychological theory that di-
vides up oral speech, we may imagine, into components such as pitch,
stress, speed, volume, intonation, resonance, and so on. These would be
aspects or functions of vocalization. The second stage would be the attempt to locate physical parts of or physical processes in the organism
which control pitch, stress, speed of utterance, and so on. We may suppose that this physiological investigation is successful. Not only is the
process in speech musculature that controls pitch, for example, picked
out, but further the neural subsystem that controls this musculature is
identified. This would be excellent progress. A psychological theory has
divided utterances into certain aspects, dimensions, or functions; and
then neurophysiological investigation has discovered the neural subsystems and associated musculature that control those functions.

So far, so good. But there is more to be done. A complete functional analysis of speech-behavior will want to take into account not
merely the physical dimensions of utterances (pitch, speed, stress,
etc.), but also the 'psychological' dimensions, such as sarcasm, wit,
rudeness, superficiality, and so on. Mr. A's retort was delivered not
only with a certain pitch and with a certain pattern of stress (e.g., 'Are
you always on time?'), but his utterance was also *sarcastic.* Suppose that
the psychologist speaks to the neurophysiologist in the following way:
'Sir, you have done splendid work in locating the neural processes
that control pitch and stress. Can you now do the same for sarcasm?'.
What should one think of this request? Is an intelligible undertaking
presented here to the neurophysiologist? If there is a neural subsystem (a 'structural realization') for the pitch of utterances, might
there also be a neural subsystem for the sarcasm of utterances—a sarcastic subsystem?

   Mr. A's utterance ('Are you always on time?') could of course be produced in circumstances in which it was not sarcastic. For example, Mr.
A has a colleague, Mr. X. To Mr. A it appears that Mr. X is habitually
punctual in keeping engagements. Mr. A finds this astonishing and impressive. One day he says to Mr. X, with admiration, 'Are you always on
time?' Here is the same sequence of words, delivered with the same
pitch, stress, and intonation. But when this utterance was delivered to
Mrs. A it was sarcastic, when delivered to Mr. X it was admiring. Could
this difference be assigned to different neurophysiological subsystems?

When Mr. A delivered his retort to Mrs. A, he might have produced a different sequence of words, e.g. 'I suppose you are never late?'. Presumably there would be some differences in the neurophysiological processes that produced the two different vocal sequences. But the two utterances would be equally sarcastic. Could there be a cerebral process that was correlated with *just* the sarcasm?

Wilkes says that the functionalism she espouses is committed to physicalism, and (as already noted) she describes physicalism as 'the attempt to correlate explanations of actions couched in psychological terms with descriptions and explanations of cerebral states, events, and processes couched in neurophysiological terms' (*Physicalism*, 29). Dennett says that 'functionalist theories' are theories of 'the sub-personal level'. He says further that 'sub-personal theories proceed by analysing a person into an organization of sub-systems . . . and attempting to explain the behaviour of the whole person as the outcome of the interaction of these sub-systems' (*Brainstorms*, 153).

Now Mr. A's sarcastic retort to Mrs. A. was a piece of behavior of 'the whole person' Mr. A. Both Wilkes and Dennett conceive of Mr. A as an organization of subsystems, and both of them presumably think that the functionalism they favor would attempt to explain the behavior of uttering a sarcasm as the result of the interaction of some of those subsystems. I am ready to acknowledge that there may be subsystems for pitch or stress, but not that there may be a subsystem for sarcasm.

The characterization of an utterance as sarcastic would be called by both Wilkes and Dennett an 'intentional description'. The aim of functionalism is to correlate intentional descriptions of behavior with extensional descriptions stated in the language of neurophysiology. The characterization of a remark as sarcastic is, of course, a description of ordinary language. And Wilkes declares that the project of physicalism (and therefore of functionalism) has 'nothing to do' with the descriptions of ordinary language (*ibid.*, 41). Functionalism does not seek to correlate the intentional terms of ordinary language with neurophysiological terms; the correlation it seeks is between the terms and descriptions of some *theory* of scientific psychology, and the terms and descriptions of neurophysiology.

Would the term 'sarcasm' be included in the conceptual apparatus of a psychological theory? Who knows? There might be a psychological theory that proposed an 'analysis' of the term 'sarcasm' into other terms; so the term 'sarcasm' would not belong to its basic conceptual apparatus. Whether any such analysis was correct or even intelligible could not be determined until it was laid before us.

Anyway, Wilkes does hold that 'whatever the detailed content of the conceptual apparatus employed by a psychological theory may prove to be, we must find there some intensional terms' (*ibid.*, 44). The idea, I think, is that intentional descriptions are required to characterize the *meaning* of behavior. Dennett expresses the same idea in saying that a description of events in the nervous system could account for the *motions* that a person made but not for *what the person was doing*. 'This latter story can only be told in Intentional terms' (*Content and Consciousness*, 78). So the descriptions of a psychological theory, since the theory is concerned with the meaning of behavior, will have to contain some intentional terms or other, but the neurophysiological explanations of 'motions' will contain no intentional terms.

What I find surprising is that the friends of structural-functional analysis believe, or hope, that this impasse can be overcome. They think that an extensional description of internal, neurophysiological, states, and events can be *upgraded*, as Dennett puts it, into an Intentional description (*ibid.*, 40). But how could this possibly be? The 'motions' can be exactly the same but the *meaning* different. On two occasions Mr. A made the same utterance. The physical dimensions, such as pitch, stress, and speed of utterance, could have been the same. Yet the meaning of the utterance was different on the two occasions. Once it was sarcastic; once it was admiring. How could a neurophysiological account of chemical changes at synapses, electrical potentials, and so on, be 'upgraded' into an explanation of how this utterance was sarcastic on one occasion and admiring on another? It would be unsatisfactory for the functionalists to object that the terms 'sarcastic' and 'admiring' will probably not belong to 'the conceptual apparatus' of a psychological theory. For, first, the functionalists concede that if those particular terms do not belong to the apparatus, some other intentional terms will: and so the same difficulty will present itself with those latter intentional terms, whatever they are. Second, Wilkes admits that when interesting and true descriptions of human behavior occur at the level of ordinary language, 'these must become part of the subject matter of psychology, a part it can reasonably be challenged to explain' (*Physicalism*, 47). So it would seem that structural-functionalism cannot be indifferent to the interesting fact that an utterance can have a striking difference in meaning on two occurrences, although having identical physical properties. And structural-functionalism can be 'reasonably challenged' to explain how the differences in the meaning of the utterance could be accounted for by some story about neural firings or electrical potentials.

My own belief is that the proponents of structural-functionalism have set themselves a problem that cannot be solved. There is no way in which neurophysiological descriptions can be 'upgraded' into explanations of meaning. That is simply looking in the wrong place. One understands that Mr. A's utterance to his wife was sarcastic, and why it was sarcastic, by knowing or surmising something of the previous course of their lives together. Probably Mrs. A had herself been late for engagements with Mr. A on several past occasions, and probably this had produced some irritation in Mr. A, consciously or unconsciously. So when on this occasion she rebukes him for being late, this evokes from him a response the meaning of which is easily understood in terms of that known or surmised background. This understanding, this explanation, of Mr. A's behavior, does not in any way relate that behavior to neural processes or structures.

The functionalists concede that understanding of this sort can be valuable at the level of ordinary language and thought. But they want something better; more scientific. What would this better explanation lay hold of? Well, it would lay hold of the actual processes in the physical organism which cause behavior. When Mr. A came out with his sarcastic retort, he had almost certainly not reviewed in his mind Mrs. A's past tardiness and his own past irritations. But the structural-functionalists believe that a record of her tardiness and his irritations must have been 'stored' in his nervous system. Mr. A did not consciously think of those past incidents and feelings; nor did he consciously conclude that a sarcastic rejoinder would be appropriate. No: he just came out with the sarcasm, 'spontaneously' (as we say). But a complete, scientific explanation of the production of that behavior would say how that knowledge of the past was 'stored' in Mr. A's brain, how it was brought out of storage into the 'operational area', and how his actual response was 'selected' from innumerable other possible responses.

Dennett neatly expresses this functionalist view when he says: 'We do many things without thinking about them, but surely we do not do these things without the brain's controlling them?' (*Content and Consciousness*, 123). This remark illustrates the impasse from which functionalism cannot escape. For *what* does the brain 'control'? Does it control merely the physical dimensions of behavioral output? Or does it also control the meaning of behavior? Mr. A might have made an apologetic response to his wife instead of a sarcastic one. Did Mr. A's *brain* choose a sarcastic reply in preference to an apologetic one? To talk in this way would be to apply an intentional description to the brain. Functionalism does not mind doing this *provisionally*. But it holds that when the functional analysis is *completed*, intentional description will have 'vanished'. Would not this imply, however, that functionalism's attempt to explain the meaning of human behavior will also have vanished?

Structural-functionalism is engaged in the amusing game of thumb-catching. The thumb is behavior at the intentional level; behavior that is meaningful and not just 'motions'. The catching-movement consists of neurophysiological descriptions and explanations. But neurophysiology cannot capture that thumb.

4

Kripke on Heat and
Sensations of Heat

One of many topics to which Professor Saul Kripke addresses himself in his immensely interesting lectures, entitled 'Identity and Necessity' and 'Naming and Necessity', is the topic of 'natural kinds'. The expression 'natural kinds' seems to be a technical one. I take it to refer to kinds of things that are found in nature. Some of the examples that Kripke gives of natural kinds are tigers, cats, whales, gold, water, and heat. One thesis of Kripke's is that natural kinds are 'originally identified' by human beings in terms of certain external marks and properties, but that scientific investigation may reveal that none of the properties by which we 'originally identified' a natural kind are essential properties of things of that kind. For example, tigers were originally identified by the properties of being large, feline, carnivorous animals, tawny yellow in color, with black stripes and white belly. But a scientific investigation of the 'internal structure' of tigers might have proved that something could have all of the 'external appearances' of a tiger and yet not be a tiger because it doesn't have the right 'internal structure'. According to Kripke we might even find out, or have found out, that 'tigers had *none* of the properties by which we originally identified them'.[1]

This contention seems to me to be exceedingly strange. My topic, however, will not be tigers. I am going to devote this paper to a consid-

---

1. Saul Kripke, 'Naming and Necessity', in *Semantics of Natural Language*, ed. D. Davidson and G. Harman (Boston: Reidel, 1972), p. 318. Hereafter this work will be cited in the text by the abbreviation '*N&N*', followed by page reference.

eration of what Kripke says about another of his examples of a natural kind, namely, the phenomenon of *heat*. Kripke asserts that heat is *identical* with the rapid motion of molecules. He asserts further that this supposed identity is a *necessary* identity. But a contention of his that I will mostly dwell on, and which I find puzzling, is the contention that it is a *contingent* property of heat that it produces in human beings a certain sensation that is called 'the sensation of heat'. In 'Naming and Necessity' Kripke says the following:

> Heat is something which we have identified, and picked out the reference of, by its giving a certain sensation, which we call the sensation of heat. We don't have a special name for this sensation other than as a sensation of heat. It's interesting that the language is this way. (*N&N*, p. 325)

> There is a certain referent which we have fixed, for the real world and for all possible worlds, by a contingent property of it, namely the property that it's able to produce such and such sensations in us. Let's say it's a contingent property of heat that it produces such and such sensations in people. . . . We've discovered eventually that this phenomenon is in fact molecular motion. When we have discovered this we've discovered an identification which gives us an essential property of this phenomenon. We have discovered a phenomenon which in all possible worlds will be molecular motion— which could not have failed to be molecular motion, because that's what the phenomenon *is*. On the other hand, the property by which we identify it originally, that of producing such and such a sensation in us, is not a necessary property but a contingent one. This very phenomenon could have existed, but due to differences in our neural structures and so on, have failed to be felt as heat. (*N&N*, p. 326)

In his lecture 'Identity and Necessity', Kripke puts forward this same view that heat has the contingent property of producing in human beings 'sensations of heat':

> We have identified the heat by the contingent fact that there happen to be creatures on this planet—(namely, ourselves) who are sensitive to it in a certain way, that is, who are sensitive to the action of molecules or to heat—these are one and the same thing. And this is contingent. So we use the description, "that which causes such and such

sensations, or that which we sense in such and such a way," to identify heat. But in using this fact we use a contingent property of heat.[2]

> We pick out heat contingently by the contingent property that it affects us in such and such a way. (*I&N*, p. 161)

Kripke dramatizes the supposed contingency of the relation between heat and 'sensations of heat' by imagining creatures who do *not* have 'sensations of heat' when exposed to heat.

> Imagine right now the world invaded by a number of Martians, who do indeed get the very sensation that we call "the sensation of heat" when they feel some ice which has slow molecular motion, and who do not get a sensation of heat—in fact, maybe just the reverse—when they put their hand near a fire which causes a lot of molecular agitation. Would we say, "Ah, this casts some doubt on heat being the motion of molecules, because there are these other people who don't get the same sensation"? Obviously not, and no one would think so. We would say instead that the Martians somehow feel the very sensation we get when we feel heat when they feel cold and that they do not get a sensation of heat when they feel heat. (*I&N*, p. 159)

Even more dramatically, Kripke imagines that the first human-like beings to inhabit the earth might have been more like Martians than like us:

> Let us suppose the laws of physics were not very different: Fires do heat up the air. Then there would have been heat even though there were no creatures around to feel it. Now let us suppose evolution takes place, and life is created, and there are some creatures around. But they are not like us, they are more like the Martians. Now would we say that heat has suddenly turned to cold, because of the way the creatures of this planet sense it? No, I think we should describe this situation as a situation in which, though the creatures on this planet got our sensation of heat, they did not get it when they were exposed to heat. They got it when they were exposed to cold. (*I&N*, p. 159).

---

2. Kripke, 'Identity and Necessity', in *Identity and Individuation*, ed. M. K. Munitz (New York: New York University Press, 1971), p. 160. Hereafter this work will be cited in the text by the abbreviation '*I&N*', followed by page reference.

This suggestion seems to me to contain the surprising implication that we ourselves may be constituted like those imaginary Martians. Perhaps the external phenomenon that produces in us 'sensations of heat' is actually cold, and the external phenomenon that produces in us 'sensations of cold' is actually heat. According to Kripke, mankind originally identified an external phenomenon as 'heat' by virtue of the fact that it had the contingent property of producing in them 'sensations of heat'. But if all of mankind is constituted like the Martians, then mankind made a gross mistake. For the external phenomenon was actually cold, not heat. And then the human science of physics compounded that mistake by discovering that the external phenomenon that produced 'sensations of heat' was the rapid motion of molecules. The physicists concluded that *heat* is identical with rapid molecular motion. But it actually was, and is, *cold* that is identical with rapid molecular motion. What a blunder!

It seems to me that a source of confusion here is the way in which Kripke uses the expression 'sensations of heat'. He says:

> When I refer to heat, I refer not to an internal sensation that someone may have, but to an external phenomenon which we perceive through the sense of feeling; it produces a characteristic sensation which we call the sensation of heat. (*N&N*, p. 323)

Now I am in perfect agreement with Kripke on one part of this remark. Like Kripke I do not refer to a *sensation* when I refer to *heat*. I have frequently encountered hot water, and also a lot of hot air. I have felt the heat of the water and the heat of the air. The water and the air could have been hot whether or not I or anyone else felt its heat. I have placed my hand on a wall and have felt that the wall was hot—that is, I felt with my hand the heat of the wall. Of course the heat of the wall was not a sensation; it was a property of the wall, and walls do not have sensations. The heat of the wall was, in Kripke's phrase, 'an external phenomenon'.

But I think there is something puzzling in Kripke's use of the words 'the sensation of heat'. He speaks of it as an 'internal sensation' and as a 'sensation *in us*'. He says that when we are exposed to the external phenomenon of heat it produces sensations of heat in us. This, however, is ambiguous. There is a distinction in language between *feeling heat* and *feeling hot*. In saying that the external phenomenon of heat produces 'sensations of heat in us', does Kripke mean that we feel heat or that we feel hot? The truth is that if on a cold day I approach a fire I will feel the heat of the fire but I may not feel hot at all. The heat of the fire is something that I perceived by feeling it. The heat is there, and was there before I perceived it, and would have been there if no one had perceived it. Its existence does not depend on sensation or perception. One could put it like this: the object of perception, the heat of the fire, is 'external' to the perception. But *feeling hot* is something else. When I feel hot, one could say that what I feel is 'internal' to my sensation or perception. *This* heat that I feel does not exist when I don't feel hot. It sometimes happens in illness that a person whose body feels hot to someone else's touch, and who has a high temperature as measured by a thermometer, does not *feel hot* but instead *feels cold*.

As I have indicated, it is not clear to me what Kripke means by his expression 'the sensation of heat'. Does he mean feeling heat or feeling hot? That is, does he mean a sensation whose object is 'external' to the sensation, or a sensation whose object is 'internal' to the sensation? Of his imaginary Martians he says something quite puzzling, namely, 'that they do not get a sensation of heat when they feel heat' (*I&N*, p. 159). Does this mean that the Martians don't feel hot when they feel heat? This might not be anything terribly remarkable; for we human beings often don't feel hot when we feel heat. Or does Kripke mean something which looks contradictory, namely, that the Martians don't feel heat when they feel heat? More probably, what he means is that when Martians draw near to a hot fire, say, they do not feel the heat of the fire.

All of this is connected with Kripke's contention that it is a 'contingent' property of heat that it produces in people 'sensations of heat'. His employment of the word 'contingent' here raises problems. According to him, the property of heat that it produces or can produce in us 'sensations of heat', is 'contingent' to a very high degree. Could it be contingent to such a degree that heat might never have produced in people 'sensations of heat'?

I think that Kripke does not want to go that far, for he says at one place that 'it might be part of the very nature of human beings that they have the neural structure which is sensitive to heat' (*N&N*, p. 326). Let us try to get clearer about this. Leaving aside speculations about 'neural structure', it is certainly true that nearly every human being often has 'sensations of heat' in both of the senses that we have distinguished.

Nearly every human being sometimes feels heat and sometimes feels hot. It may be, for all I know, that there are a few human beings who are not capable of having 'sensations of heat' at all, or at least for certain periods. Just as there actually are some human beings who are incapable of feeling pain. Of course they are highly *abnormal*. And human beings who were incapable of 'sensations of heat' would be equally abnormal. I think it is safe to say that it is part of the nature of a normal human being to be capable of 'sensations of heat', as well as to have sight and hearing. This is a truth about the concept of a normal human being. It is not a contingent fact.

So in what respects is it a 'contingent' property of heat that it is able to produce in human beings 'sensations of heat'? First, as Kripke says, it could have been that there were no human beings. Second, it seems to be some kind of nonsense to suppose that there might have been human beings in the world, none of whom were *normal* human beings, that is, none of whom had, for example, sight or hearing or 'sensations of heat'—although it might have been that the world was inhabited solely by creatures who were like human beings in some important respects. Third, since human beings do exist, and have existed for thousands of years, it is not at all a 'contingent' property of heat that it should produce in them 'sensations of heat'. It is not a contingent matter that when normal human beings are exposed to the heat of fires or of sunlight, they should normally feel the heat and also should sometimes feel hot.

It seems to me that Kripke presents a queer picture of how human beings 'originally identified' heat. He says that 'we' originally identified it as something that produced in us 'a certain sensation' that 'we call the sensation of heat' (*N&N*, p. 325). He says: 'So we use the description, "that which causes such and such sensations, or that which we sense in such and such a way," to identify heat. But in using this fact we use a contingent property of heat' (*I&N*, p. 160). We use that description to originally identify heat, but that description does not give an account of what the word 'heat' means. Kripke says:

> Nevertheless, the term "heat" doesn't *mean* "whatever gives people these sensations." For first, people might not have been sensitive to heat, and yet the heat still have existed in the external world. Secondly, let us suppose that somehow light rays, because of some difference in their nerve endings, *did* give them these sensations. It

would not then be heat but light which gave people the sensation which we call the sensation of heat. (*N&N*, p. 325)

Who is the 'we' that is supposed to have originally identified heat in the way described by Kripke? I am sure that none of the people presently in this room did it. I am sure that I, for example, never did pick out 'a certain sensation' and then went on to 'identify' heat as that which produces that sensation in me. When would I have done this?

What is more likely is that I grew up in a community of people who already had the present common use of the words 'heat', 'hot', 'not so hot', 'warm', 'warmer', 'cold', 'colder', and so on. I gradually learned from them that whole system of words. Perhaps I was warned not to get into the bath water yet 'Because it's too hot', and then later was told that I could get into it now 'Because it's cooler'. Undoubtedly I learned to make correct comparative judgments of heat and cold, such as 'This rock is hotter than that one', or 'This one was hot and now it's cold'. Probably I made some mistakes in applying the words and was corrected by the adults who were around. But eventually my discriminations of hot and cold, hotter and colder, came into agreement with those of the grown-up speakers.

Now someone might want to say, 'Surely you could not have achieved this unless you had had sensations of heat and sensations of cold!' Well, that is true if it means that I would not have learned to make correct judgments of heat and cold if I had not been able to feel the heat and the cold of things around me. In this sense of the words 'a sensation of heat', to have a sensation of heat just is to feel the heat of something, such as the air in a room, or sunlight, or a rock, or a stove. A sensation of heat, in this sense, just is the perception of an external phenomenon, namely, heat. When we have sensations of heat, in this sense, we are perceiving heat itself, and not inferring or conjecturing the presence of some unknown thing that causes 'sensations of heat in us'; just as when we see the trees themselves and do not infer their existence from the occurrence of 'sensations of sight'.

Thus, it is quite impossible that the thing we perceive when we have 'sensations of heat' could have turned out to be light or sound. Long before anything was known about the rapid motion of molecules, the name 'heat' was given to that external phenomenon which is directly perceived, which can be comforting or painful, which also boils water and cooks meat. It would be absurd to think that people did not know what heat was until science discovered a correlation between heat and the rapid motion of molecules.

A remark repeated by Kripke again and again is that heat is *identical* with rapid molecular motion. I find this a puzzling assertion. It looks more like a metaphysical proposition than a scientific one. I don't doubt that as the water in a pan becomes hotter the motion of the water molecules increases in rapidity, and as the water cools the rapidity of the molecular motion decreases. Although science could establish this correlation, how could it establish that heat is *identical* with rapid molecular motion? Actually, I don't even understand the assertion either that heat is, or that it is not, 'identical' with rapid molecular motion. Or rather, I think I do understand it if 'identity' here just means the same as 'correlation'. But if 'identity' is supposed to mean something that is *in addition to* correlation, then I am completely puzzled as to what sort of scientific observation could determine either that heat is, or that it is not, identical with rapid molecular motion. Therefore, I doubt whether it is meaningful to say either that this supposed identity holds or that it doesn't hold; and, *a fortiori*, I doubt that it is meaningful to say that it holds *necessarily*.[3]

My main concern, however, is not with this identity claim, since I know nothing about the scientific work that Kripke believes to have

---

3. Kripke is presumably talking about the derivation of the Boyle-Charles's law from the kinetic theory of gases. Ernest Nagel, in his *The Structure of Science* (New York: Harcourt, Brace, and World, 1961), chap. 11, provides a careful treatment of this example of scientific development. Nagel's interpretation of the matter seems to be different from Kripke's. Nagel nowhere says that what was established was that the temperature of a gas is *identical* with the mean kinetic energy of the gas molecules. On the contrary, Nagel says that the deduction of the Boyle-Charles's law from the kinetic theory of gases 'depends on the additional postulate that the temperature of a gas is proportional to the mean kinetic energy of its molecules' (*ibid.*, p. 355). Nagel says further: 'As was noted in discussing the reduction of thermodynamics to mechanics, the Boyle-Charles' law cannot be deduced from the assumptions of statistical mechanics unless a postulate is added relating the term "temperature" to the expression "mean kinetic energy of molecules". This postulate cannot itself be deduced from statistical mechanics in its classical form' (p. 372). The postulate 'must be added to statistical mechanics as an independent assumption if the gas law is to be deduced' (*ibid.*).

To say that the derivation of the gas law from statistical mechanics required the additional postulate that the temperature of a gas is proportional to the mean kinetic energy of its molecules would appear to be quite different from saying that it was discovered that the temperature of a gas is *identical* with the mean kinetic energy of its molecules. I only know what I read and am not competent to assess Nagel's interpretation. I merely find it interesting that an informed philosopher of science presents an account of this scientific achievement that apparently differs considerably from Kripke's.

proved this supposed identity. I am concerned with Kripke's contention that prior to a certain scientific discovery, mankind 'identified heat' as something that has the 'contingent' property of producing in people 'sensations of heat'. I have already said that this is wrong: it is not a contingent fact that normal people normally perceive heat *as* heat, when exposed to it.

Let us return to Kripke's Martians, who are supposed to have our 'sensations of heat' when exposed to cold and our 'sensations of cold' when exposed to heat (*I&N*, p. 159). I doubt that this is a coherent description. Previously we distinguished two different meanings of the expression 'a sensation of heat'. In the first meaning, 'a sensation of heat' just is the perception of the external phenomenon of heat, for example, the heat of hot air, or the heat of a fire. On Kripke's own account the Martians do not have 'sensations of heat' in this sense. They do not feel the heat of a fire. In this same sense they do not have 'sensations of cold', for, on Kripke's account, they do not feel the coldness of ice or of the frigid air.

In what sense, then, do the Martians have 'sensations of heat' and 'sensations of cold'? What about 'sensations of heat' in the sense of feeling hot, where the heat that one feels is 'internal' to the sensation? Similarly, there is a sense of the expression 'sensation of cold', or of 'feeling cold', where the cold that one feels is 'internal' to the feeling. The most that one could attribute to the Martians is feeling hot and feeling cold, in this sense.

What sort of behavior on the part of the Martians would justify us in attributing to them 'sensations of heat and cold' in this sense? Are we to imagine that when they enter a hot room or stand near a hot fire they begin to massage themselves and to put on more clothing? But this would be unsuitable behavior for the Martians. Massaging one's body and donning more clothing is warming because it increases the heat of the body. If the Martians adopted those measures they would show themselves to be sensitive to heat as heat, which they are not supposed to be. This description of the Martians would seem to be contradictory. On the one hand, they are not sensitive to heat as such; on the other hand, they are sensitive to and grateful for the increase of bodily heat produced by putting on more clothing.

Similarly, when the Martians come into a freezing room we are to imagine that they begin to feel hot. What will their behavior be? Will they remove some of their clothing? No, for this would indicate that they were sensitive to the decrease of bodily heat that is produced in this way. Would they take a cold shower? No, for this would indicate that they felt and enjoyed the coldness of the water. But, by hypothesis, they are not supposed to feel the coldness of cold air or water. What possible behavioral reaction of the Martians to the freezing air of the room would show that they felt hot, but at the same time would be compatible with the hypothesis that they do not perceive the cold of cold air or of cold water or of ice, or of anything else that is cold?

Although it was right to distinguish feeling heat from feeling hot there is a conceptual connection between them, which presents itself when we think through these examples. If the Martians really do feel hot, then we have a right to expect that they will take measures to cool themselves. If one feels hot, exposing oneself to still greater heat cannot be called cooling oneself. Similarly, if the Martians really feel cold we have a right to expect that they will take measures to warm themselves. And if one feels cold, exposing oneself to greater cold cannot be called warming oneself. In thinking through Kripke's examples we have to give our language its ordinary use; otherwise we will end up just babbling.

What Kripke's hypothesis does is to cut the conceptual connection between a sensation and the natural expression of that sensation in behavior. To do this is to cease to employ the concept of that sensation. If one feels hot, a part of the normal behavioral expression of that sensation is trying to cool oneself. A Martian who is supposed to feel hot cannot try to cool himself by exposing himself to greater heat, for this isn't trying to cool oneself. Nor can he try to do it by exposing himself to cold air or cold water, for by hypothesis the Martian is not capable of perceiving the coldness of things. The same holds, *mutatis mutandis*, if the Martian is supposed to feel cold.

It seems that the only remaining manifestation of the sensations of feeling hot or of feeling cold that is available to the Martians is for them to utter the words 'I feel hot' or 'I feel cold'. But the behavior of the Martians is so abnormal that they could not be credited with an understanding of those words. Thus the Martians would be unable to provide any manifestation of their having sensations of heat or cold, in either sense of those terms, either in linguistic or in nonlinguistic behavior. Indeed, their behavior would be so bizarre that we could not apply that language to them.

I conclude that Kripke's description of the Martians is not coherent. It certainly is not enough just to *say* that *they* have 'sensations of heat' where *we* have 'sensations of cold', and vice versa. Nor is calling them 'Martians' a stroke of magic that makes everything all right. Kripke's description of the Martians seems exciting until one tries to work it out in detail, whereupon it collapses.

I have confined myself to Kripke's remarks about heat. As for tigers, I have only a modest acquaintance with them; but I will venture to say that it is impossible, in every sense of the word, that scientists might have discovered that tigers had *none* of the properties by which people normally identify tigers. I am quite familiar with household cats, and am prepared to hazard that it is equally impossible that 'cats might turn out to be automata, or strange demons' (*N&N*, p. 318). Since these examples are intended to illustrate Kripke's theory of the mode of 'reference' that characterizes names of natural kinds, the fact that the examples are pretty preposterous entitles us to be doubtful of the correctness of Kripke's theory.

5

Kripke and the Standard Meter

1

In his lectures entitled 'Naming and Necessity'[1] Professor Saul Kripke puts forward some original and interesting ideas about contingency, necessity, naming, designation, reference, and meaning. He illustrates his themes with various examples. In a previous paper I studied his example of *heat*.[2] In the present essay I will consider his remarks about *the standard meter*.

In his lectures Kripke focuses on a remark that Wittgenstein makes about the standard meter. Wittgenstein says:

> There is *one* thing of which one can say neither that it is one meter long, nor that it is not one meter long, and that is the standard meter in Paris.—But this is, of course, not to ascribe any extraordinary property to it, but only to mark its peculiar role in the language-game of measuring with a meter-rule.[3]

In response to this Kripke says: 'This seems to be a very "extraordinary property", actually, for any stick to have. I think he must be wrong' (p. 274).

1. Saul Kripke, 'Naming and Necessity', in *Semantics of Natural Language*, ed. D. Davidson and G. Harman (Boston: D. Reidel, 1972). Page number references are given in parentheses in the text.
2. Norman Malcolm, 'Kripke on Heat and Sensations of Heat', Chapter 4 in this volume.
3. Ludwig Wittgenstein, *Philosophical Investigations*, ed. G. E. M. Anscombe and Rush Rhees, trans. G. E. M. Anscombe (Oxford: Blackwell, 1967), 50.

I know scarcely anything about the standard meter in Paris. I have not used it to measure anything, and I know of no one who has. Furthermore, I know nothing about the actual history of the creation of the metric system.

It is easy to imagine, however, that the history was something like the following: Let us suppose that at one time there were different units of length employed in different countries and even within the same country. People in science and industry found this state of affairs increasingly inconvenient. An international committee studied the matter and recommended the establishing of a new system of measurement that would be employed throughout the world. This recommendation was accepted by many countries. The committee was empowered to create a new system, which it proceeded to do. It decided that the basic unit of length of this system was to be called 'one meter', and it designated a particular rod, to be kept in Paris, as the standard meter or *Urmeter*. Each country that was a party to the agreement took for itself a rod that coincided in length with the Urmeter. Then in each country a number of rods were produced equal in length to the national meter rod of that country; in comparison with these still others were made, and so on, until in each country there were thousands of rods and sticks of different materials, used as meter-rules. In the process of manufacturing meter-rules in the various countries some discrepancies might occur and, consequently, some disagreements in metrical measurements. The international agreement provided that if and when such disagreements occurred, uniformity would be restored by comparing various meter rods with the Urmeter, the original meter in Paris. This would be the final authority, the court of last resort.

In the institution of the metric system, as here imagined, the Urmeter has a unique role. It serves solely as an object for comparison. Other objects are measured against it; it is not measured against anything.

We can imagine a complication that might arise. Suppose that the material of which the Urmeter was composed was highly sensitive to fluctuations of temperature and so frequently contracted or expanded. Consequently there began to be discrepancies in metric measurements throughout the world. The international committee on standards of measurement decided to designate a rod of less sensitive material as the new Urmeter. When the rod that had formerly been the Urmeter was compared with the new Urmeter, it was found to measure sometimes less than one meter, sometimes more, depending on temperature.

Although we can imagine such a state of affairs, we can also imagine that it did not occur. We can suppose that when the metric system was brought into being, the Urmeter was made out of a material known to be relatively uninfluenced by moderate changes of temperature. The Urmeter might even have been placed in a vault that was kept at a constant temperature. No troublesome discrepancies in metric measurements in science or industry were noted. The Urmeter continued to reign as the single, final standard of metric length. It remained as a stable, enduring object with which other things could be compared—which was the point of creating the Urmeter.

Let us suppose that this latter state of affairs is the actual one. Can one *say* that the Urmeter is one meter in length? Well, there might be someone who had heard that *a* standard unit of length was kept in Paris, but didn't know which unit of length it was. He might ask: 'Is the standard unit of length in Paris a yard long or a meter long?'. Another person could say to him: 'It is one meter long'. In those circumstances that would be an informative remark.

But anyone who understands the institution of metric measurement will realize that one cannot say that the Urmeter has been *determined by measurement* to be one meter in length. By 'one cannot say this' I mean that it is nonsense. In that institution, in that 'language-game', there is not such a thing as *measuring* the Urmeter. When Wittgenstein said that 'there is *one* thing of which one can say neither that it is one meter long, nor that it is not one meter long, and that is the standard meter in Paris', I am pretty sure that the foregoing is what he meant. If this is so, and if Kripke thinks Wittgenstein is wrong about *that*, then Kripke is the one who is wrong.

2

Let us consider some of the things that Kripke says about the Urmeter. He designates it by the letter 'S'. He raises the question of whether the statement 'Stick *S* is one meter long' is 'a necessary truth' (p. 274). It isn't very clear what Kripke means by this question. It is obvious that some rod other than *S* could have been chosen to be the Urmeter—a rod of different material or one that was shorter or longer than *S*. The chairman of the international committee might have arbitrarily picked up a rod from a pile of rods of different lengths and have said, 'Let's choose this rod as the Urmeter', and the other members might have agreed. Whether or not it happened like that, it is plainly a contingent matter that *that* particular rod or stick, *S*, was designated as the Urmeter.

But this obvious point is not what Kripke has in mind. What he does say is puzzling. He says that when the length of stick *S* was stipulated to be 'one meter', this definition did not *give the meaning* of 'one meter' but instead *fixed the reference* of 'one meter'. The meaning of this distinction is certainly not transparent. Kripke says the following of a man who uses as the definition of 'one meter', 'One meter is the length of stick *S*': 'He uses it to fix a reference. There is a certain length which he wants to mark out. He marks it out by an accidental property, namely that there is a stick of that length' (p. 274). According to Kripke, the definition is used to 'fix the reference' of the phrase 'one meter'. What, according to him, is 'the reference' that is fixed for this phrase? It is not any physical stick or rod. It is 'an abstract thing' (p. 274). It is 'a certain length'. It is an 'accidental property' of this abstract thing, a certain length, that stick *S* is of that length.

Kripke's phrase, 'a certain length', is curious. *What* length? Suppose the chairman of the international committee said, 'I have a certain length in mind that I want the expression "one meter" to refer to'. The other members say, 'What length?'. The chairman looks at several rods, and finally picks one up and says, 'The length of this one is what I had in mind'. The others say, 'That's fine with us'. So the rod the chairman picked up became the Urmeter. Here was a case in which the chairman had 'a certain length' in mind, which he wanted to be designated as 'one meter'.

There could, however, be a different case. Suppose the chairman said that he did not have any particular length in mind which he wanted to be designated as 'one meter'. He added, jokingly, 'Any length that is longer than my arm and shorter than my bed will be OK'. The other members also say that they have no particular length in mind. The committee decides to blindfold the chairman and let him reach into a pile of rods that happens to be there. Whichever rod he takes hold of will be the Urmeter. So that was how it was done. In this case there was *no* 'certain length' that the committee 'wanted to mark out'.

Now Kripke might retort that in saying of someone who adopts the definition, 'One meter is the length of stick *S*', that 'There is a certain length which he wants to mark out', he did not mean that this person had a certain length in mind *before* he decided to use that definition. Kripke might say that all that is required is that just at the time when the person adopts that definition he intends the phrase 'one meter' to refer to 'a certain length'.

In reply I would ask, *which* 'certain length' is it to which the person intends the phrase 'one meter' to refer when he adopts the definition, 'One meter is the length of stick *S*'? In the act of adopting this rule he is stipulating that 'one meter' is to refer to the length of stick *S*. He could have adopted a different rule. Contingency does come in there. But in adopting this definition he is specifying that the 'certain length' to which 'one meter' is to refer is none other than the length of stick *S*. If he were to give a different specification of the 'certain length' to which 'one meter' is to refer, then he would not be 'baptizing' stick *S* as the Urmeter.

This being so, what is 'contingent' about the definition, 'One meter is the length of stick *S*'? Nothing that I can see. Of course a different definition of 'one meter' could have been adopted. But we should not confuse the genuinely contingent proposition, ' "One meter" was defined as "the length of stick *S*" ', with the definition, 'One meter is the length of stick *S*', or 'Stick *S* is one meter long'.

Consider what I think is a parallel example. It is a rule of chess that the bishop can move only on diagonals. Of course a different rule could have been adopted—one that permitted the bishop to move vertically and horizontally as well as diagonally. Even if this game were called 'chess', it would be a different game from *our* chess. There is nothing 'contingent' about the rule for the bishop in our chess. It would be nonsense to say that in some 'counterfactual situations' the bishop could move vertically or horizontally, unless what was meant by this was just that in some 'counterfactual situations' a game similar to but different from our chess might be played. Likewise, to say, as Kripke does, that in some 'counterfactual situations' stick *S*, the Urmeter, would be, or might be, more or less than one meter long, is nonsense, unless it just means that in those counterfactual situations an institution of a metric system similar to but different from *our* present institution of the metric system, would be, or might be, established.

Kripke says the following of stick *S*, the Urmeter:

> In some counterfactual situations the stick might have been longer and in some shorter if various stresses and strains had been applied to it. So we can say of this stick the same way as we would of any other of the same substance and length, that if heat of a given quantity had

been applied to it, it would have expanded to such and such a length. Such a counterfactual statement, being true of other sticks with identical physical properties, will also be true of this stick. (P. 275)

Kripke goes on to assert that 'even if S is used as the standard of a meter, the *metaphysical* status of "S is one meter long" will be that of a contingent statement' (p. 275).

Suppose it were discovered that the interior of the vault in which the Urmeter is kept had risen to an abnormally high temperature. A physicist calculates that the Urmeter has expanded to such and such a length. He says, half seriously, 'The Urmeter is no longer one meter long'. What would happen? Various things might happen. One thing that might happen is that no one paid any attention. The Urmeter continued to be the court of last resort in serious disagreements about metrical measurements. 'Stick S is one meter long' was retained as the rule that defines the term 'one meter'.

Another thing that might happen is that the international committee became so worried about possible future discrepancies in measurements that they designated another stick, R, as the Urmeter. They then measured S against R and found that S was more than a meter long. But it is easy to see that what happened here is that the committee made a change in the institution of the metrical system. They canceled the rule, 'S is one meter long', and substituted the rule, 'R is one meter long'. S was dismissed from the role of Urmeter. The possibility of this eventuality does *nothing*, however, to show that when S is being *used* as the standard meter, the status (whether 'metaphysical' or not) of 'S is one meter long' is that of a contingent statement. This would be like arguing that the rule, 'The bishop can move only diagonally', is a contingent statement, because at some future time the international chess federation might stipulate a new rule, which permits the bishop to move horizontally or vertically.

3

As previously noted, Kripke says that when a person stipulates that 'one meter' is to be the length of stick S he is 'using this definition not to *give the meaning* of what he called the "meter", but to *fix the reference*' (p. 274). Kripke says there is a 'distinction between "definitions" which fix a reference and those which give a synonym' (p. 275). I would not wish to say that the committee, or whoever did it, 'gave a synonym' of 'one meter' when they stipulated that 'one meter' was to be 'the length of stick S'. Perhaps the term 'one meter' was first introduced into the language at that time; in that case the phrase 'the length of stick S' was not an already existing synonym of the term 'one meter'. Furthermore, as the institution of the metric system began to operate, it would not be true that the people all over the world who began to use the term 'one meter', and who learned to measure with meter-rules, regarded the phrase, 'the length of stick S', as a 'synonym' for 'one meter'. Most of them would never have heard of stick S, the Urmeter in Paris. The two phrases are not, and never were, synonymous in ordinary discourse.

It would seem to me, however, that it is quite a proper use of language to say that when the committee laid down the rule, 'One meter is the length of stick S', it 'determined the meaning' of the term 'one meter'. When the committee laid down that rule, did it also 'fix the reference' of the term 'one meter'? Kripke uses the expression, 'the reference' of the term 'one meter', in such a queer and obscure way, that this question has no clear meaning when it is asked in respect to Kripke's own use of the words, 'the reference' of 'one meter'. But in an ordinary way of speaking, it would seem to me to be all right to say that when the committee laid down the rule, it 'fixed the reference' of the term 'one meter'. So it could be said *both* that the stipulated rule determined the meaning of 'one meter' and that it fixed the reference of 'one meter'. But it isn't as if there were *two* things that the stipulation did. The stipulation established the meaning of 'one meter' as the length of S, and the stipulation made the term 'one meter' refer to the length of S. But these come to the same thing, namely, that 'one meter' was *defined* as the length of S. There may be a distinction in some cases between definitions that fix a reference and definitions that determine the meaning of a term. I won't attempt to go into that. But in the particular case of the stipulated definition of 'one meter', such a distinction would appear to be nonexistent.

4

One source of Kripke's idea that the stipulated definition of 'one meter' is a *contingent* statement is his notion that it is an 'accidental property' of a 'certain length' that there is a stick of that length. There were various things about the establishing of the metric system that were undoubtedly contingent. First, it might not have been established at all. Second, a stick of a length different from the length of stick S might have been chosen as the Urmeter. Third, the stick S might, for one reason or another, have been replaced by another stick of a different material or of a different length, the second stick then being 'baptized' as the Urmeter. Thus, it is at least triply contingent that 'one meter' is the length of stick S. However, given the institution of the metric system as it was established, and given that stick S was designated as the Urmeter and continues to have that role, then the rule 'One meter is the length of stick S' is not a contingent statement. This is to say that, given that institution and that unique role for S, it makes no sense to try to determine by measurement whether S is or is not one meter long—which is probably what Wittgenstein meant.

Now Kripke says that there is an 'object' (p. 309) that *is* 'a certain length'. It is 'that object' which is designated by the term 'one meter', or, in Kripke's words, is 'the reference' of the term 'one meter'. The designation of 'that object' by this term was achieved by adopting the definition, 'One meter is the length of stick S'. The 'object' that was so designated, according to Kripke, does not *have* 'a certain length'; it is *identical* with 'a certain length'. The alleged 'accidental property' that 'this object' has is not that it is identical with 'a certain length'. The accidental property of 'this object', according to Kripke, is that stick S *had* 'that certain length' at the time the definition was adopted.

I think this is wrong. In the first place it is utterly strange to speak of the term 'one meter' as designating, denoting, referring to, or naming an 'object'. In contrast, it is correct and intelligible to say that the expression, 'the standard meter', or 'the Urmeter', does refer to or designate an object, namely, the stick S in Paris. If, however, we do talk in Kripke's way, and if we say that the 'object' referred to by the term 'one meter' is 'a certain length', then it is wrong to think that it is an accidental property or contingent mark of '*that* object' (which is identical with 'a certain length') that stick S had *that* length. For if stick S had been of a different length when the definition was adopted, then *the object* would have been *different!* It cannot be a contingent property of 'the object' in question that stick S was of '*that* length,' since if S had been of a different length 'the object' designated by the term 'one meter' would have been different. The *identity* of the so-called 'object' depended solely on the length of S. A difference in the length of S would have yielded a different 'object'. This being so, the fact that S had the length it had was an essential and not an accidental property of 'the object'. A different length, a different 'object'.

Kripke seems to have something like the following picture (although this is only my conjecture) of what transpired when stick S was designated as the Urmeter. He speaks as if the person or persons who performed the 'initial baptism' in some sense had hold of 'a certain length' or had 'a certain length' in mind. They then noticed that stick S happened to have that precise length. So it was an 'accidental property' of the 'object' ('a certain length') which they had in mind, that stick S had precisely that length.

But we have already seen that the 'baptizers' need not have had any certain length in mind. If they did not, then they could not have noted that stick S was of '*that* length'. Nor could they have determined that stick S was of '*that* length' by *comparing* stick S with '*that* length'.

Kripke speaks as if stick S was compared with an 'object' which is supposed to be 'the reference' of the term 'one meter'. In fact, the unique role that was assigned to S when it was designated as the Urmeter was that S was not to be compared with anything, but that any number of sticks and rods might be compared with it.

I have argued that in relation to the actual operation of the institution or 'language game' of measurement with a meter stick, the sentence 'One meter is the length of S' is not a contingent statement. Do I hold then that this sentence expresses a 'necessary truth'? I would not say this either, especially if a 'necessary truth' is supposed to be something that is 'true in all possible worlds'. Certainly there is no requirement to hold that if the sentence is not a contingent statement then it must be a necessary statement. To think that this sentence should be characterized as either a contingent statement or as a necessary statement seems to me to be looking at it in a wrong way. The sentence, 'One meter is the length of S', is correctly characterized as being, in relation to the institution of metric measurement, the *definition* of 'one meter' and also as a *rule* for the use of the term 'one meter'. One can also rightly say that this sentence was used to make a *fiat* or a *decree*.

Kripke says that the term 'one meter' was meant to designate 'a certain length in all possible worlds' (p. 275). It seems extravagant to say that the decree was a decree for 'all possible worlds'. Probably, the person or persons who made the decree did not envisage anything whatever about 'all possible worlds'.

To think of the sentence, 'One meter is the length of *S*', in its use to define 'one meter', as being a 'statement' or as expressing a 'proposition', is almost bound to lead one astray. For then one will think that this 'statement' is either true or false. And if one thinks it is true one will be led, as Kripke was, to inquire into *which* brand of truth it has, contingent or necessary?

In 'Naming and Necessity' Kripke puts forward a theory about how names and terms are made to refer to things and objects. According to this theory a thing, or a kind of thing, is 'originally identified' by a contingent property of the thing or of the kind of thing. In speaking of 'natural kinds', and using as an illustration the phenomenon of *heat*, Kripke argues that heat was originally identified by a contingent property, namely, the property of producing in people sensations of heat. In my previous essay on Kripke I tried to show that it is a mistake to think it is a *contingent* property of heat that when normal people are exposed to heat they normally have sensations of heat.

Although Kripke does not regard 'one meter' as a term referring to a 'natural kind', he puts forward a similar thesis about it, holding that this term refers to an 'object' which *is* a certain length, and also holding that a *contingent* property of this object was used to fix the reference of the term 'one meter', namely, the contingent property that stick *S* was of *that* length. In the present essay I have tried to show that this is wrong too.

Kripke presents acute criticisms of theories about names, references, designations, and so on, that have been put forward by other philosophers. Judging, however, by two of the principal illustrations of his own theory, namely, *heat* and *the standard meter*, that theory too won't hold much water. One may be reminded here of Kripke's nice observation that being *wrong* 'is probably common to all philosophical theories' (p. 280).

6

Wittgenstein: The Relation of Language to Instinctive Behavior

1

'Language did not emerge from reasoning'. This remark from *On Certainty* (*OC* 475) presents an important theme of Wittgenstein's later writing. The idea is most plausible in respect to simple linguistic expressions of fear, pain, surprise, desire. A small child exhibits unlearned, instinctive, behavior of fear. A dog rushes at it and it recoils with fear, just as a cat would. It would be absurd to attribute to either child or cat the thought, 'This beast may be dangerous, so I had better take avoiding action'.

Wittgenstein's suggestion is that the child is taught or simply picks up from adults, words and sentences that are added to its repertoire of fear-expressive behavior. In a well-known passage in the *Philosophical Investigations* concerning the transition from non-linguistic to linguistic expressions of pain, Wittgenstein remarks that when a child learns linguistic expressions of pain it learns 'new pain-behaviour' (*PI* 244). The learned verbal expressions of pain or fear are no more due to thinking or reasoning than are the instinctive preverbal behaviors. Wittgenstein calls these first person utterances, *Äusserungen*, to indicate that they are *immediate expressions* of pain, fear, surprise, desire, and so on, and are not the result of thought.

2

This conception of certain linguistic expressions as replacements for unlearned reactions was seen by Wittgenstein to extend to some of the sentences that we use to refer to other persons. Not only 'I'm in pain' but also 'He's in pain', can take the place of instinctive behavior. In *Zettel* Wittgenstein observes that 'it is a primitive reaction to tend, to treat, the part that hurts when someone else is in pain, and not merely when oneself is' (*Z* 540). Plainly there are instinctive reactions of shock, concern, sympathy, when one sees that another person is injured. We observe something of this sort in lower animals too. In the *Zettel* passage Wittgenstein asks himself what he means by saying that these reactions are 'primitive'; and he answers: 'Surely that this way of behaving is *prelinguistic*: that a language-game is based *on it*, that it is the prototype of a way of thinking and not the result of thinking' (*Z* 541). Wittgenstein is disagreeing with a 'rationalistic' explanation of this behavior—for example, the explanation that we have a sympathetic reaction to an injured person 'because by analogy with our own case we believe that he too is experiencing pain' (*Z* 542). The actions of comforting or trying to help that go with the words 'He's in pain', are no more a product of reasoning from analogy than is the similar behavior in deer or birds. Wittgenstein goes on to say that

> being sure that someone is in pain, doubting whether he is, and so on, are so many natural, instinctive, kinds of relationship towards other human beings, and our language is merely an auxiliary to, and further extension of, this behaviour. Our language-game is an extension of primitive behaviour. (For our *language-game* is behaviour.) (Instinct.) (*Z* 545)

This same conception is set forth, in more general terms, in *Vermischte Bemerkungen*:

> The origin and the primitive form of the language-game is a reaction; only from this can the more complicated forms grow.
> Language—I want to say—is a refinement; 'in the beginning was the deed'.[1]

1. Ludwig Wittgenstein, *Vermischte Bemerkungen*, ed. G. H. von Wright in collaboration with Heikki Nyman, 2d ed. (Frankfurt: Suhrkamp, 1978), p. 65. Published under the title *Culture and Value*, with English translation by Peter Winch (Oxford: Blackwell, 1980), p. 31.

3

Wittgenstein says here that not only does language replace prelinguistic behavior, but also that it serves as an extension, refinement, or elaboration of that behavior. What does this mean? An example is the way in which exclamations such as 'It hurts' or 'The pain is here' can, first of all, simply take the place of the instinctive behavior of caressing, protecting, comforting, the painful part. But the *language* of sensation provides finer descriptions of sensation than would be possible with purely non-linguistic behavior. One says, 'It still hurts but not as much as it did yesterday'; or 'There is a slight pain in my hip but not enough to bother me'. These reports could not be conveyed in prelinguistic behavior.

As another example consider natural human reactions to heat and cold, such as doffing and donning garments, fanning oneself, huddling near a fire, and so on. The exclamations, 'Hot!', 'Cold!', are learned in connection with such preverbal behavior, and come to be used themselves as responses to heat and cold. But language provides an expansion and refinement far beyond these simple verbal equivalents of preverbal behavior. Predictions, comparisons, warnings, in regard to the heat and cold of objects, which could not be conveyed in wordless behavior, become possible. The language of the thermometer yields more precise discriminations of heat and cold than could be expressed in nonverbal behavior. But of course the thermometer would never have been taken to be a measure of heat and cold if there had not been a rough agreement between the contraction and expansion of mercury in a tube and the natural behavioral responses of human beings to heat and cold.

4

As a more difficult example, let us consider the use of the word 'cause' and of other causal expressions. Philosophers often assume that this causal language originates in observations of constant sequences of events. But this view is too intellectual. It implies that when one event is followed by another we remain in doubt whether the two events are related as cause and effect until we have satisfied ourselves by further observations that an event of one kind is always in all instances conjoined with an event of another kind: whereupon we call the one, *cause,* the other, *effect*. On this view the *thought* of a universal rule, and a *doubt* as to whether the rule is satisfied by the events in question, is present at the very beginning of our employment of causal expressions.

In remarks written in 1937[2] Wittgenstein presents an entirely different conception. Suppose that a child runs into another child, knocking him down. The latter might react by leaping up and hitting or kicking the other one. He would be 'reacting to the cause' of his falling. Wittgenstein says: 'Calling something "the cause" is like pointing and saying: "He's to blame!" ' ('Cause and Effect', p. 410). The child would not be doubting or wondering what made him fall. He would not wait to observe what happens in other cases. Nor could he be said to *assume* that in similar cases the same thing occurs. Wittgenstein remarks:

> There is a reaction which can be called 'reacting to the cause'.—We also speak of 'tracing' the cause; a simple case would be, say, following a string to see who is pulling it. If I then find him—how do I know that he, his pulling, is the cause of the string's moving? Do I establish this by a series of experiments? (*Ibid.*, p. 416)

This 'reacting to the cause' can be called 'immediate'. This means, first, that there is no uncertainty, guessing, conjecturing, inferring, concluding. Second, calling it an 'immediate reaction' emphasizes the aspect of *action*—striking back, chasing away the cat that has hold of the string, pointing in anger at the one who broke the toy. Causal expressions, such as 'He knocked me down', 'The cat is pulling it', 'She broke it', are grafted on to these immediate reactions.

Later on there develops a use of causal expression where doubt, conjecture, testing, experiments, theory, enter in. According to Wittgenstein's conception these are 'second-order features' (*ibid.*, p. 420). Wittgenstein says:

> The primitive form of the language-game is certainty, not uncertainty. For uncertainty could never lead to action. (*Ibid.*)

> The basic form of the game must be one in which we act. (*Ibid.*, p. 421)

---

2. Wittgenstein, 'Cause and Effect: Intuitive Awareness', *Philosophia* 6 (Sept.–Dec. 1976), 391–408. Selected and edited by Rush Rhees, English translation by Peter Winch. (I am deeply indebted to Rush Rhees for leading a faculty seminar at King's College in 1979–80 on the topic of Wittgenstein's writings on causation, and also to my other colleagues at King's College who participated in the discussions.)

To suppose that *wondering* whether this caused that, or questioning in one's mind whether the two events are constantly conjoined, comes in advance of, or along with, the first employment of causal words, is putting the cart before the horse. The child who retaliates against the one that crashed into him does not do this because he 'knows' or 'believes' that this caused his fall. He simply does it. It is an instant reaction, like brushing away an insect that is tickling one's skin. One does not make experiments to determine whether the tickling sensation is caused by the insect.

When Wittgenstein says that the primitive form of the language-game with the word 'cause' is 'certainty', he does not mean that the child affirms in his mind the proposition that the other one certainly knocked him down, or that the child has a *perception* or *intuitive awareness* of the causal connection between his being crashed into and his falling down. No. Wittgenstein means that the hitting back at the other child is *instinctive*. This instinctive behavior is what Wittgenstein calls 'reacting to the cause'. The 'certainty' he is talking about is a certainty in behavior, not a certainty in propositional thought.

Doesn't the child's reaction at least presuppose that he has *the concept* of cause and effect? No. In the first place, it is misleading to speak of '*the* concept' of cause and effect, as if there were an *essence* of causation, a set of necessary and sufficient conditions, a hidden definition of causation that lies behind the differing uses of causal expressions. In the second place, instinctive reactions of this sort would be one *source* of the learning of causal expressions. Sentences, such as 'He knocked me down', 'He caused me to fall', would be linked to the instant reaction. The understanding of some causal terms would grow out of such reactions, and would not be presupposed by them. Just as a child's crying out with pain when injured would be one source of its acquisition of the use of the word 'pain' and would not presuppose that it has 'the concept' of pain.

Wittgenstein's idea is that the child's first learning of causal expressions consists in learning to use them along with, or in place of, unlearned reactions. Being in doubt about the cause of something, learning to investigate by tests and experiments, would be a subsequent addition.

A similar thing occurs in the first learning of names of objects. Wittgenstein remarks that 'children do not learn that there are books, that there are armchairs, etc. etc., but they learn to fetch books, sit in armchairs, etc.' (*OC* 476). He imagines someone saying: 'So one must know that the objects exist whose names one teaches a child by ostensive definition'. Wittgenstein replies: 'Why should the language-game rest on knowledge?' (*OC* 477). And he asks: 'Does a child believe that milk exists? Or does it know that milk exists? Does a cat know that a mouse exists?' (*OC* 478).

A cat watches a mouse hole. It would be natural to say that the cat knows, or believes, that a mouse may come out of the hole. But what does this come to? Are we attributing to the cat the propositional thought, 'A mouse may appear'? No. We are only placing this behavior in the larger pattern of cat-seeking-mouse behavior. An infant reaches for its milk bottle. Does it 'believe' that what is in the bottle is milk? One could say this. But what would it mean? Just that there is this behavior of reaching for the bottle from which it has been fed in the past; plus, perhaps, the fact that it will reject the bottle if what it tastes is chalk water. This is *just doing*. In order to understand it we do not have to suppose that this doing rests on some *underlying* belief. The belief here is nothing other than this behavior in these circumstances; not a *source* of the behavior. In the case of the infant, words and sentences will gradually emerge from such behavior. Not so with the cat.

5

Wittgenstein's conception is sharply at odds with some current views. Noam Chomsky, for example, regards a child's language learning as a highly intellectual performance. A child is bombarded with what Chomsky calls 'primary linguistic data':

> On the basis of such data, the child constructs a grammar—that is, a theory of the language of which the well-formed sentences of the primary linguistic data constitute a small sample. To learn a language, then, the child must have a method for devising an appropriate grammar, given primary linguistic data. As a precondition for language learning, he must possess, first, a linguistic theory that specifies the form of the grammar of a possible human language, and, second, a strategy for selecting a grammar of the appropriate form that is compatible with the primary linguistic data.[3]

3. Noam Chomsky, *Aspects of the Theory of Syntax* (Cambridge: M.I.T. Press, 1965), p. 25.

The child approaches the data with the presumption that they are drawn from a language of a certain antecedently well-defined type, his problem being to determine which of the (humanly) possible languages is that of the community in which he is placed. Language learning would be impossible unless this were the case. (*Ibid.*, p. 27)

To acquire language, a child must devise a hypothesis compatible with present data—he must select from the store of potential grammars a specific one that is appropriate to the data available to him. (*Ibid.*, p. 36)

On Chomsky's view each normal child is an intellectual marvel right from the start. Before an infant can hold his milk bottle he is already in possession of a theory concerning the general form of every possible human language (as if there were such a thing). When the adults around him utter words this child immediately starts forming and testing hypotheses to determine which of the possible languages is the actual language of the community in which he happens to be placed. Chomsky says: 'Language learning would be impossible unless this were the case'. *Mirabile dictu!*

Suppose a sailor whose native language is French or Russian is cast ashore on a Pacific island whose inhabitants speak an alien tongue. Since the sailor believes that this island was a Japanese possession for a good many years, he forms the hypothesis that perhaps the language of these people is Japanese. In his travels he has picked up a few words and sentences of Japanese; so he tries out his little bit of Japanese on the inhabitants in order to find out whether they respond with any understanding. It won't be easy, but at least he can make a stab at confirming or disconfirming his hypothesis.

Could the infant do this? Could he address the adults around him with remarks in Japanese, French, or Russian? No; he doesn't know any spoken language. So he will have to formulate and test his hypotheses solely *in his mind.* He will think to himself, 'Was that utterance I just heard a request, or a statement, or a prediction, or was it merely a swear word?' But what evidence could there be that an infant understands these differences?

According to Chomsky, 'The child approaches the data with the presumption that they are drawn from a language of a certain antecedently well-defined type'. So does this infant think to himself, 'I presume that these people speak a subject-predicate language'; or, 'I assume that in this language adjectives agree with nouns in gender and number'?

Suppose there were an especially remarkable child (or, perhaps, an especially backward one) who did *not* 'approach the data' with any assumptions or preconceptions, but despite this handicap did gradually learn the language of his community, just like older children. Chomsky would say, 'It is impossible that there should be such a child'. How does Chomsky know this? Has Chomsky conducted tests with infants who make such assumptions, and infants who don't, and found that only those of the first group do succeed in learning language? Of course not. Chomsky would have no way of determining whether any given infant belongs to one group or to the other. His claim about what a child *must* do is obviously not based on any tests whatever.

J. A. Fodor correctly draws out an implication of Chomsky's view and fearlessly endorses it. The implication is that a child cannot learn a language unless it *already has* a language. Fodor holds that both perception and learning require the forming and confirming of hypotheses, and that this in turn requires processes of 'computation'. But computation can only be carried out in a system of representation—that is, in a language. Fodor says: 'Computation presupposes a medium of computation: a representational system'.[4] Fodor argues explicitly that a person cannot learn a language unless he already has a language:

> Learning a language (including, of course, a first language) involves learning what the predicates of the language mean. Learning what the predicates of a language mean involves learning a determination of the extension of these predicates. Learning a determination of the extensions of the predicates involves learning that they fall under certain rules (i.e. truth rules). But one cannot learn that P falls under R unless one has a language in which P and R can be represented. So one cannot learn a language unless one has a language. (*Language of Thought*, pp. 63–64)

The unlearned language that one possesses, presumably from birth, is called 'the language of thought'. It is innate, inner, and private. It is an 'internal code'. One does learn the predicates of a natural language, such as Spanish or German. But according to Fodor, 'for every predicate in the natural language it must be possible to express a coextensive

4. Jerry A. Fodor, *The Language of Thought* (Hassocks, Sussex: Harvester Press, 1975), p. 27.

predicate in the internal code' (*ibid.*, p. 85). 'One can't learn a conceptual system richer than the conceptual system that one starts with' (*ibid.*, p. 97).

These are astonishing contentions. How could one find out whether the innate system of representation that Fodor postulates does actually exist? Certainly not by introspection; for Fodor does not hold that the representations and computations that occur in the innate system are 'consciously accessible' (*ibid.*, p. 49).

A map is a system of representation. One can use a map to make computations, e.g. 'If we continue along the Strand from here it is only four blocks to Trafalgar Square'. It is a matter of observation that newcomers to London tend to lose their way unless they employ maps of the city. One can see whether a person on the street is or isn't consulting a map.

Furthermore, a map can be used *incorrectly*. This is true of *any* system of representation. It doesn't follow from the fact that a person arrived at his wanted destination that he used his map correctly. The symbols of a map and its method of projection can be understood or misunderstood. Computations based on the map can be right or wrong. None of this could apply to the innate, inner, private, representational system that, according to Fodor, must exist. Therefore, whether its existence can be *verified* is not really the issue. Whatever Fodor is talking about, the important point is that it cannot be a *representational system*.

Fodor thinks it is reasonable to suppose that the 'internal language' has a 'vocabulary' (*ibid.*, p. 123). If there is a vocabulary the items that compose it should have *meaning* and should be *understood*. How can either of these things be true of a system that is inner and private? A child grows up in a community of speakers and learns, by imitation and training, the language of the community. This language contains expressions that have a function in some contexts of life and not in others. Another expression is employed in different activities and different circumstances. A normal child gradually masters these differences, not in the sense of being able to describe them, but in the sense of conforming with them in its use of words. When this happens the child is said to 'understand the meaning' of those words. It is only in comparison with the practices of the community of speakers in which the child is reared that the child's utterances are correct or incorrect. The 'internal language' that Fodor postulates could not be subject to such comparison, and therefore the items of its 'vocabulary' could have no employment that was either correct or incorrect—which means that they are not items of a language or of a system of representation.

It is no surprise to learn that, for Fodor, the medium in which the supposed innate language of thought operates is the nervous system. He says: 'The nervous system "speaks" an internal language' (*ibid.*, p. 122). As if neural processes could contain symbols, representations, descriptions. Is a nervous system a member of a community of language-users? Does it apply symbols to objects and situations? Does it sometimes make mistakes and have to be corrected until its practices accord with those of the adult nervous systems of its language-community? Can it be said to understand, or to misunderstand, the items of its 'vocabulary'? The nervous system of a human being is indeed innate. But to say that neural processes constitute a 'language of thought' or a 'representational system' is to use these phrases not merely misleadingly but vacuously.

In contrast, Wittgenstein's conception of the role of instinctive behavior does not attribute to the human infant an innate representational system, nor any theories, assumptions, or hypotheses—attributions that are initially preposterous and ultimately devoid of content.

6

Wittgenstein presents a conception that is even more striking than what we have so far considered. Not merely is much of the first language of a child grafted onto instinctive behavior—but the whole of the developed, complex, employment of language by adult speakers embodies something resembling instinct. To explain this I will refer to some of Wittgenstein's responses to the declarations of G. E. Moore.

Wittgenstein's last writing, *On Certainty*, is a meditation on Moore's so-called defense of common sense. Moore declares that he knows with certainty that he is a human being, that his body has existed continuously since his birth, that the earth existed for a long time before he was born, that he has often perceived material things, and so on. Moore began his paper 'Certainty' with the following remarks:

> I am at present, as you can all see, in a room and not in the open air;
> I am standing up, and not either sitting or lying down; I have clothes

on, and am not absolutely naked; I am speaking in a fairly loud voice, and am not either singing or whispering or keeping quite silent; I have in my hand some sheets of paper with writing on them; there are a good many other people in the same room in which I am; and there are windows in that wall and a door in this one.[5]

Moore goes on to assert that it would be ridiculous for him, in his circumstances, to say such a thing as 'I *think* I've got some clothes on', or 'I not only think I have, I know that it is very likely indeed that I have, but I can't be quite sure'. Moore declares that he *knows* that he has clothes on, and knows all of those other things that he enumerated (*ibid.*, p. 228). In his 'Proof of an External World' he insists that he *knew* that he was holding up one hand and then the other:

> How absurd it would be to suggest that I did not know it, but only believed it, and that perhaps it was not the case! You might as well suggest that I do not know that I am now standing up and talking—that perhaps after all I'm not, and that it's not quite certain that I am! (*Ibid.*, pp. 146–47)

7

There seems to be an important insight in Moore's assertions; yet it is not easy to say what it is. Certainly it would have been astonishing if Moore, standing before his audience, had said, 'I think this is a hand, but I could be mistaken', or 'I believe I have clothes on but it isn't absolutely certain'.

If my wife and I were about to go out to dinner, and she called to me from another room, 'Do you have your clothes on?', she would be taken aback if I replied in all seriousness, 'I think so but I may be wrong'. Why is this? Haven't I been wrong about lots of things? So why shouldn't I be cautious here? This uncertainty would be shocking because we do not understand what being mistaken, or discovering that one was mistaken, would be like in such a matter as that (see *OC* 32).

Of course there could be circumstances in which uncertainty would be understandable. Suppose I had been knocked unconscious and when I regained consciousness I was tightly bound and blindfolded. If

---

5. G. E. Moore, *Philosophical Papers* (London: Allen and Unwin, 1959), p. 227.

my companion, who was in the same condition, whispered to me, 'Do you have clothes on?', I might whisper back, 'I think so but I may be wrong'. Being in doubt, being mistaken, is intelligible here. If the blindfold were removed I would ascertain whether I have clothes on. But if Moore, lecturing to his audience, were to look at his arms and legs, would he be ascertaining whether he has clothes on? Surely not; any more than in picking a piece of lint from my jacket would I be verifying that I am wearing a jacket. As Wittgenstein remarks: 'Does my telephone call to New York strengthen my conviction that the earth exists?' (*OC* 210).

If Moore had declared to his audience that he did *not* have clothes on, was not standing up, did not have two hands, etc., the people there would have regarded him not as *mistaken,* but as *mentally disturbed* (*OC* 155). Why is this? Apparently because we expect an adult speaker of the language, who is in possession of his faculties, to be able in normal circumstances to say straight off, without looking for evidence, whether he has clothes on, or whether he is sitting or standing.

This helps to bring out the fact that Moore is wrong in saying that he *knows* these things. For when a person contends that he is not merely convinced of something but *knows* it to be so, we expect him to be able to produce evidence in support of this distinction. But Moore was in no position to do this. As Wittgenstein says, if what a person believes 'is of such a kind that the grounds which he can give are no surer than his assertion, then he cannot say that he knows what he believes' (*OC* 243). 'My having two hands is, in normal circumstances, as certain as anything that I could produce in evidence for it. That is why I am not in a position to take the sight of my hand as evidence for it' (*OC* 250).

But Wittgenstein's remark that my having two hands is 'as certain' as anything I could bring forward as evidence for it, might be misleading. Is it *certain* that I have two hands? Who is supposed to be saying or thinking this; and in what circumstances? One can easily describe a natural context for the sentence, 'It is certain that I have two hands'. Suppose both of my hands were infected and I went to hospital for surgery. As I regained consciousness I heard one nurse ask another, 'Were his hands amputated?' After a moment of panic it seems to me that I can feel my fingers moving inside the bandages. Reassured, I say to myself, 'It is certain that I have both hands'. Whether I am right or wrong this would be a natural use of those words.

The case is exactly the same here as with Moore's assertion, 'I *know* that that's a tree', which he reiterated in philosophical discussion. Wittgenstein said of this:

> 'I know that that's a tree'. Why does it strike me as if I did not understand the sentence?, though it is after all an extremely simple sentence of the most ordinary kind? . . . As soon as I think of an everyday use of the sentence instead of a philosophical one, its meaning becomes clear and ordinary. (*OC* 347)

Outside of ordinary contexts neither 'I am certain' nor 'It is certain' (that I have two hands) has a clear meaning. Nor can a person who is going about his affairs in ordinary life be said to assume, or take for granted, or presuppose, that he has two hands. Wittgenstein remarks:

> No one ever taught me that my hands don't disappear when I am not paying attention to them. Nor can I be said to presuppose the truth of this proposition in my assertions, etc., (as if they rested on it) whereas it only gets some sense from our other asserting. (*OC* 153)

What does Wittgenstein mean by saying that this proposition gets its sense from 'our other asserting'? A clue is to be found in another remark, where he is trying to *find* an underlying sense for Moore's curious insistence that he *knows* that *this* is a hand:

> Doesn't 'I know that that's a hand', in Moore's sense, mean the same or something similar to: I can make statements like 'I have a pain in this hand' or 'this hand is weaker than the other' or 'I once broke this hand', and countless others, in language-games where a doubt as to the existence of this hand does not come in? (*OC* 371)

Doubt does not come in! That is where the emphasis should be put. It isn't that in normal life a person is certain, or convinced, or knows, or assumes, or takes for granted, or presupposes, that he has two hands. It is simply that he makes statements about his hands without any doubt as to their existence occurring to him or to others. He uses the word 'hand' without a second thought. And it isn't only that he uses this word in *statements* about his hands—he *acts*. A child responds to requests such as 'Hold out your hands', 'Wash your hands', and so on, without considering whether he has hands. This immediate, unthinking response cannot be said to show that he knows, or is certain, that he has hands. 'Knowledge' and 'certainty' have no application here. Wittgenstein says that the young child 'learns to react in such-and-such a way; and in so reacting it doesn't so far know anything' (*OC* 538). This learned but unthinking acting also characterizes the use of words by adults, of the word 'hand' and of other names of things. It is 'our *acting* which lies at the bottom of the language-game' (*OC* 204).

An adult has acquired a confident use of many words. But isn't it an empirical fact that *this* word is used like *this*? (*OC* 306). And since it is an empirical fact, shouldn't I have empirical grounds for my 'certainty' that the word is used like that? But, as Wittgenstein notes:

> The strange thing here is that when I am quite certain of how the words are used, have no doubt about it, I can still give no *grounds* for my way of acting. If I tried I could give a thousand, but none of them as certain as the very thing they were supposed to be grounds for. (*OC* 307)

8

Absence of doubt manifests itself throughout the normal life of a human being. It appears, first, in advance of any learning: for example, in the spontaneous behavior of reacting to a cause. This behavior is 'instinctive' in the primary sense of the word. Second, it appears in the young child when it is taught to respond to orders such as 'Sit in the chair', 'Hold out your hands', and so on, before the child can itself employ words. Third, it appears in the behavior, due to teaching, of employing the names of objects. At these second and third levels, the confident way of acting and speaking could be called 'instinctive' in a secondary sense.

The absence of doubt, at all three levels, can be called 'instinctive' because it isn't *learned*, and because it isn't the product of thinking. In the original reacting to something as a cause, there is no thought of whether a similar result will follow upon a similar event. Nor in the sympathetic response to another's injury is there any reflection as to whether this other person has 'the same thing' that I have when I'm in pain. The child who has not yet begun to speak but has reached the stage of responding to orders, such as 'Sit on a chair', could be said to 'know' that this thing is a chair and that the couch, stool, or cushion is not a chair. The same could be said of a dog. In neither case does this knowingly imply the overcoming of doubt or the testing of a hypothesis. In both cases the knowledge is nothing other than correct behavioral responses produced by training. The knowledge is not something that underlies and explains the behavior.

One of the most striking illustrations of what I am calling the 'instinctive' element in the employment of language and in language-like activities, is the way in which people who have been given some instruction in a procedure (such as continuing a mathematical series, or drawing a design, or building a brick wall) will, when told to carry on from there, spontaneously and on their own continue in the *same* way. It would seem that from the original instruction those people could branch out in an indefinitely large number of directions, each one going a different way. It is true that they *could*. But they don't! Almost all of them will go on in a way that the others will agree is the *same* way. This 'agreement in reactions' is impressive. And it cannot be *explained* by saying that they have 'intuitively grasped the rule', or something of the sort. This confident going on in the same way, without any doubt, cannot be given any rational foundation. This is a reason for calling it 'instinctive'. Without this kind of natural agreement, this instinctive going on in the same way, there could not be language.

A boy who grows up on a farm is taught that the farm animals need to be fed in the morning, and this becomes one of his daily chores. Now if the animals had ceased to exist for several hours during the night, perhaps they wouldn't be hungry and wouldn't need to be fed. Does the thought of such a possibility occur to the boy? No. Does this mean that he *assumes* that the animals continued to exist throughout the night? On the basis of what could we attribute this assumption to him? On the fact that he does act this way every day, without raising any questions? But why couldn't he act that way *without* an assumption? The case here is the same as in the following example of Wittgenstein's: 'Why do I not satisfy myself that I have two feet when I want to get up from a chair? There is no why. I simply don't. This is how I act' (*OC* 148). 'There is no why'! There is no explanation. I don't, for example, make an inductive inference from past experience. Wittgenstein says: 'The squirrel does not infer by induction that it is going to need stores next winter as well. And no more do we need a law of induction to justify our actions and predictions' (*OC* 287).

9

As I previously noted, an obsession with 'rationality' is characteristic of much of current philosophical thought. For example, Fodor says:

> Perception must involve hypothesis formation and confirmation because the organism must somehow manage to infer the appropriate task-relevant description of the environment *from* its physical description together with whatever background information about the structure of the environment it has available. (*Language of Thought*, p. 50)

If I am sitting in a chair and decide to go for a walk, I need first to get out of the chair. According to Fodor, I must *infer* this 'appropriate task-relevant description'. Why is there a *must* here? Isn't it enough if I simply rise from the chair *without* inferring that this is the appropriate action? Do I need to form a hypothesis about the way to proceed, any more than would a dog?

10

What is striking is not only that one's first learning of words is an outgrowth of unthinking, instinctive behavior, but that something of the same kind permeates and surrounds all human acting and all use of language, even at sophisticated levels. The chemist who is conducting an experiment may be in doubt about the outcome of the experiment, but not about the existence of his laboratory. A person who is doing an arithmetical calculation might wonder whether he multiplied correctly, but not whether the figures on the paper changed themselves into other figures (*OC* 337). This freedom from doubt has not been won by any tests or any reasoning.

Wittgenstein conceives of the absence of doubt that exists at so many points in the daily course of our lives as not something 'hasty or superficial' but as 'something that lies beyond being justified or unjustified; as it were, as something animal' (*OC* 358, 359). It is too fundamental to be either 'unjustified' or 'justified'. It underlies any mastery of words in which a procedure of justification could be framed.

This fundamental thing is *so* fundamental that it is difficult, or perhaps impossible, to describe it in words. One would *like* to characterize it in mental terms—to call it knowledge, or belief, or conviction, or certainty, or acceptance, or confidence, or assumption. But none of these expressions fit. All of them have their appropriate application *within* various language-games. Whereas Wittgenstein is trying to call attention to something that underlies all language-games.

But can't one give a characterization at least in *negative* terms of this fundamental thing? Wittgenstein attempts this in many passages. A formulation he frequently resorts to is 'the absence of doubt'. For example, in conversation I say, 'This hand is weaker than the other', or 'I once broke this hand', without (as Wittgenstein puts it) 'a doubt as to the existence of this hand coming in' (*OC* 371). And he says:

> The fact that I use the word 'hand' and all the other words in my sentence without a second thought, indeed that I should stand before the abyss if I wanted so much as to try doubting their meanings—shows that the absence of doubt belongs to the essence of the language-game. (*OC* 370)

Now it is true that if a previously normal adult began to be in constant doubt about the meanings of ordinary words, not only could he not continue to carry on the everyday employment of language, but also his behavior would fall into disarray. But is it right to say of me right now that I 'am not in doubt' as to whether this is called a 'hand'? This is a formulation I have resorted to in trying to expound Wittgenstein. But is this the way in which the expressions 'I am not in doubt' or 'He is not in doubt' are used in everyday life? Surely not. One normally says this only in a situation where a doubt has been voiced or felt or anticipated—and for some reason. For example: One person says that he is in doubt as to whether Mr. A will come to the meeting since he was absent from the two previous ones. Another person replies: 'I know that he didn't come those other times; but I have no doubt that he will come today because he told me explicitly that he would'. Here a ground for doubt is met by a ground for not doubting. The expression 'I don't have any doubt' is typically used to counter a presented or anticipated reason for doubt. And who, in my present circumstances, has any reason to doubt that this is called a 'hand'?

Wittgenstein says: 'I would like to reserve the expression "I know" for the cases in which it is used in normal linguistic exchange' (*OC* 260). Of course the same should hold for 'I believe', 'I am certain', 'I agree', 'I assume', and also 'I do not doubt'.

11

There are indications in *On Certainty* that Wittgenstein is dissatisfied with every attempt to characterize this fact that is so fundamental to language, thought, and action. Suppose that a customer tells a greengrocer that he wants ten apples, and the shopkeeper proceeds to count them out. Wittgenstein says:

> If the shopkeeper wanted to investigate each of his apples without any reason, in order to play safe, why doesn't he have to investigate the investigation? And can one speak here of belief (I mean belief as in religious belief, not conjecture)? Here all psychological terms merely lead us away from the main thing. (*OC* 459)

In order to have 'absolute certainty' must not the shopkeeper try to determine not only that these things are apples, but also that what he is doing is trying to find out whether they are apples, and in addition that he is really counting them? And if the shopkeeper doesn't do this, is this because he 'believes', or 'knows', or is 'certain', or is 'convinced', or 'assumes', or 'has no doubt', that these are apples and that he is counting them? No. All psychological terms, says Wittgenstein, lead us away from 'the main thing' (*die Hauptsache*).

In later passages Wittgenstein asks himself whether he knows or only believes that his name is L. W., and whether he knows or only believes that the law of induction is true? In regard to the latter he says that it appears to him to be nonsense to say, 'I know that the law of induction is true', and that it would be 'more correct' to say 'I believe in the law of induction' (*OC* 500). Yet apparently he is dissatisfied with this too, for he goes on to remark: 'Am I not getting closer and closer to saying that in the end logic cannot be described? You must look at the practice of language, then you will see it' (*OC* 501). *Logic cannot be described!* I take this to mean that it is not appropriate for Wittgenstein to say either that he 'knows', or 'believes', or is 'certain', or is 'convinced', or 'assumes', or 'does not doubt', that his name is L. W., or that this is called a 'hand', or that the law of induction is true. None of these terms are correct.

What does it mean to say: 'You must look at the practice of language, then you will see it'? *What* do you see? Well, you see *the unhesitating behavior* with which a person signs his name at the end of a letter or gives his name to a bank clerk; or uses the word 'hand' in statements; or makes inductive inferences; or does calculations; and so on. What you see is this unhesitating way of *acting*. This is the 'logic' of language that cannot be described with psychological words. It is too 'primitive', too 'instinctive', for that. It is *behavior* that is *like* the squirrel's gathering nuts or the cat's watching a mouse hole. This is why Wittgenstein says it is something *animal* (*OC* 359).

Just now I have spoken of this human behavior as 'unhesitating', and previously as 'confident'. But isn't this a strained use of these words? When I sign my name to a check in the normal way, is it correct to say that I do it 'confidently' or 'without hesitation'? It seems not. If, with advancing senility, I sometimes forget my name, or sometimes write it unconfidently, then an observer could report of me, 'This time he wrote his name confidently, without any hesitation'. Or if I had been given a drug that is supposed to produce amnesia, an observer might report, with surprise, 'Why, he stated his name quite confidently!' But the way in which a normal adult normally comes out with his own name and with the names of familiar objects cannot be called either 'confident' or 'unconfident', 'hesitating' or 'unhesitating'.

12

Wittgenstein's remark, 'Am I not getting closer and closer to saying that in the end logic cannot be described? You must look at the practice of language, then you will see it' (*OC* 501), may strike one as remarkably similar to an important theme of the *Tractatus*, namely, that there are things that cannot be *said* but *show* themselves. Is this theme of the *Tractatus* reemerging in Wittgenstein's last writing?[6]

I do not have the space to give this topic the treatment it deserves, but I will make a brief comment. According to the *Tractatus* something can be 'said' only if it is a *contingent* proposition—that is, only if its negation is a logical possibility. If you try to say what is logically necessary your remark is 'nonsense' (*Unsinn*). You are not contrasting one state of affairs with another conceivable state of affairs.

Throughout Wittgenstein's later writings he is describing what he calls 'the grammar' of concepts. His remarks are called 'grammatical'

---

6. Thomas Morawetz, in his *Wittgenstein and Knowledge* (Hassocks, Sussex: Harvester Press, 1980), p. 51, says that in *OC* 501, 'There are echoes of Wittgenstein's *Tractatus*'.

because they are attempts to describe how a certain *expression* in the language is actually used. In a sense, a true grammatical remark is a 'truism' since it merely spells out some feature of our familiar use of an expression. But in philosophy we get confused about the language we speak, and so a truistic grammatical remark, when brought to bear upon a particular confusion, can sometimes be illuminating.

A true grammatical remark expresses a *logically necessary truth*. Take the sentence, 'If you *know* that *p*, then *p* is *true*'. It isn't that the verb 'to know' *had* to be used that way. But it *is* normally so used that if one person says 'Jones knew that *p*', and another person concludes, 'So *p* was true!', the latter is making a logically valid inference.

Would Wittgenstein, in his later period, have thought that whenever a philosopher says, 'If you know that *p*, then *p* is true', he is uttering 'nonsense'? I think not. It would be a matter of how the philosopher is *taking* this sentence. If what he wants to say is that there is a certain 'mental state' called 'knowing', which is such that if a person knows that *p*, then the fact that *p* is contained in or guaranteed by that 'mental state', then Wittgenstein would say, 'Nonsense!' (see *Z* 408; *OC* 356). But if the philosopher only meant that this is how the verb 'to know' *is used*, Wittgenstein would not say 'Nonsense!'; nor would he hold that this philosopher was trying to say something that could not be 'said'. No longer does he hold the view that any remark that expresses something non-contingent is 'nonsensical' and must finally be 'thrown away' (*Tractatus*, 6.54).

On Certainty is full of grammatical remarks. An example is this: 'The child learns by believing the adult. Doubt comes *after* belief' (*OC* 160). Wittgenstein is trying to express, in this remark, something that is necessarily true about the concept of doubting—namely, that a person's behavior and utterances can be rightly described as 'doubting' only if they occur against a background of things that the person *accepts*.

The difficulty confronting Wittgenstein in *On Certainty* is *not* that what he is trying to state is a logical or conceptual necessity. It is instead a problem concerning *the words* in terms of which the necessary truth can be stated. Is, for example, the word 'accepts', that I used just now, the right word? Can it be said that the small child 'accepts' that what he is told to sit on is a 'chair'? Isn't this too sophisticated a term to apply to him at this stage? Nor can one say that he 'agrees' that it is a chair, nor that he 'believes' this, nor even that he 'does not doubt' it. As previously noted, if a child has not yet begun to speak, but has learned to respond with discrimination to the orders, 'Sit on a chair' and 'Sit on a stool', we are ready to say that the child 'knows' that a chair is a chair and that a stool is not a chair. We are ready to say the same of a dog. The word 'knows' merely refers here to that learned discriminative behavior, not to some mental state that *explains* the differential response.

We have the inclination to suppose that all mastery of language, as well as all meaningful behavior, is based on and emerges from mental states or attitudes that should be expressible in psychological terms. But what we find is that all of the psychological terms either redescribe, or else presuppose, *ways of acting*. It is these ways of acting that provide the foundation for the psychological concepts. They are 'the main thing' (*die Hauptsache*), which *shows* itself when one reflects on the practice of language, but which itself is not supported by any mental process or structure.[7]

7. This paper was presented as the J. R. Jones Memorial Lecture, University College of Swansea, May 1981. (I am grateful both to Bruce Goldberg and Rush Rhees for their criticisms of an earlier draft of this essay.)

7

Wittgenstein and Idealism

Recently some philosophers have proposed that the later philosophy of Wittgenstein tends toward idealism, or even solipsism. The solipsism is said to be of a peculiar kind. It is characterized as a 'collective' or 'aggregative' solipsism. The solipsism or idealism is also said to be 'transcendental'. In the first part of this paper I will be examining a recent essay by Professor Bernard Williams,[1] in which he presents what he takes to be the grounds for such an interpretation of Wittgenstein. After that I will try to offer convincing evidence that no tendency toward any form of idealism is to be found in Wittgenstein's later philosophy.

1

Professor Williams starts off by referring to the solipsism of the *Tractatus*. The solipsistic passages in that work have perplexed many readers. Some have even doubted that any genuine solipsism is present there at all. However, from the propositions that 'The world is *my* world' (5.62) and that 'I am my world' (5.63), it follows that 'I am the world'—which surely is an assertion of solipsism. From this, together with 'The world and life are one' (5.621), it follows that 'I am life'. At 6.431 it is said that 'So too at death the world does not alter but ceases'.

---

1. Bernard Williams, 'Wittgenstein and Idealism', in *Understanding Wittgenstein*, Royal Institute of Philosophy Lectures, vol. 7, 1972–73, ed. G. Vesey (New York: St Martin's Press, 1974).

Now, if *I* am life, then *my* death is the end of life. And since life and the world are one, *my* death is the end of the world. It would be hard to deny that this is a severe solipsism. Furthermore, 5.62 declares that 'What solipsism wants to say (*meint*) is entirely correct; only it cannot be *said*, but shows itself'.

One's understanding of the solipsism of the *Tractatus* is complicated by the fact that the *I* that is talked about in the foregoing propositions is not something *in* the world. Thus, this *I* is not L. W., nor any other human being, nor any mind or soul. It is not anything *in* the world, nor is it anything outside of the world, for there is nothing outside. Then *what* is it and *where* is it? The answer is that it is the boundary of the world. 'The subject does not belong to the world, but is a boundary of the world' (5.632). Here it is said to be *a* boundary (*eine Grenze*)—which might suggest that there could be more than one boundary. But what was surely meant is that the subject ('the metaphysical subject') is *the* boundary (*die Grenze*)—which is how Wittgenstein actually puts it in 5.641.

The assertion that the subject is 'the boundary' of the world is a pretty dark saying. My guess is that it means that if there were no subject there would be no world. I think here of the relationship of the boundary of a circle to a circle. The boundary is neither within the circle nor outside it: but if there were no boundary there would be no circle. A circle *presupposes* a boundary. This is actually how Wittgenstein puts the matter in the *Tractatus Notebooks* (p. 79): 'The subject is not a part of the world but a presupposition of its existence'.

It would perhaps be right to call this a form of 'transcendental idealism'. The *I* is a necessary condition (presupposition) of the existence of the world; but not being *in* the world, it is not itself a possible object of experience or knowledge, and in this sense is 'transcendental'.[2]

2. Ludwig Wittgenstein, *Tractatus Logico-Philosophicus*, trans. D. F. Pears and B. F. McGuinness (New York: Humanities Press, 1961). The remarks on solipsism in the *Tractatus* are exceedingly compressed, even for the *Tractatus*. Some thoughtful interpreters of those remarks believe that Wittgenstein was not actually stating a solipsistic position. I disagree; but also I apologize for my peremptory treatment of the matter, my excuse being that it is not my topic in this essay. The bare way in which I have sketched the position may make it appear that Wittgenstein's adoption of solipsism was ridiculous and dogmatic. I believe it was ingenious and profound.

The most fundamental step in the development of solipsism in the *Tractatus* is the observation that 'There is no thinking, representing subject' (5.631). In the *Tractatus Notebooks* (p. 80), this idea is expressed in the remark that 'The I is not an object'. A basic doctrine of the *Tractatus* is that each significant proposition is ultimately analyzable into a grouping of 'names', each of which designates an object. To say that 'The I is not an object' means

2

Professor Williams acknowledges the criticisms of solipsism that occur in Wittgenstein's later work. He speaks of 'The well-charted moves
in the later work from "I" to "we" . . .' and of 'the emphasis in the later
work on language's being an embodied, this-worldly, concrete social activity, expressive of human needs . . .' ('Wittgenstein and Idealism',
79). However, he goes on to say:

> My chief aim will be to suggest that the move from 'I' to 'we' was not
> unequivocally accompanied by an abandonment of the concerns of
> transcendental idealism. . . . Rather, the move is to something
> which itself contains an important element of idealism. That ele-
> ment is concealed, qualified, overlaid with other things, but I shall
> suggest that it is there. I shall suggest also that this element may

---

that the word 'I' is not a *name* and so does not appear in the final analysis of any sentence
in which it occurs. For example, the pronoun 'I' will not appear in the final analysis of 'I am
angry', nor in the final analysis of any first-person psychological sentence. What about third-
person psychological sentences, such as 'He is angry'? It is sufficiently obvious that if 'I' is
not a name, neither is 'He'. The sentences 'I am angry' and 'He is angry' differ in meaning;
but the difference cannot consist in the two pronouns designating numerically different objects, i.e., numerically different 'thinking, representing subjects'.

Where then can the difference in meaning of those two sentences lie? It must lie in the
predicates. The predicate 'angry' must differ in meaning in the first-person and third-person
sentences. Let us say that in the first-person sentence 'angry' refers to something genuinely
'mental', while in the third-person sentence it refers to *physical behavior*. Thus, 'I am angry' is
equivalent to 'There is anger', whereas 'He is angry' is roughly equivalent to 'The behavior of
that body is similar to the behavior of *this* (my) body when there is anger'. According to this
model, first-person psychological sentences do truly assert the existence of thoughts, feelings,
sensations, whereas third-person sentences only assert the existence of physical behavior. This
is a form of solipsism, although a no-self solipsism. Let us call this *psychological solipsism*.

How do we get from psychological solipsism to *world solipsism*? There is an easy transition
by way of *phenomenalism*, which is the doctrine that propositions about physical things and
events are analyzable in terms of propositions about sensations and sense-impressions. There
is evidence from Wittgenstein's *Philosophische Bemerkungen* (ed. Rush Rhees [Frankfurt:
Suhrkamp, 1964], pp. 51, 84), and also from Friedrich Waismann's record of conversations
with Wittgenstein (*Wittgenstein und der Wiener Kreis*, 45) that at an early stage Wittgenstein accepted phenomenalism. The conjunction of psychological solipsism and phenomenalism
yields world solipsism, i.e., 'I am the world', which of course cannot be said but shows itself.

The foregoing is a very skimpy outline of the case for interpreting the *Tractatus* as pre-
senting a no-self solipsism. I derived this interpretation of the *Tractatus* from reading the
doctoral dissertation of my friend and Cornell colleague, Professor Richard Miller. Miller's
interpretation has been recently published: Richard W. Miller, 'Solipsism in the *Tractatus*',
Journal of the History of Philosophy 18 (January 1980).

help to explain a particular feature of the later work, namely a per-
vasive vagueness and indefiniteness evident in the use Wittgenstein
makes of 'we'. (79)

Perhaps there is a form of transcendental idealism which is suggested, not indeed by the confused idea that the limits of *each* man's
language mean the limits of *each* man's world, but by the idea that the
limits of *our* language mean the limits of *our* world. (82)

First of all, I am surprised by the assertion that Wittgenstein's use of
'we' is vague and indefinite. Williams himself notes how Wittgenstein
frequently compares the 'language-games', 'forms of life', and 'world-
pictures' of various groups of human beings who differ in their upbringing and interests, and how he uses such comparisons to indicate
the possibility of different concepts.

To give an example, not mentioned by Williams, Wittgenstein imagined a society of people who measure tracts of land and determine
boundaries solely by pacing off distances, and who have no interest in
employing measuring tapes or surveyors' instruments. It appears right
to say that those people have a different *concept* of 'exactness' in measurement to the one *we* have. The 'we' here would obviously refer to the
great majority of people in Western cultures who would not dream of
fixing property lines by merely pacing off distances. It would be the 'we'
of one actual segment of mankind, contrasted with another (imagined)
human society.

In an example from *On Certainty*, to which Williams does refer,
Wittgenstein imagines a people who are guided in their actions by the
pronouncements of oracles in preference to the propositions of
physics. Wittgenstein remarks: 'Is it wrong for them to consult an oracle
and be guided by it?—If we call this "wrong" aren't we using our language-game as a base from which to *combat* theirs?'[3] The 'we' here includes Wittgenstein and all others who would rather put their trust in
physical principles than in oracles. The 'we' refers to one human group
in contrast with another.

Wittgenstein does indeed use 'we' with a shifting reference. For example, in the *Investigations* he speaks of the philosophical temptation to
hold that the sentence, 'Red exists', is nonsense, 'because if there were
no red it could not be spoken of at all'. He goes on to remark:

3. Wittgenstein, *On Certainty* (Oxford: Blackwell, 1969), 608, 609.

What we really *want* is simply to take 'Red exists' as the statement: the word 'red' has meaning. Or perhaps better: 'Red does not exist' as ' "Red" has no meaning'. Only we do not want to say that that expression *says* this, but that *this* is what it would have to be saying *if* it meant anything. But that it contradicts itself in the attempt to say it— just because red exists 'in its own right'.[4]

This 'we' refers to all of those philosophers, including Wittgenstein himself, who feel the temptation that he is describing. In the following remarks 'we' has a different reference:

When philosophers use a word—'knowledge', 'being', 'object', 'I', 'proposition', 'name'—and try to grasp the *essence* of the thing, one must always ask oneself: is the word ever actually used in this way in the language-game which is its original home?
What *we* do is to bring words back from their metaphysical to their everyday use. (*PI* 116)

In this example, unlike the previous one, 'we' refers to Wittgenstein and to any other philosophers who are trying to follow the method of his later philosophy, in contrast to, say, the method of the *Tractatus*. But in both cases the 'we' refers to actual groups of human beings.

Wittgenstein certainly gives different references to 'we'. But there is nothing vague or indefinite about it. Williams thinks that the supposedly 'curious use that Wittgenstein makes of "we" ' ('Wittgenstein and Idealism', 85), may be explained by Williams's hypothesis that there is a tendency toward transcendental idealism in Wittgenstein's later philosophy. Williams says:

While the 'we' of Wittgenstein's remarks often looks like the 'we' of our group as contrasted with other human groups, that is basically misleading. . . . Thus, while much is said by Wittgenstein about the meanings *we* understand being related to *our* practice, and so forth, that *we* turn out only superficially and sometimes to be one *we* as against others *in* the world, and thus the sort of *we* which has one practice as against others which are possible in the world. . . . One finds oneself with a *we* which is not one group rather than another in

4. Wittgenstein, *Philosophical Investigations*, ed. G. E. M. Anscombe and Rush Rhees, trans. G. E. M. Anscombe (Oxford: Blackwell, 1967), 58. Hereafter cited as *PI*.

the world at all, but rather the plural descendant of that idealist *I* who also was not one item rather than another in the world. (92)

The new theory of meaning, like the old, points in the direction of a transcendental idealism. (95)

Although the reference that Wittgenstein gives to 'we' often changes from one remark to another, his use of 'we' is not on that account 'vague', 'indefinite', or 'curious'. A moderate amount of attention and thought suffices to make it clear to a reader what the reference of 'we' is in each case. And in each case the reference is to some actual human group, society, or culture. Consider the following remark from *Zettel*:

> A tribe has two concepts, akin to our 'pain'. One is applied where there is visible damage and is linked with tending, pity, etc. The other is applied to stomach-ache, for example, and is tied up with mockery of the complaining one. 'But then do they really not notice the similarity?'—Do we have a single concept everywhere there is a similarity? The question is: Is the similarity *important* to them? And need it be so? And why shouldn't their concept 'pain' split ours up?[5]

Wittgenstein is imagining a society of people who have a word, 'W', to which they respond in two different ways when one of their group complains of 'W', depending on whether the complaining person has or hasn't suffered some visible injury. If he has, they respond with concern and help. If he has not, they regard the complaining one with indifference, or even with contempt and ridicule. We may suppose that a complaining person spontaneously exclaims 'W!' in both cases, and that his primitive behavior in both cases is like the behavior that surrounds our use of the word 'pain' in the first person present tense. But the marked difference in reaction of those who observe the complaining one, depending solely on whether there is visible injury, justifies Wittgenstein's remark that the tribe 'has two concepts, akin to our "pain" '. This may strike us at first as strange and irrational. 'Don't they notice the similarity?' Of course they do. But they also notice *the difference*! Their difference in response will perhaps seem *less* unintelligible if we remember that we too have some tendency to react with *more* pity, concern, anxi-

5. Wittgenstein, *Zettel*, ed. G. E. M. Anscombe and G. H. von Wright, trans. G. E. M. Anscombe (Oxford: Blackwell, 1967), 380. Hereafter cited as *Z*.

ety, and help where there is visible bodily damage (after a child has a fall, say) than where there is none. So this difference affects our reactions too. But we don't draw as sharp a line as they do.

Now when Wittgenstein asks, 'Do we have a single concept wherever there is a similarity?', who is the 'we'? Clearly it refers to everyone, including you and me, who do not draw as sharp a line as do the people of the tribe that Wittgenstein imagined. An actual human group is being compared with an imagined one. The point of the comparison is to show how the same behavioral phenomena could give rise to different concepts. How another group could be more struck by a difference in circumstances than we are.

In Wittgenstein's writings the reference of 'we' is precise. The reference is always to some actual human group or society, in contrast with another real or imagined one. I do not find 'a *we* which is not one group rather than another in the world' but is instead 'the plural descendant of that idealist I' of the *Tractatus*. I am unable to gather from Williams's essay what it is that leads him to think either that a transcendental *I* has been replaced by a transcendental *we* or that some form of idealism is obscurely present in Wittgenstein's later thought.

3

Williams's interpretation of Wittgenstein seems to be influenced by a worry about what Williams calls 'the *evaluative* comparability of different world-pictures' ('Wittgenstein and Idealism', 87). He remarks that, on Wittgenstein's view, different world-pictures 'are accessible to one another, to some extent, but that does not say anything, or anything much, about whether one could compare them with regard to adequacy' (87–88).

According to Wittgenstein, the concepts of reason, justification, evidence, proof, certainty, doubt, are *relative* to various language-games and forms of life. Illustrations of this point can be more, or less, obvious. To take an obvious example: suppose there is a tribe which has a technique of counting (say, from 1 to 100) that is taught and employed in the life of the tribe. But this tribe has no arithmetic. For certain purposes these people make arrangements of stones. Let us suppose that they arrange three vertical rows with six stones in each row. They want to determine the number of stones in this group and they do this by counting the stones one by one. Now *we*, who have arithmetic, could look at the arrangement, note that there are three rows with six in each row, and say: 'Three times six is eighteen; so there are eighteen stones here'. The people of the tribe cannot speak or think in that way. That three times six is eighteen cannot be, for them, a reason, justification, or proof that the arrangement contains eighteen stones. Our arithmetic provides us with reasons and proofs that are meaningless to them. Is there a hint of idealism in this? Not at all. The stones could be there, and there could be eighteen of them, even if no human beings or other creatures were, or ever had been, present. This relativity of reasons, justification, proof, to language does not yield idealism.

Now what about Williams's question as to whether different language-games, forms of life, world-pictures, can be compared 'with regard to adequacy'? The question seems to assume that there could be such a thing as 'adequacy' in some absolute sense. But 'adequacy' is obviously relative to interests, problems, purposes. If these are not taken into account it has no meaning to ask whether one method of doing something is more or less adequate than another. If we were to declare to the members of the tribe, who have counting to one hundred but no arithmetic, that our arithmetical calculations are swifter, are better for dealing with large numbers, and are more reliable than counting, they could reply (or rather, someone could reply for them) that they are in no hurry, they don't deal with large numbers, and as for reliability isn't it possible to make mistakes in calculation as well as in counting? For their limited purposes and interests, counting is adequate. It would be silly to insist that calculating is better for them.

It is to be noted that there is no equality between them and us in respect to 'accessibility' of language-games: for they have no arithmetic, and so cannot compare it with their counting; whereas we have both. Since we use both techniques we can make an 'evaluative comparison'; and this comparison enables us to see that for the concerns of the tribe, counting is a satisfactory technique, not to be judged inferior to calculation. The point is the same as with the previously imagined people who determine areas of land lots solely by pacing. Perhaps they are not troubled if different pacers obtain different results. Or perhaps there is an official who does the pacing for all of them. In either case they don't get into squabbles about boundaries. It would be foolish to assert that they ought to adopt the more refined technique of surveying. Their concept of 'same area' is good enough for their life.

4

But probably these examples are too easy for dealing with Williams's worry about the comparative adequacy of different language-games. Wittgenstein's example of the tribe that has two concepts similar to our 'pain' presents a harder case. If there is no visible swelling, bruise, or laceration, those people regard a person's groans and writhings as pretence, malingering, or illusion. Apparently those people have no concept of an invisible cause of physical pain. To us this seems strange and even absurd. We would want to bring them over to our point of view, perhaps explaining to them that there are various internal organs, veins, intestines, which when infected, injured, blocked, swollen, can produce physical pain. We give them reasons for changing their view. Suppose those people go along with us in conceding that there are these internal parts and that they can become impaired. But suppose they hold that this doesn't produce physical pain but merely complaining behavior?

This difference between them and us would be an example of what Wittgenstein calls a difference in 'world-pictures', not merely a difference in language-games, as in our previous easier examples. The attitude of the other community would seem incomprehensible to us, and we would feel that they were not just wrong but crazy. This is like the case of the people who rely on oracles in preference to physics. Of those people Wittgenstein asks: 'If we call this "wrong" aren't we using our language-game as a base from which to *combat* theirs?' (*OC* 609). And he adds: 'I said I would "combat" the other man—but wouldn't I give him *reasons*? Certainly; but how far do they go? At the end of reasons comes *persuasion*' (*OC* 612). We can imagine how the attempt at persuasion would go. 'Why should pain be produced solely by visible injury? Why shouldn't a diseased or damaged internal organ also produce pain?' And much more. But this other man might resist our reasons and persuasion. He might reply: 'How do you *know* that internal physiological conditions cause pain and not merely pain-like behavior? How can you prove it? Why shouldn't pain be produced solely by external damage?'

This arguing back and forth might get nowhere. The real difference in world-pictures would not lie in evidence and argument but in different ways of *acting*. The people of the other community do not respond with concern and help unless there is visible bodily damage;

whereas we do not draw that sharp line in our behavior toward persons who complain of pain. The fundamental conflict would consist, not in reasoning, but in action and reaction. We would be convinced that our perception of reality is superior to theirs, and that we know something which they don't know. But our preference for our view of the matter is, in the end, something that cannot be justified. As Wittgenstein puts it:

> Giving grounds, . . . justifying the evidence, comes to an end;—but the end is not certain propositions' striking us immediately as true, i.e. it is not a kind of *seeing* on our part; it is our *acting*, which lies at the bottom of the language-game. (*OC* 204)

> At the foundation of well-founded belief lies unfounded belief. (*OC* 253)

In our present example, the 'unfounded belief' would be our belief, or we would call it *certainty*, that people can and do suffer physical pain even without visible bodily damage. This belief or certainty is displayed in our actions and reactions. It is not the result of reasoning; it could be called 'instinctive'. Wittgenstein makes some remarks that can be applied to this case.

> Now I would like to regard this certainty, not as something akin to hastiness or superficiality, but as a form of life. (*OC* 358)

> But that means I want to conceive it as something that lies beyond being justified or unjustified; as it were, as something animal. (*OC* 359)

> I want to regard man here as an animal; as a primitive being to which one grants instinct but not reasoning. As a creature in a primitive state. Any logic good enough for a primitive means of communication needs no apology from us. Language did not emerge from reasoning. (*OC* 475)

> It is a help here to remember that it is a primitive reaction to tend, to treat, the part that hurts when someone else is in pain; and not merely when oneself is. (*Z* 540)

> But what is the word 'primitive' meant to say here? Presumably that this sort of behaviour is *pre-linguistic*: that a language-game is based *on it*, that it is the prototype of a way of thinking and not the result of thought. (*Z* 541)

Each of *us* normally has an instinctive reaction of concern when someone behaves as if in pain, usually in disregard of whether there is perceptible bodily damage. The people of the tribe imagined by Wittgenstein do not have this same primitive reaction. They respond with concern only when they perceive bodily injury. This difference in natural response would give rise to different language-games with the word 'pain'. Two different uses of the word 'pain' would be based on two sharply different forms of primitive behavior—on two different 'forms of life'. One difference in the two 'grammars' of the word 'pain' would be the following: If a young member of that tribe were to declare in all sincerity, 'I really was in pain yesterday even though I had no bodily injury', he might be told by his elders: 'You merely *thought* you were in pain'. In contrast, the grammar that *we* give to the word 'pain' does not permit such a sentence as 'You thought you were in pain but you really were not'. Wittgenstein has invented a fictitious natural history (*PI* 230) in the light of which we are enabled to see the possibility of a different concept of pain.

5

I wish to return to Williams's question about 'the evaluative comparability of different world-pictures'. We surely have a strong inclination to think that our concept of pain, the grammar that the word 'pain' has in our language, is correct, and that the concept of pain employed by the fictitious tribe is mistaken. But what can this mean? In relation to *what* is our concept more correct than theirs? Do we want to say that our concept more accurately portrays the actual nature of pain? Wouldn't this be like thinking that it follows from 'the nature of negation' that a double negative is an affirmative? About *this* Wittgenstein remarks:

> There cannot be a question whether these or other rules are the correct ones for the use of 'not'. (I mean, whether they accord with its meaning.) For without these rules the word has as yet no meaning and if we change the rules, it now has another meaning (or none), and in that case we may just as well change the word too. (*PI* 147n.)

Similarly, it cannot be a genuine question whether our rules for the use of the word 'pain' are more correct than are those of the fictitious tribe.

Their use of the word is both like and unlike our use. Insofar as it is unlike we can rightly say that they give a different meaning to the word. On the other hand, their use of the word has much in common with ours: to that extent, they don't give it a different meaning. Neither they nor we can be said to have a more accurate conception of the nature of pain. It is not as if these two societies had both observed the nature of pain and drawn different conclusions, ours right and theirs wrong, or theirs right and ours wrong.

Williams raises a question about the 'accessibility', by which I presume he means the 'intelligibility', of concepts that differ from our own. I think this would be different in different cases. There is nothing perplexing about the people who determine the number of objects in an arrangement solely by counting, nor about the people who measure land boundaries solely by pacing. We see in both cases that their methods are satisfactory for them, and also that if their interests widened they could be trained in arithmetical calculation or in new methods of measuring. Their methods are included in our methods. There is no baffling instinctive difference between them and us.

But the case is different with the fictitious tribe whose members respond with concern and help only when there is visible injury. Wittgenstein remarks that 'concepts other than though akin to ours might seem *very* queer to us: deviations from the usual *in an unusual direction*' (Z 373). That is how it is with the fictitious tribe. How strange that they should use visible injury to mark off pain from the absence of pain! We cannot imagine ourselves responding this way in all cases. I would apply to this example Wittgenstein's remark: 'We are here describing a language-game that *we cannot learn*' (Z 339).

Is this strange concept of pain intelligible ('accessible') to us? Two things can be said about this. It *is* intelligible in the sense that we can *describe* their language-game with the word 'pain'—how they react, how they speak, how they differ from us. But there is also a sense in which neither those people nor their use of the word 'pain' is intelligible to us; and this consists in there being a striking difference between them and us at the level of instinctive reaction. It would go against the grain for us to feel pity and concern, in the presence of pain-behavior, *only* where there was visible injury.

This difference between them and us at a primitive, instinctive level does not indicate that our world-picture, form of life, or language-game is better, more true, than theirs. To suppose that it was would indeed be using our own language-game as a base from which to combat theirs.

Williams remarks that when it comes to comparing different world-pictures 'with regard to adequacy', Wittgenstein 'tends to say things which cast great doubt' on the possibility of 'whether there is some objective basis from which one "we" could come to recognize the greater truth of what was believed by another "we"' ('Wittgenstein and Idealism', p. 88). Williams appears to think that there should be an 'objective basis'. But what could that be? Our concept of pain has a certain grammar; the concept of the imagined tribe a different grammar. The difference between the two is rooted in different instinctive reactions, in different forms of life. Wittgenstein rightly says that our language-game 'is not based on grounds. It is not reasonable (or unreasonable). It is there—like our life' (*OC* 559). The same holds for the language-game of the imagined tribe. Each 'we' finds the language-game of the other 'we' strange, absurd. What more can be said? To suppose that there is an 'objective basis' in terms of which one language-game could be judged to be more adequate or more 'true' than the other, is to suppose that the true concept of pain is stowed away somewhere like the standard meter, available for comparison when differences arise between merely human concepts. But we may be certain that there are no principles of justification which lie outside of all human conceptual frameworks and world-pictures.

6

What bearing has all this on 'idealism'? We employ a particular concept of pain; the imagined tribe employs a different one. Their concept contains the condition that attributions of pain are justified only if there is visible injury. Thus their use of the word 'pain' will be surrounded by a use of the words 'justification', 'reason', 'evidence', 'proof', that is different from ours. This difference has wide ramifications. For example, costly medical research into causes of bodily pain when there is no visible injury is supported in our society; whereas the imagined people would consider such an activity as nonsensical; they would look on it with the same attitude of incredulity that many of us take toward astrology. They would not regard the presence of pain in the absence of visible bodily damage as anything that could be explained by empirical investigation—just as many of us would not take seriously any purported scientific backing for the presence of 'astral influence'.

Previously I said that, on Wittgenstein's view, the concepts of reason, evidence, justification, proof, are 'relative' to language-games. This now seems to me to be an understatement. For the way in which those words are used is *part* of a language-game, not just 'relative' to it. And the concept of pain that a group has, *is* their language-game with the word 'pain', not something 'relative' to that language-game.

Williams says, quite correctly:

> It looks as though the question, whether something is empirically explicable or not, is itself relative to a language; for such explanation, and *a fortiori*, particular forms of scientific explanation, are just some language-games among others. (89)

But Williams draws a conclusion from this which I cannot follow. He says:

> Thus our view of another world-picture, as something accessible, and empirically related, to ours, may just be a function of our world-picture. . . . Thus we lose hold at this level on the idea that they are *really* accessible. Once that alarm has broken out, we may indeed even begin to lose the hard-earned benefits of 'we' rather than 'I'. For if our supposed scientific understanding of the practices of other groups is to be seen merely as how those practices are *for us*, and if our experience of other forms of life is inescapably and non-trivially conditioned by our own form of life, then one might wonder what after all stops the solipsist doubt, that my experience which is supposedly of other individuals and the form of life which I share with them, cannot fail to be an experience only of how things are *for me*. (89–90)

Let us assess these remarks in terms of the example of the concept of pain of the imagined tribe. As I said previously, we can *describe* the language-game of those other people. In this sense it is 'accessible' to us. It is trivial to say that this description is formulated in *our* language. How else could we formulate it? But this does not imply that we may be failing to see their practice as it really is. The failure of understanding would be, as I said, not at the level of description, but at the deeper level of instinctive action and reaction. We can describe this difference *too*. What makes those people incomprehensible to us is that we cannot imagine ourselves instinctively rejecting all pain-behavior as expressive of pain if it is not accompanied by visible injury.

It is a huge non sequitur to infer that this opens the way to first-person solipsism. What 'stops the solipsist doubt' is the realization that language cannot be the creation of an individual thinker but must involve activities and reactions that are shared by a group, whose members *agree* in the application of words within those activities, which agreement is the measure of the right or wrong use of language by individual speakers of that group.

But probably Williams does not really mean that the 'relativity' of concepts to language-games threatens us with *first-person* solipsism. For he goes on to put his point in what he says is another way—although actually it is a very different point. He says:

> The point can be put also like this, that there is the gravest difficulty . . . in both positing the independent existence of culturally distinct groups with different world-views, and also holding that any access we have to them is inescapably and non-trivially conditioned by our own world-view. For the very question from which we started, of the existence and relative accessibility of different world-views, becomes itself a function of one world-view. In fact what we have here is an exact analogue, at the social level, of aggregative solipsism. (90)

Thus the real threat, according to Williams, is not first-person solipsism, but 'aggregative solipsism'. But is 'aggregative solipsism' a meaningful expression? Solipsism in its original, stern sense, is the idea that no person other than myself can understand what I mean by my words, because my words obtained their meaning from my inner, private, ostensive definitions. But if this idea is untenable, as Wittgenstein has sufficiently demonstrated, what room is there for solipsism in any form? Each one of us grows up in a linguistic community and gradually comes to share in the uses of language that are embedded in the activities and reactions of that community. There can be no place for solipsism *within* the common use of language of an 'aggregate'. In this sense, 'aggregative solipsism' is a contradiction in terms.

Presumably Williams wants to say that there is a solipsism *between* different aggregates. To speak of 'solipsism' here should mean that one community cannot *understand* the different world-pictures and language-games of another community. But as I have said, there is an ambiguity here. We can understand the use of the word 'pain' of the imagined tribe, in the sense that we can *describe* it. I cannot see what Williams means in saying that our description is '*non-trivially* conditioned' by our own use of the word 'pain' and our related form of life. It is completely trivial to say that we describe their use of the word in terms of our own, and that we compare it with our own. Yet we do perceive the difference between their use and ours.

What we find puzzling, even incomprehensible, are *those people*. The trouble is *not* that we cannot *explain* why they instinctively react as they do. For that matter, we cannot explain why *we* react as we do in *not* demanding visible injury as a rigid condition for applying the word 'pain'. Such attempts at explanation do not belong to our philosophical job. As Wittgenstein says:

> Our interest certainly includes the correspondence between concepts and very general facts of nature. . . . But our interest does not fall back upon these possible causes of the formation of concepts; we are not doing natural science, nor yet natural history—since we can also invent fictitious natural history for our purposes. (*PI* 230)

What was gained by the invention of the fictitious tribe was the realization that there could be a concept of pain that deviated from ours. This helps to free us from the assumption that our concept is 'absolutely the correct one'; but also it helps us to understand our own concept better; for we are now able to perceive how it is rooted in our own form of life—that is, in our instinctive, unlearned, reaction of concern in the presence of the pain-behavior of other persons, independently (for the most part) of whether there is visible injury.

There is nothing in all of this that hints at either solipsism or idealism. In fact, quite the contrary. For in describing forms of life, world-pictures, language-games, real or imaginary, that differ from our own, we are enabled to reflect on our own concepts and to see them objectively: we distance ourselves from our concepts and view them from outside, as it were. There is no analogue here of the doctrine of *Tractatus* that 'the limits of *my* language means the limits of *my* world'. Williams suggests that this has been replaced, in Wittgenstein's later philosophy, by the doctrine that 'the limits of *our* language means the limits of our world' (82). I see nothing in this except the tautology that our language is our language. One of the great endeavors of

Wittgenstein's later philosophical work is to show how we can detach ourselves from our own concepts by making them objects of study, through comparison with other imagined concepts and corresponding forms of life. In this way we can also contemplate world-pictures other than our own.

Nor, as I said previously, is there any basis whatever for Williams's suggestion that in Wittgenstein's later philosophy a 'transcendental "we"' replaces the 'transcendental "I"' of the *Tractatus*. Contrary to what Williams says, 'we' in the later writings always refers to an actual group *in* the world which is being compared in its practices and language-games with some other group that is actually, or imagined to be, *in* the world. There is no *we* that is 'the boundary' of the world—no *we* that is 'the plural descendant of that idealist *I*' of the *Tractatus*, as Williams supposes (92). Nor is there a language which is *the* language that defines *the* limits of thought—but only different language-games, real or imagined.

7

But now I will turn to a difficulty that seems to me to present a temptation to think that Wittgenstein's later philosophy implies a form of idealism—a temptation that is greater than any suggested by the points brought forward by Williams, insofar as I understand his paper. I refer to the fact that the word 'know', like any other word, has its place in a language-game. Indeed, this word is used by us in a number of different language-games. Sometimes 'I know' is offered as a guarantee that confirming evidence can be produced. Sometimes the force of 'I know' is to *exclude* further tests, evidence, confirmation, as being *irrelevant*.

Leaving aside such differences, it seems that 'know' is always governed by this rule: if I know that *p* then *p* is true. Philosophers sometimes mistakenly take this to mean that if I know that *p* then I *cannot* be mistaken. Actually it should mean only this: If I know that *p* then I *am not* mistaken.

But to proceed to the apparent idealistic consequence: If I am trained in a language-game in which the word 'know' is used, then if I say, 'I know that *p*', using my sentence in conformity with the conventions of that language-game, including (let us suppose) a backing of evidence that is deemed in that language-game to be adequate or even overwhelming—does it not follow that *p* is true? Isn't that what the language-game tells us to say? Doesn't this language-game *define* my statement as being true? If so, the nature of reality, what is the case, is determined by human language. This is a conclusion that surely deserves the name of idealism.

I think that a concern with this problem is prominent in *On Certainty*. It is particularly conspicuous in Wittgenstein's study of the expression, 'I cannot be mistaken'. Previously I said that 'I know that *p*' entails, not 'I cannot be mistaken', but only 'I am not mistaken'. However, 'I cannot be mistaken', 'I can't be in error about that', certainly are sentences of ordinary language. Wittgenstein raises an interesting question about how those sentences are used:

> The sentence 'I can't be making a mistake' is certainly used in practice. But we may question whether it is then to be taken in a perfectly rigorous sense, or is rather a kind of exaggeration which perhaps is used only with a view to persuasion. (*OC* 669)

I think the answer is that it is used in both ways. Wittgenstein certainly concludes that it has a rigorous sense. He says: 'There are, however, certain types of case in which I rightly say I cannot be making a mistake, and Moore has given a few examples of such cases' (*OC* 674). Some of Moore's examples would be: 'I have clothes on'; 'I am standing up'. Normally, 'I know', would not be used in such cases. But we can imagine circumstances in which another person would be in doubt whether Moore's statements were true, and there Moore could rightly say, 'I *know* I have clothes on', the sense of Moore's assertion there being the same as, 'I can't be mistaken as to whether I have clothes on'.

Wittgenstein gives his own examples:

> If someone believes that he has flown from America to England in the last few days, then, I believe, he cannot be making a *mistake*. And just the same if someone says that he is at this moment sitting at a table and writing. (*OC* 675)

> I might ask: '*How* could I be making a mistake about my name being L. W.?' And I can say: I don't see how it would be possible. (*OC* 660)

What does it mean to say that 'I can't be making a mistake' is used 'rigorously' in these examples? Wittgenstein understands it to mean that a 'mistake' is *logically* excluded. He distinguishes between 'subjective certainty' and 'objective certainty' in the following remark:

> With the word 'certain' we express complete conviction, the total absence of doubt, and thereby we seek to convince other people. That is *subjective* certainty. But when is something objectively certain?—When a mistake is not possible. But what kind of possibility is that? Mustn't a mistake be *logically* excluded? (*OC* 194)

But are we not now confronted with a 'linguistic' idealism? If when I say that my name is N.M., or that I am seated and writing, or that I am living in England, or that I have never been to the moon, and so on—I can't be *mistaken*; and if 'I can't be mistaken' is used here in a rigorous sense to mean that a mistake is logically excluded—then doesn't it follow that the *truth* of my statement is *guaranteed* by this correct use of the expression 'I can't be mistaken'? It is not merely that *I* say that I can't be mistaken: the actual use in ordinary language of the word 'mistake' does not admit of its correct application to those statements of mine. If the language-game with the word 'mistake' forbids its application to those statements, does it not by the same stroke establish them as true? Here again we seem to be presented with the consequence that the conformity of reality with certain statements is secured by a language-game.

There is a tiny hint in Williams's essay that he interprets Wittgenstein in this way. In talking about 'the evaluative comparability of different world-pictures', he speaks of 'those elements in the world-picture which purport to be truth-carrying' (88). He doesn't say to what 'elements' he is referring: so I can only guess at his meaning. I can, however, see the temptation to regard the use of 'I know that *p*', and of 'I can't be mistaken', in their appropriate language-games, as 'truth-carrying'. These might be some of the 'elements' that Williams has in mind.

I wish to show, however, that this is a misinterpretation of Wittgenstein. First of all, the statement, 'I know that *p*', even when one is perfectly *justified* in making it, is not 'truth-carrying'. Wittgenstein says:

> It would be wrong to say that I can only say 'I know that there is a chair there' when there is a chair there. Of course it isn't *true* unless there is, but I have a right to say this if I am *sure* there is a chair there, even if I am wrong. (*OC* 549)

The same holds for the statement, 'I can't be mistaken'. Suppose I have to give my name to an official. For some reason he suspects that I am suffering from some delusion about my identity, and says 'Are you sure that that is your name?'. I might reply, 'Come now! I can't be mistaken about my name'. Wittgenstein remarks: 'I have a right to say "I can't be making a mistake about this" even if I am in error' (*OC* 663). Even if I am completely justified in saying, 'I know that my name is N.M.', or in saying, 'I can't be mistaken about that', it does not follow that my name is N.M. For me a mistake about my name can rightly be said to be 'logically excluded', in the sense that *I* can't conceive of anything that I would regard as evidence that my name is not N.M.—but from this it doesn't follow that that is my name. We have a temptation (I know that I have been influenced by it) to think that 'the impossibility of being mistaken' is a super-strong concept, which when correctly applied is 'truth-carrying'. But in fact it is a down-to-earth expression, containing no magic. ' "I can't be making a mistake" is an ordinary sentence, which serves to give the certainty-value of a statement. And only in its ordinary use is it justified' (*OC* 638). But how is this ordinary sentence used? One thing it does is to exclude a particular *kind* of *failure* (*OC* 640). I can make a mistake in a calculation, or about what day it is, or mistake that person across the street for someone else, and so on. But could I be 'mistaken' about my name, or whether I am in England, or have been to the moon, or am now sitting down? If I *were* wrong in *these* cases it could not be called a 'mistake'. Wittgenstein says:

> In certain circumstances a man cannot make a *mistake*. ('Can' is here used logically, and the proposition does not mean that a man cannot say anything false in those circumstances.) If Moore were to pronounce the opposite of those propositions which he declares certain, we would not just not be of his opinion, but would regard him as mentally disturbed. (*OC* 155)

Being *mentally disturbed* is quite a different thing from *being mistaken*. Wittgenstein remarks that 'it would be completely *misleading* to say: "I believe my name is L.W." And this too is right: I cannot be making a *mistake* about it. But that does not mean that in this I am infallible' (*OC* 425). The important point here is that if I say that '*p*' is true, then even if it is one of those cases in which I can't be *mistaken* it doesn't follow that '*p*' is true.

> When we say 'Certain propositions must be excluded from doubt', it
> sounds as if I ought to put these propositions—for example, that I
> am called L.W.—into a logic-book. For if it belongs to the descrip-
> tion of a language-game, it belongs to logic. But that I am called
> L.W. does not belong to any such description. The language-game
> that operates with people's names can certainly exist even if I am
> mistaken about my name—but it does presuppose that it is nonsen-
> sical to say that the majority of people are mistaken about their
> names. (*OC* 628; see also 519)

> On the other hand, however, it is right to say of myself 'I cannot be
> mistaken about my name', and wrong if I say 'perhaps I am mistaken'.
> But that doesn't mean that it is senseless for others to doubt what I
> declare to be certain. (*OC* 629)

> It is simply the normal case, to be incapable of mistake about the des-
> ignation of certain things in one's mother tongue. (*OC* 630)

In the overwhelming number of cases, adult speakers are not wrong
about their names, or about this being called a 'chair', or that a 'tree'.
This is a general fact about human ability, without which the practice of
giving names could not exist. Being wrong has to be an exception. This
has the consequence that one's statements in such matters will have
weight—will normally be relied on by others.

This general fact cannot, however, prevent the occurrence of events
so extraordinary that they would leave me dumbfounded. Suppose that
I made a casual remark to my wife about being in England now—whereupon she looked at me with amazement and exclaimed, 'You are not in
England, but in Ithaca, New York, USA! Don't you feel well?' Going to
the window I saw, or seemed to see, familiar scenes of Ithaca. Some
Ithaca friends came into the room and assured me, with apparent sincerity and concern, that although there had been talk of my moving to
London, in fact I am still in Ithaca. What would be my reaction? Probably I would feel that I no longer understood anything—that indeed I
had gone crazy! Certainly I would *not* say, 'Well, I guess I made a mistake' (see *OC* 420).

Wittgenstein imagines a similar case:

> What if something *really* unheard-of happened?—If I, say, saw houses
> gradually turning into steam without any obvious cause, if the cattle
> in the fields stood on their heads and laughed and spoke compre-

hensible words; if trees gradually changed into men and men into trees. Now, was I right when I said before all these things happened 'I know that that's a house' etc., or simply 'That's a house' etc.? (*OC* 513)

We move about in our language-games with confidence. We name things, report events, give descriptions. In an overwhelming number of cases we are entirely free from any doubt about what to say. Furthermore, our language is blended with action. We *act* with complete certainty. But this ease and confidence in speech and action is possible only because the world and life go on in regular ways—because, as it were, things 'behave kindly' (*OC* 615). Wittgenstein says:

> Certain events would put me into a position in which I could not go on with the old language-game any more. In which I was torn away from the *sureness* of the game. Indeed, isn't it obvious that the possibility of a language-game is conditioned by certain facts? (*OC* 617)

This conception is surely contrary to idealism. If the logical possibility of language, and therefore of thought and judgment, depends on regularities in the world and life, then it cannot be that reality is *created* by language, thought, judgment.

Then there is the other anti-idealistic feature of Wittgenstein's thinking, which I have already mentioned but will repeat. Suppose that the world and life go on evenly, in the sense that the stability of language is not undermined by wild irregularities. Among the language-games we master are those that employ the expressions, 'I know', 'It's certain', 'I can't be mistaken'. When the presuppositions and requirements of those language-games are satisfied, then one is *entitled* to say, with confidence, 'I know that so-and-so', 'I can't be mistaken'. But nevertheless, *one might be wrong*. Being contradicted by other evidence is not one of those unheard-of occurrences that would destroy language. Thus, even if one says with *complete* justification, 'I know it to be so', reality, the facts, may give one a surprise. This is perhaps the meaning of Wittgenstein's remark:

> It is always by grace of nature that one knows something. (*OC* 505)

8

The 'Intentionality' of Sense-Perception

My topic comes from an essay by Professor G. E. M. Anscombe, 'The Intentionality of Sensation', first published in 1965 and republished in volume 2 of her *Collected Papers*.[1] This essay is a splendid piece of philosophical work, rich in ideas. I am puzzled, however, by its principal thesis, which is that verbs of sense-perception 'are intentional or essentially have an intentional aspect' (p. 11).

The terms 'intentional' and 'intentionality' have been given a technical use in philosophy. Various concepts are said to possess the character of 'intentionality': for example, intentionally doing something, aiming at something, worshipping something, thinking about something, trying to do something. The technical term 'intentionality' is taken from the ordinary word 'intention'. According to Anscombe, the ordinary concept of intention, or of acting intentionally, has three features that pertain to the technical notion of 'intentionality'. They are the following:

'First, not any true description of what you do describes it as the action you intended' (p. 4). (You borrowed five pounds from your friend, but you did not intend to borrow his *last* five pounds.)

'Second, the description under which you intend what you do can be vague, indeterminate'. (You intended to fish from a bridge instead of from a bank, but not from a bridge of some specific length.)

---

1. Oxford: Blackwell, 1981. Page numbers refer to this edition.

'Third, descriptions under which you intend to do what you do may not come true'. (You intended to take a chisel out of the tool box but you took a screwdriver by mistake.)

According to Anscombe, if a concept has the foregoing features, or analogous features, it is an 'intentional' concept: it has the property of 'intentionality' (*ibid.*) She gives an example that employs the concept of *aiming at* something. I quote: 'A man aims at a stag: but the thing he took for a stag was his father, and he shoots his father' (p. 9). This example satisfies the first feature of the concept of intention: there is a true description of what the hunter aimed at (his father) which is not a true description of what he intended to aim at. The feature of indeterminacy is also present: the hunter aimed at a stag, but not at a stag of some particular age. The third feature is also present: he aimed at a stag, but the existing thing in the situation, at which he aimed, was not a stag.

What the man aimed at, in the sense that his aiming had the foregoing three features, is called by Anscombe 'the intentional object' of his aiming (p. 6). She defines an 'intentional verb' as a 'verb taking an intentional object' (*ibid.*). In the sense in which it is true that the hunter aimed at a stag, the intentional object of his aiming is 'given', as Anscombe puts it, by the phrase 'a stag', not by the phrase 'his father'.

Anscombe introduces another technical term, 'material object'. In the sense in which the statement 'He aimed at his father' is true, the material object of his aiming is given by the phrase 'his father'. This, Anscombe says, is not because he shot his father, but 'because the thing he took for a stag actually was his father' (p. 10). The hunter aimed at something he took for a stag: in this sense he aimed at a stag, which is to say that a stag was the intentional object of his aiming. The thing he took for a stag was his father, which is to say that his father was the material object of his aiming.

We should avoid confusing this use of the phrase 'material object' with its more familiar philosophical use. In this latter use, trees, rocks, chairs, etc., are called 'material objects', whether or not they are objects of perception or thought. But in Anscombe's use of the phrase, something is a 'material object' only if it is an object *of* perception, or *of* worship, or *of* thinking, and so on.

Professor Anscombe's main thesis is that verbs of sense-perception are intentional verbs: they require intentional objects. She concentrates on the verb 'to see', and I will do the same. Anscombe says: 'there must be an intentional object of seeing'; 'an intentional object is necessarily involved in seeing' (p. 17). In other words, she contends that when 'see' is used as a verb of visual sense-perception it not only takes an object (which I do not question) but also that it necessarily takes an *intentional* object (which I do question).

I agree that 'see' sometimes takes an intentional object, and also sometimes takes a material object. For example, a man points at a house and exclaims, 'I see a flame in the window!'. (He thinks the house is on fire.) But a moment later he realizes that what he took for a flame was a reflection (of sunlight) in the window glass. He might then say: 'I saw a flame, but it was actually a reflection'. In this latter sentence he was using 'saw' as an intentional verb. As he there used 'saw', it took an intentional object. But he might also have said: 'I saw a reflection that I took for a flame'; or, 'I saw a reflection as a flame'. In either of these latter sentences the material object of 'saw' was a reflection.

I have just given an example in which 'saw' took an intentional object, and also an example in which it took a material object. What I doubt is Anscombe's assertion that an intentional object is *necessarily* involved in seeing. Why should we believe this? Anscombe says:

> While there must be an intentional object of seeing, there need not always be a material object. That is to say "X saw A" where "saw" is used materially, implies some proposition "X saw—" where "saw" is used intentionally; but the converse does not hold. (P. 17)

It does seem to follow from the way Anscombe has defined the expression 'material object', that when there is a material object of seeing there necessarily is an intentional object of seeing. She introduced the expression 'material object' in the context of the example of aiming, where what the hunter took for a stag was actually his father. Anscombe says:

> We can ask what he was doing—what he was aiming at—*in that* he was aiming at a stag: this is to ask for another description "X" such that in "He was aiming at X" we still have an intentional object, but the description "X" gives us something that exists in the situation. For example, he was aiming at that dark patch against the foliage. The dark patch against the foliage was in fact his father's hat with his father's head in it. (P. 10)

Thus, the given intentional object (the stag) being non-existent in the situation, we looked for another intentional object until we found one that did exist. Then the phrase giving that intentional object, and any other true description of the existent thing in question, gives the material object of "He aimed at . . ." (*Ibid.*)

This way of defining the material object of the aiming presupposes there being an intentional object of the aiming. When this terminology is applied to *seeing*, it will also be true by definition that a material object of seeing presupposes an intentional object of seeing. If there is no intentional object there is no material object.

But might there be cases of seeing where there is no intentional object and, *ipso facto*, no material object of seeing? Anscombe's distinction between an intentional and a material object of seeing *seems* to rely on the notion of *taking* something, X, *for* something, Y. The hunter aimed at something (a dark patch against the foliage) which he took for a stag, although it was actually his father. So both the dark patch and the stag were intentional objects of his aiming (one existing, the other not); and his father was the material object of his aiming.

In my example of seeing, a man saw a flickering light in the window and took it for a flame, although it was actually a reflection. Both the flickering light and the flame were intentional objects of his seeing (one existing, the other not); and the reflection was the material object of his seeing.

In Anscombe's example of aiming, and in my example of seeing, a person *took* something, X, *for* something, Y. But cannot one see something, X, without taking it for something, Y? If I see a horse is it necessarily true that I see something I take for a horse? There are cases where this *is* true. I see an animal far away in the distance: I take that distant animal for a horse, and it turns out to be a horse. Or: I saw a dark shape moving through the trees; I took that dark shape for a horse, and it was a horse. Also there could be a case where I took a distant animal, or a dark shape moving through the trees, for a horse, and it was not a horse but a cow.

Suppose, however, that when walking in thick woods I came out into a little clearing and to my surprise saw a horse grazing there only a few feet away. I was not in doubt as to what it was. If it were said that in this case too I saw something I took for a horse, that would be a wrong description of the situation. I saw a horse right in front of me a few feet away: it was not a case of *taking* something *for* a horse!

In her essay Anscombe compares two opposing philosophical positions about the nature of sense-perception. One position she calls the 'ordinary language' view; the other position she calls the 'sense-datum' or 'sense-impression' view (p. 11). She says there are points for and against each of these positions. According to her a point in favor of 'the sense-impression philosophy' is the following:

> The minimum description that must be possible if someone can see something, will be of colours with their variations of light and darkness. One cannot say "Colour, light and dark? No question of any such things", in response to a *present* enquiry about what one sees. (P. 15)

I am not sure what Anscombe means by saying that 'the minimum description' of what one sees in seeing something is of colors in variations of light and darkness. If she means it is necessarily true when one sees something that one sees colors, that seems to be wrong. It is perhaps true that when one is perplexed about what one is seeing, is at a loss to make it out, one could if pressed say something of this sort: 'I see a reddish brown shape against the green of the foliage'. One might then be told: 'That reddish brown shape you see is a horse'. Here one was responding, as Anscombe says, 'to a *present* enquiry about what one sees' (present tense).

But in the case of an inquiry about what one *saw* (past tense) even in the immediate past, one may not be able to give an answer in terms of colors. Suppose I return from town and report that I saw a lot of people in the streets. If asked, 'What colors of various shades and shapes did you see, such that those shades and shapes of color were people?', I might not be able to give an answer in those terms. I might reply: 'It wasn't like that! I didn't notice any shades and shapes of colors; I just saw a lot of people; they were all around me as I walked through the streets'. Suppose the following was then said to me: 'You *must* have seen colors in various shades and shapes, even if you didn't notice them, or noticed them but don't remember them'. Why should we believe this *must?*

In her example of the hunter's aiming at a stag, when no stag was there, Anscombe says rightly that we are entitled to ask: What was the man aiming at *in that* he was aiming at a stag? So also, in my example of a man's seeing a flame in the window when no flame was there, we are entitled to ask: What did the man see *in that* he saw a flame? But in the cases of coming upon a horse in the clearing, and of seeing a lot of people in the streets, there is no demand for the question, 'What did you see *in that* you saw a horse; and what did you see *in that* you saw a lot of people?'. Nor can it be said of those situations that I must have seen something that I *took for* a horse, and something that I *took for* people.

According to Anscombe 'the sense-impression philosophy' has a correct understanding of the Platonic dictum, 'He who sees must see something'. The sense in which this dictum is true, she says, 'is that if someone is seeing, there is some content of his visual experience' (p. 15). She moves from this to her assertion that 'the minimum description' of what one sees is of colors with their variations of light and darkness. Granting that when one sees there is some content of one's visual experience it does not, however, have to be true that colors, or variations of light and darkness, always belong to the content of visual experience. Cannot we say that 'the content' of one's 'visual experience' is given by a true description of what one sees? Of course there are different kinds of descriptions of what one sees, and therefore different kinds of things can be meant by 'the content' of one's visual experience. But since 'a horse' would have been a true description of what I saw when I came out of the woods, then *a horse* was the content of my visual experience. I do not think that there *must* have been some *other* true description, 'X', of the content of my visual experience, such that I *took* X *for* a horse.

It might be said that, even so, my example of suddenly coming upon a horse in a clearing is still an example of taking something for a horse, namely, taking *a horse* for a horse. But this claim would merely reflect the dogmatic insistence that seeing *necessarily* is taking something for something. Can it be said that whenever I see a tube train pulling into an underground station, I *take* the train *for* a train? If someone regularly rides on underground trains, can it be said of him that every day when he watches a train pulling in, and prepares to board it, 'He takes it for a train'? Certainly not. Nor can it be said of him, 'He does not take it for a train'. Neither thing could normally be said of the daily passenger.

Only in special contexts does seeing involve taking something for something. When I walk along the Strand I do not take the people I see about me for people, nor do I take the red buses for buses. When I enter a room do I take the chairs for chairs, or the carpets for carpets? Only in certain circumstances would it make sense to say that. As Wittgenstein remarks in the *Investigations*: 'One doesn't "*take*" what one knows as the cutlery at a meal *for* cutlery; any more than one ordinarily tries to move one's mouth as one eats, or aims at moving it'.[2] I do not see my furniture *as* furniture; nor of course do I see it as something *other* than furniture. Neither *seeing as* nor *taking for* comes into play here.

Let us return to the three features of intentional action that, according to Anscombe, are expressed by the concept of intentionality. The first is: 'Not any true description of what you do describes it as the action you intended'. What would be the analogue for seeing? It would not be this—'Not any true description of what you see describes what you see'—for that is self-contradictory. Would it be this—'Not any true description of what you see describes what you see it *as*, or what you *take* it *for*'? This is true. But it applies only to seeing that is seeing as or taking for. This first feature of intentionality does not apply to every use of 'see' as a verb of sense-perception.

The second feature of intentional action is: 'The description under which you intend what you do can be vague, indeterminate'. The analogue for seeing would presumably be this—'The description under which you see what you see can be vague, indeterminate'. Now in the example of my having seen a horse in a clearing it is true that my description of what I saw ('a horse') did not mention various visible properties of the horse, such as its height or color. But this does not help to show that 'saw' was used there as an intentional verb. Anscombe offers 'thinking of' and 'hitting' as examples of intentional and nonintentional verbs respectively; and she presents the following contrast: 'I can think of a man without thinking of a man of a particular height; I cannot hit a man without hitting a man of some particular height' (p. 6). This is true. But there is a use of 'see' in which I could not have seen a horse in a clearing without having seen a horse of some particular height and color. In this sense, 'seeing' is no more an intentional verb than is 'hitting'.

The third feature of intentional action is: 'Descriptions under which you intend to do what you do may not come true'. Here it is difficult to think what the analogue for seeing might be. It could hardly be this—'Descriptions under which you see what you see may not *come* true'—since in many cases of reported seeing there is no question of any description *coming* true. (When I said, 'I saw a horse', I was not making a prediction.) Perhaps the analogue for seeing would be this—'De-

2. Ludwig Wittgenstein, *Philosophical Investigations*, ed. G. E. M. Anscombe and Rush Rhees, trans. G. E. M. Anscombe (Oxford: Blackwell, 1967), Part 2, p. 195.

scriptions under which you see what you see may not *be* true'. I am uncertain how this should be understood, but I surmise it would be as follows: 'Descriptions under which you see something may not be true descriptions of what you see'. This formulation is satisfied when either you see X *as* Y, or when you see X and *take* it *for* Y—for in some of these cases X may not be Y. This formulation, however, seems to have no application when seeing is neither seeing as nor taking for.

Some philosophers have held that seeing is *always* seeing *as*. And H. A. Prichard, in arguing that it is *impossible* to see bodies (i.e., three-dimensional material things) held that when we *think* we see bodies what really happens is that we see colors which we (mistakenly) take for bodies.[3] I mention Prichard as an illustration of the strength of the temptation to think that seeing material things is always seeing something, X, that one takes for something, Y.

I know of no grounds for attributing to Professor Anscombe either the view that seeing is always seeing as, or the view that seeing is always taking for, or the view that it is always one or the other. If she held such views then I would understand *why* she holds that 'an intentional object is necessarily involved in seeing'. But I doubt that she holds any of those views. Thus I am in the dark as to what might have led her to think that 'an intentional object is necessarily involved in seeing', or more generally, that verbs of sense-perception 'essentially have an intentional aspect'. Insofar as I understand the matter, it appears to me that, in their actual use, verbs of sense-perception sometimes take intentional objects, and sometimes not.

I suspect that the thinking which underlies the contention that there must be an intentional object of seeing, may be presented by the following argument:

> When I reported, "I saw a horse", I might subsequently be convinced by evidence that there was no horse there. Being thus convinced I might then say, "Isn't it queer that I saw a horse, even though no horse was there?". If I said this, then I *would* be using "saw" to take an intentional object. The intentional object would be given by the description "a horse". The possibility of having been mistaken, and of becoming convinced of it, is necessarily present whenever one gives a report of what one saw. The possibility of the above sort of retraction

3. H. A. Prichard, 'Perception', in his *Knowledge and Perception* (Oxford: Clarendon Press, 1950).

is thus *implicit* in every report of visual experience. In this sense, see-ing necessarily has an intentional aspect.

There are several objections to this argument. First, in numberless cases where one reports that one saw an X, no evidence that there was no X there is presented or even considered. There is, therefore, no occasion for one to withdraw to the statement, 'I saw an X but there was no X there'. Second, even if apparent evidence was produced that no X was there, the person who made the original visual report might not re-spond by withdrawing to an intentional use of 'saw'. One possible re-sponse would be to be dumbfounded—too dumbfounded to know what to say or think. Another possible response would be for the person to *refuse* to accept the apparent counter-evidence, and to insist that there was an X there.

Thus, the foregoing argument for claiming that a fallback position, a withdrawal to an intentional use of 'saw', is always potentially present seems to be wrong. I cannot think of any other plausible argument for the claim that seeing necessarily has 'an intentional aspect'. And I do not believe that in or behind every report of visual experience there lurks an intentional object. I do not see any support for the 'sense-datum' or 'sense-impression' philosophy in the alleged intentionality of sense-perception.

9

Subjectivity

1

In his book *The View from Nowhere*,[1] Thomas Nagel says that 'the subjectivity of consciousness is an irreducible feature of reality' (p. 7). He speaks of 'the essential subjectivity of the mental' (p. 17), and of 'the mind's irreducibly subjective character' (p. 28). 'Mental concepts', he says, refer to 'subjective points of view and their modifications' (p. 37):

> The subjective features of conscious mental processes—as opposed to their physical causes and effects—cannot be captured by the purified form of thought suitable for dealing with the physical world that underlies the appearances. Not only raw feels but also intentional mental states—however objective their content—must be capable of manifesting themselves in subjective form to be in the mind at all. (Pp. 15–16)

These are puzzling statements. How is Nagel using the term 'subjective'? In everyday life we characterize some beliefs, opinions, attitudes, as subjective, and others as objective. An opinion that was idiosyncratic or whimsical, or reflected personal prejudice, or was biased, or was an expression of paranoia, or ignored the evidence, could be called a 'subjective' opinion. A belief or judgment that was impartial, unprejudiced,

---

1. Thomas Nagel, *The View from Nowhere* (New York: Oxford University Press, 1986).

and based fairly on the available evidence, could be called 'objective'. If a citizen's attitude toward community proposals (such as building hospitals, laying sewers, or increasing taxes) was exclusively concerned with how his own interest would be affected, his thinking on these matters could be called 'subjective' or (less politely) 'self-centered'. Another citizen's thinking might be more objective. A view that weighed long-term interests as well as short-term goals could be called 'more objective' than a view that considered only the one or the other. A person might be persuaded to adopt an objective view in place of his previously subjective one. So in daily life some opinions and attitudes are deemed subjective and other ones objective; and a particular individual's view of a proposal or situation may change from a subjective one to an objective one, or vice versa.

Hence, when Nagel declares that 'the mind' or 'the mental' or 'consciousness' is 'essentially subjective', and that 'mental concepts' refer to 'subjective points of view', I feel that I have lost whatever grip I had on the terms 'subjective' and 'objective'—and I flounder. That is uncomfortable—so I seek to regain my footing by trying to piece together Nagel's meaning.

When Nagel speaks of 'the mental' and of 'mental concepts', one might take him to be referring to concepts that in philosophical writing are frequently called 'psychological concepts'—such as the concepts of fear, anger, belief, thinking, seeing, intention. This interpretation is approximately correct; but it needs an amendment. Nagel's theme is about 'the mental' only insofar as it is *conscious*: conscious fear, conscious anger, conscious belief. He is not dealing with such phenomena as *unconscious* anxiety, prejudice, or depression. His position is that all conscious psychological phenomena are 'essentially subjective'.

There may be a clue to Nagel's meaning in his remark that 'mental concepts' refer to 'subjective points of view'. Perhaps he means that conscious psychological phenomena can occur only when there is 'a point of view'. The phrase 'a point of view' figures in Nagel's well-known essay 'What Is It Like to Be a Bat?'.[2] He states there that 'an organism has conscious mental states if and only if there is something that it is like to *be* that organism—something it is like *for* the organism' (p. 160). Nagel calls this 'the subjective character of experience' (*ibid.*):

2. Thomas Nagel, 'What Is It Like to Be a Bat?', *Philosophical Review* 83 (1974). Reprinted in *Readings in Philosophy of Psychology*, vol. 1, ed. Ned Block (London: Methuen, 1980). My page citations refer to this volume of *Readings*.

> We believe that bats feel some versions of pain, fear, hunger, and lust.
> . . . But we believe that these experiences also have in each case a spe-
> cific subjective character, which it is beyond our ability to conceive.
> (P. 161)

> Whatever may be the status of facts about what it is like to be a human
> being, or a bat, or a Martian, these appear to be facts that embody a
> particular point of view. (Pp. 162–63)

The 'subjective character of experience' seems to require the presence
of 'a point of view'. According to Nagel, a phenomenon such as lightning 'has an objective character that is not exhausted by its visual appearance' (p. 163). There is something to lightning other than just the
way a flash of lightning looks. But when it comes to someone's conscious experience of *seeing* lightning, then the reference to 'a point of
view' is essential:

> It is difficult to understand what could be meant by the *objective* char-
> acter of an experience, apart from the particular point of view from
> which its subject apprehends it. After all, what would be left of what it
> was like to be a bat if one removed the viewpoint of the bat? (Pp.
> 163–64)

Nagel says that 'even to form the *conception* of what it is like to be a bat
. . . one must take up the bat's point of view' (p. 167n.).

Nagel seems to have been persuaded by Wittgenstein that 'mental
concepts do not refer to logically private objects of awareness' (*View
from Nowhere*, p. 37). Nagel thinks that instead they refer to 'subjective
points of view' (*ibid.*). An example might be the following: suppose I
have a conscious fear of falling from high places. Nagel allows that this
fear does not belong to me alone; others may have the same fear; this
fear that I have is not 'a logically private object'. But if many people can
have that *same* fear, can feel it—what is subjective about it?

Nagel's thought may be the following: although there is nothing
unique or unsharable in this fear I have, there is something in *my* feeling that fear which *is* exclusively mine—namely, *my point of view*. When
an experience occurs there is not only the experience, but there is also,
says Nagel, 'the particular point of view from which its subject apprehends it' ('Bat', p. 163). Nagel seems to think that an 'experience', unlike the physical phenomenon of lightning, 'does not have, in addition

to its subjective character, an objective nature that can be apprehended from many different points of view' (p. 164). He says:

> If the subjective character of experience is fully comprehensible only from one point of view, then any shift to greater objectivity—that is, less attachment to a specific viewpoint—does not take us nearer to the real nature of the phenomenon: it takes us farther away from it. (*Ibid.*)

So perhaps *experiences* do not even have an 'objective' character: 'Does it make sense, in other words, to ask what my experiences are *really* like, as opposed to how they appear to me?' (*ibid.*, p. 166). Obviously, we are confronted with a very confusing topic: the seas of language are running high. In these latter statements from his 'Bat' essay, Nagel *seems* to be expounding 'the logical privacy of experience'. For it appears that he wants to hold that 'the subjective character of experience' is fully comprehensible only 'from *one* point of view' (my emphasis); to hold that there is no sense in speaking of what my experiences are like, apart from 'how they appear to *me*' (my emphasis).

On the other hand, Nagel was at pains in the 'Bat' essay to reject this interpretation:

> I am not adverting here to the alleged privacy of experience to its possessor. The point of view in question is not one accessible only to a single individual. Rather it is to a *type*. It is often possible to take up a point of view other than one's own, so the comprehension of such facts is not limited to one's own case. There is a sense in which the phenomenological facts are perfectly objective: one person can know or say of another what the quality of the other's experience is. They are subjective, however, in the sense that even this objective ascription of experience is possible only for someone sufficiently similar to the object of ascription to be able to adopt his point of view—to understand the ascription in the first person as well as in the third, so to speak. (P. 163)

The idea is that by virtue of being human it is possible for me to grasp the point of view of another human being; but not the point of view of a member of some very different species, such as a bat or a reptile.

It is difficult to know how much of the thinking of the 'Bat' essay is carried over into Nagel's book. Certainly the emphasis on 'a point of view' is retained. Nagel says:

> When we conceive of the minds of others, we cannot abandon the es-
> sential factor of a point of view; instead we must generalize it and
> think of ourselves as one point of view among others. (*View from
> Nowhere*, p. 20)

It is unclear, however, whether the phrase 'a point of view' in this remark
refers to a single individual, or to a type or species. Nagel is discussing
here 'the problem of other minds' which, he says, is 'the conceptual
problem, how I can *understand* the attribution of mental states to others'
(*ibid.*, p. 19). As Nagel's wording indicates, it is necessary for the statement of this familiar philosophical problem that it be expressed in *the
first person singular*. Accordingly, the remark just quoted from p. 20
should also be stated in the first person *singular*, as follows: When *I* conceive of the minds of others, I cannot abandon the essential factor of a
point of view; instead I must generalize it and think of *myself* as one point
of view among others.

The expression 'a point of view' is being used in an unusual way. I am
to think of *myself* as a point of view. Am I a point of view? In the ordinary
use of the expression, a point of view is something that a person sometimes *has*, not *is*. It would be premature to conclude anything significant from this remark of Nagel's. Other passages will, I believe, support
the hypothesis that, on Nagel's conception, a person *is* a point of view.
But I leave this aside for the moment.

Nagel's idea seems to be that whenever any person has a conscious
thought, desire, or intention, that person is, or is operating from, 'a
point of view'. Nagel tends to treat the expressions 'subjective character',
'subjective form', and 'point of view', as roughly equivalent. He says:
'Not only raw feels but also intentional mental states—however objective
their content—must be capable of manifesting themselves in subjective
form to be in the mind at all' (*ibid.*, pp. 15–16). Nagel seems to have the
notion that any conscious sensation, or any consciously held intention
(no matter how trivial), or any conscious mental process (no matter how
humble), must involve 'a point of view'. It is not just opinions, or beliefs,
or views (in the ordinary sense), that require a point of view. Anything
'in the mind at all'—such as suddenly recalling an errand, or feeling a
pang of hunger—demands a point of view. Of course, this is not how the
expression 'a point of view' is used in daily language. The conception
that every conscious mental phenomenon requires 'a point of view' still
lies in darkness. It will take some digging to bring it into the light.

2

It may be rewarding to do this digging in the area where Nagel speaks variously of 'the concept of "I" ', 'the concept of the self', 'the concept of myself', and 'the identity of the self'.

When Nagel uses the phrase 'the concept of myself' and 'the concept of "I" ' (*ibid.*, p. 35), one might suppose that he regarded them as equivalent to the phrase 'the concept of Tom Nagel'. It may be that sometimes this is so; but it is sometimes not so. Nagel believes that he can use the sentence 'I am TN' to express a 'fundamental' truth about the world, something 'extremely non-trivial' (*ibid.*, p. 57). This indicates that for him the phrases 'the concept of "I" ' and 'the concept of TN' do not always have the same meaning or same reference.

It is true that the use of the word 'I' is very different from the use of the name 'TN', or of any name or description. But does Nagel think that when he uses the sentence 'I am TN' to state a supposedly fundamental truth, he is using 'I' and 'TN' to refer to different things: I suspect that this is what he thinks.

The matter is complicated by the fact that Nagel thinks the word 'I' can be used in two sharply different ways. First, there is the use of 'I' in ordinary speech. At a party someone asks, 'Which of you is TN?', and Nagel replies 'I am TN'. Here, says Nagel, 'There is no inclination to believe that such statements express anything remarkable: ordinary objective facts about the speaker make them true or false' (*ibid.*, p. 59). No dramatic philosophical thought is expressed. But Nagel thinks the sentence 'I am TN' *can* be used by him to state a noteworthy philosophical truth. And he need not be speaking *to* anyone other than himself. How is this done? Nagel explains:

> To arrive at this idea I begin by considering the world as a whole, as if from nowhere, and in those oceans of space and time TN is just one person among countless others. Taking up that impersonal standpoint produces in me a sense of complete detachment from TN, who is reduced to a momentary blip on the cosmic TV screen. (*Ibid.*, p. 61)

Before continuing with Nagel's explanation, I will say that this 'considering the world as a whole' is not an easy idea to grasp. A person might consider the world as a whole in regard to wheat production, or growth of population, or consumption of petroleum. But I wonder what one would be doing in 'considering the world as a whole, as if from nowhere', and *not* in regard to petroleum consumption, or food supply, or birthrate—or, in short, *not in regard to anything!* That would seem to be an empty kind of considering. But let that pass.

To continue with Nagel's explanation: the interesting thing that happens (or seems to happen) when this 'considering the world as a whole' occurs, when one 'apprehends the world from without rather than from a standpoint within it' (*ibid.*)—what happens is that there emerges a 'special form of reference of "I" ' (*ibid.*, p. 60). What strikes Nagel in this situation is the following thought:

> So far as what I am essentially is concerned, it seems as if I just *happen* to be the publicly identifiable person TN—as if what I really am, this conscious subject, might just as well view the world from the perspective of a different person. The real me occupies TN, so to speak; or the publicly identifiable person TN contains the real me. From a purely objective point of view my connection with TN seems arbitrary. (*Ibid.*, pp. 60–61)

Nagel's image is that of someone or something, an *I*, that has the whole world in its view, including all of the individuals in the world. As this *I* casts its gaze over the world, its attention focuses on one of those individuals, and it exclaims with a cry of recognition—'That's me! I am TN!'

This reminds one of something that happens in real life. Looking at a photograph of a group of people, you point at one of those figures and exclaim with surprise, 'That's me!' You were outside of the photograph, and looking into it you recognized yourself. Of course you could have been mistaken. The picture was taken years ago, and you no longer resemble much that figure in the picture.

But Nagel is speaking of viewing, not a photograph, but the whole world. And he isn't surprised to find TN there, since his conception postulates that everyone is there:

> This centreless world contains everybody, and it contains not only their bodies but their minds. So it includes TN, an individual born at a certain time to certain parents, with a specific physical and mental history, who is at present thinking about metaphysics. (*Ibid.*, p. 56)

What does it mean to speak of a 'centreless' world? It means that Nagel is imagining that there could be a description of the whole world, and a description of a special kind—one in which neither the word 'I' nor any other indexical expression will occur. This description of the world will include a description of TN, but will not contain any 'I' sentences. Leaving out 'I' sentences will make the description of TN 'objective', including them would make it 'subjective'.

Nagel thinks that he can give the word 'I' a double *reference*. He can make it refer to an 'objective self', and also to a 'subjective self'. The objective self views the world from outside—that is, from *nowhere*, since there is no place outside of the world. The subjective self, in contrast, is located in the world. Of the centerless conception of the world, Nagel says:

> It includes all the individuals in the world, of every kind, and all their mental and physical properties. In fact it *is* the world, conceived from nowhere within it. But if it is supposed to be this world, there seems to be something about it that cannot be included in such a perspectiveless conception—the fact that one of those persons, TN, is the locus of my consciousness, the point of view from which I observe and act on the world. (*Ibid.*, p. 56)

It looks as if Nagel is speaking of two different things, one called 'I', the other called 'TN'. This *I* is normally located in TN. But occasionally it steps out of TN, even out of the world. That is when it views the world from outside. When the *I* inhabits TN it is a 'subjective self'. When it steps outside to view the world as a whole, including TN in its view, it is an 'objective self'.

It is my impression that the subjective self and the objective self, of Nagel's conception, are not two different things, but one thing playing two different roles. This one thing is the *I*, the self, the subject. Objective self and subjective self are different roles or functions of one and the same *I*. But TN and the *I* surely seem to be different things. Nagel says of his conception:

> The picture is this. Essentially I have no particular point of view at all, but apprehend the world as centreless. As it happens, I ordinarily view the world from a certain vantage point, using the eyes, the person, the daily life of TN as a kind of window. But the experiences and the perspective of TN with which I am directly pre-

sented are not the point of view of the true self, for the true self has
no point of view and includes in its conception of the centreless
world TN and his perspective among the contents of that world.
(*Ibid.*, p. 61)

Here the *I* is pictured as dwelling within the person TN—using TN's
eyes and ears to take in information; using TN's limbs to get from one
place to another. This *I* is not, however, chained to TN by any logical
necessity:

So far as its essential nature is concerned, it could base its view of the
world on a different set of experiences from those of TN, or even
[on] none at all coming directly from a perspective within the world,
for in itself it has no such perspective. (*Ibid.*, p. 62)

There is a striking resemblance between Nagel's *I* and the *I* of which
Descartes says:

Examining attentively that which I was, I saw that I could conceive
that I had no body, and that there was no world nor place where I
might be; but yet I could not for all that conceive that I was not. (*Discourse*, Part IV)

The *I* of which Descartes there speaks is certainly not *Descartes*; and the
I of which Nagel speaks is not TN. See how strangely Nagel separates
his *I* from TN: 'Much of my conception of the world comes directly
from what TN delivers to me. I have had to rely heavily on TN's experience, language, and education' (*View from Nowhere*, p. 62). A friend of
mine, Robinson, speaks that way about his uncle. He says: 'Much of my
conception of the world comes directly from what my uncle delivers to
me. I have had to rely heavily on my uncle's experience, language, and
education.'
    Nagel does not regard his *I* as the only *I* there is:

The objective self that I find viewing the world through TN is not
unique: each of us has one. Or perhaps I should say each of you is
one, for the objective self is not a distinct entity. Each of us, then, in
addition to being an ordinary person, is a particular objective self,
the subject of a perspectiveless conception of reality. (*Ibid.*, pp.
63–64)

The remark that the objective self 'is not a distinct entity' is somewhat obscure. Not distinct *from what?* I can see that 'the objective self' is not a distinct entity from 'the subjective self': for these two expressions refer to two different ways in which the *I*, of Nagel's conception, functions. Strictly speaking, Nagel should not have used the words, 'The objective self that I find viewing the world through TN . . .'—for when the *I* is viewing the world through TN, it is not playing the objective role but the subjective one. Subjective self and objective self are merely different functions of the same *I*.

But isn't Nagel's *I* distinct from TN? Surely it is. For the actual human being, TN, does not view the world through the eyes of TN 'as a kind of window'. Sometimes TN looks at the weather *through* a window; but never *through* his eyes. TN is not inside TN, looking out. The *I* or 'self' that is said to 'use' the eyes of TN for viewing the world cannot be TN himself. When Nagel says that the person TN 'is the locus of my consciousness, the point of view from which I observe and act on the world' (*ibid.*, p. 56), it would seem that the *I* of which this is supposed to be true must be something other than the person TN; something that just happens to be residing in TN, and to be using TN as a vehicle for observing the world and acting on it.

One thinks here of the driver of a huge lorry. He sits high up in the cab, and from that 'vantage point' he observes the road and the traffic, and he maneuvers his great vehicle by manipulating the controls with his hands and feet. But this comparison is not fair, since the *I* that occupies the human being, TN, does not have eyes or ears, hands or feet. One wonders how an *I* that is so severely handicapped can observe or act at all!

As I remarked previously, it appears that what has come on stage in Nagel's book is the Cartesian *ego*, which surfaces in philosophy from time to time. Its presence in Nagel's book is obscured by the fact that when Nagel speaks of 'the idea of myself' (*ibid.*, p. 38), or of 'the concept of the self' (*ibid.*, p. 40), sometimes he seems to be talking about the concept of a *person*, and sometimes about the *I* or *Self* that resides in a person and uses that person as its vantage point. When in search of 'the self', Nagel says:

> One of the conditions that the self should meet if possible is that it is
> something in which the flow of consciousness and the beliefs, desires,
> intentions, and character traits that I have all take place—something

beneath the contents of consciousness, which might even survive a
radical break in the continuity of consciousness. (*Ibid.*, p. 45)

Here there is a subtle switching between the person TN and the *Self* that
occupies TN. When Nagel speaks of the desires, and so on, that 'I have',
presumably he is referring to the desires of the human person TN. TN is
the 'something' in which all that 'takes place'—he is not something 'beneath' the contents of consciousness. In this passage 'the self' is both
TN and not TN. The self that is not TN is concealed beneath those desires and that flow of consciousness. Nagel says that 'the self is something
that *underlies* the psychological continuities' (*ibid.*, p. 38, my emphasis).
'I believe that whatever we are told about continuity of mental content
between two stages of experience, the issue logically remains open
whether they have the same subject or not' (*ibid.*). Part of what Nagel is
doing with this remark is disagreeing with philosophical theories that attempt to analyze the concept of personal identity in terms of psychological continuity. I have no dispute with his rejection of such theories. But
the assertion that no matter what the continuity between two stages of
experience, 'the issue logically remains open whether they have the
same subject'—is a staggering thought. What does it mean?

Robinson told me that yesterday at lunch he read about the football
game to be played that evening, and promptly decided to attend it; but
that an hour later, when it began to rain, he changed his mind. Here
was 'continuity of mental content' between Robinson's initial decision
and his subsequent revoking of it. Is there any doubt that it was Robinson, the human being, who first made a decision and later changed his
mind? Surely not. Yet Nagel *seems* to be saying that it 'logically' remains
in doubt whether it is 'the same subject' who made those two decisions.
It seems, therefore, that 'the same subject', of which Nagel speaks, is
something *other* than the man Robinson. *The same subject*, if there is one,
would presumably be the *Self*, the *I*, that uses the person, Robinson, as
its point of view.

In real life when it is a matter of identifying *people*, we employ a host of
criteria such as name, sex, physical appearance, residence, family, native
language, nationality, profession, knowledge, memories, abilities—and
also passport, driving licence, fingerprints, birthmark, tattoo. In trying to
identify a person we do not employ all of these criteria at once, but different ones in different circumstances. Frequently we succeed in identifying people, sometimes easily, sometimes with difficulty. Sometimes we

make mistakes. But if it ever were a question of determining whether the *Self* or *I* or *Subject* that was supposedly 'beneath' Robinson's two decisions was *the same one* in both decisions, how would one proceed? What would one look for? (Does the *Self* have a native language, a birthmark, a passport?) What considerations would count, one way or the other? And what *difference* would it make, to Robinson or to anyone else?

There are additional indications that Nagel thinks he can use 'I' to designate an entity that is distinct from TN. He says:

> What I am is whatever is in fact the seat of the person TN's experiences and his capacity to identify and re-identify himself and his mental states, in memory, experience, and thought, without relying on the sort of observational evidence that others must use to understand him. (*Ibid.*, p. 41)

Here Nagel wants the word 'I' to refer to something that is not the person TN, but is 'the seat' of TN's experiences and capacities. Nagel employs different images to characterize the *I* that must be distinguished from the visible and tangible TN. The *I* 'underlies' TN's psychological continuities; it is 'the seat' of TN's experiences; it is 'beneath' the contents of TN's consciousness; in itself it has no point of view, but when its locus is TN it uses 'the eyes, the person, the daily life of TN as a kind of window', through which it views the world; it is 'a self that views the world *through* the perspective of TN' (*ibid.*, p. 65).

The *I* that is characterized in these ways is called 'the objective self'. The notion that there is an objective self that can be called 'I' is what enables Nagel to express 'the philosophical realization that I am TN' (*ibid.*). Nagel says that in order to express this significant thought, 'The "I" must refer in virtue of something larger whose inclusion in the world is not obvious, and the objective self qualifies for the role' (*Ibid.*).

Nagel can use the sentence 'I am TN' to express something remarkable, by virtue of employing the word 'I' to designate something that might never have been present in the world, and might never have had its locus in TN. 'Here *I* am, located in TN! Extraordinary! *I* might have been nowhere; or *I* might have been located in a different person'. As Nagel says, it can seem 'amazing that I am in fact attached to it [the world] at any particular point' (*ibid.*). Probably Descartes felt a similar astonishment at the 'realization' that 'this I (*moi*) . . . by which I am what I am' is lodged in *Descartes* (*Discourse*, Part IV).

There is a respect, however, in which Nagel's 'objective self' is very different from Descartes's *moi*. Descartes held that the *I* or *me* that is lodged in Descartes is essentially a thinking thing, and would be a thinking thing even if it were not lodged there or anywhere. But it is a reiterated theme of Nagel's that the psychological concepts apply to something only if it has 'a point of view'. And he also holds that the objective self in its own nature 'has no point of view' (*View from Nowhere*, p. 61). Of the objective self, Nagel says:

> So far as its essential nature is concerned, it could base its view of the world on a different set of experiences from those of TN, or even [on] none at all coming directly from a perspective within the world, for in itself it has no such perspective. It is the perspectiveless subject. (*Ibid.*, p. 62)

When the *Self* or *I* is 'viewing' the world 'from nowhere', it has no perspective, no point of view. If, as Nagel certainly seems to hold, consciousness and mind are possible only where there is a point of view, then the perspectiveless 'self' has neither consciousness nor mind. No mental concepts will apply to it. If the *I*, in its pursuit of objectivity, could really step away from every point of view, then it would become a mindless thing—which would appear to be a self-defeating achievement.

3

At the beginning of this essay I expressed perplexity about the meaning of Nagel's claim that consciousness, experience, mind, and conscious psychological phenomena in general are essentially 'subjective'. I noted that this use of the word 'subjective' departs from its ordinary employment. The terms 'subjective' and 'objective' are commonly applied to beliefs, opinions, views, attitudes. In everyday language we *distinguish* between beliefs or views, in terms of whether they are subjective or objective, or more one than the other. Is Nagel saying that when in our everyday thinking we judge someone's view of a certain matter to be quite objective, we are wrong—since by virtue of being a *view* it has to be subjective? His use of the term 'subjective' poses a problem for our understanding.

In pursuing this matter I found in Nagel's terminology a link be-
.ween the word 'subjective' and the phrase 'a point of view'. It appears
that the 'subjectivity' of the 'mental' amounts to the necessary presence
of 'a point of view'. The linking of these two expressions is not immediately helpful, since Nagel's use of the phrase 'a point of view' is eccen-
tric. Does deciding to buy a loaf of bread, or suddenly feeling a chill,
require a point of view?

The best clue to Nagel's use of both expressions is provided, I think,
by a study of his treatment of 'the concept of "I" ' and 'the concept of
the self'. Nagel's use of these expressions is thoroughly metaphysical.
He is convinced that he can use the word 'I' to refer to something that
is not the publicly identifiable person TN, but that does normally reside
in TN. The person TN is the point of view from which an *I* or *Self* or *Subject* observes and acts on the world. The conception is perhaps best expressed by saying that a particular person is a point of *viewing*, for the
Self or *I* that inhabits that person.

Nagel's conception deepens perplexity. One feels bombarded by
questions such as the following: (1) If the *I* that normally resides in TN
were to move out, would TN lose consciousness? (2) Nagel says that the
I that occupies TN 'receives the experiences' of TN (*ibid.*, p. 62). Does
this mean that a single experience of TN is had *twice*—that in TN there
are *two* experiencing subjects? Or does TN *have* the experience and the
I only *apprehend* it? (3) If TN is the point of view from which the *Self* or
I observes and acts on the world, does not TN *himself* observe and act on
the world; or do TN and the *I* do it in unison? One hopes that they will
not fall into disagreement.

What about the theme of the 'subjectivity' of experience, of mind,
of all conscious psychological phenomena? When in ordinary life we
tell someone that a belief or impression of his is 'subjective', this often
comes to saying, 'That is just *your* impression, not anyone else's'; or
'That impression is *peculiar* to *you*'. Now Nagel surely does not want to
claim that two or more people cannot have the *same* impression (or
belief, or sensation). For he has been convinced by Wittgenstein (perhaps reluctantly) that impressions, beliefs, sensations, experiences, in-
tentions, are not 'logically private' possessions of the people who have
them. Nagel should acknowledge that it is common enough for two
people to have the *same* thought, experience, intention. What can he
mean then by his insistence on the 'subjectivity' of all 'mental concepts'?

This claim is connected with Nagel's obscure notion of 'a point of view'. In the everyday use of this expression, many people can share the *same* point of view on some proposal or concern. So what is necessarily 'subjective' about a point of view? The answer is that Nagel is not employing the phrase 'a point of view' in any ordinary sense. He is trying to give this phrase a philosophical meaning, perhaps without fully realizing it. In this meaning a person (and maybe also a bat) *is* a point of view, occupied by a unique *Self* or *I*. The *I* or *Subject* that occupies one person, and thus one point of view, is supposed to be numerically distinct from the *I* that occupies another person. An *I* 'observes the world' from a particular person. This is its point of *viewing*. Even when two persons have the same point of view (in the ordinary sense), the observing *I* in one person will be numerically different from the observing *I* in another person. What is 'peculiar', 'unique' (and thus 'subjective'), in each point of view, is the *I* that looks out from each such 'vantage point'. This appears to be the meaning of Nagel's theme of 'the subjectivity' of experience and mind.

Does this theme make any sense? It would if there were criteria of identity for an *I*. I remarked previously that we employ many different criteria for identifying *persons*, different ones being used in different circumstances. When we are uncertain about the identity of a person, sometimes we succeed in determining his identity, sometimes we make mistakes. But in regard to the identity of an *I* that supposedly occupies the point of view of a person, we could be neither right nor wrong. After a bout of severe amnesia Nagel might be able to identify himself as TN— but not as *I*. 'I am TN' could announce a discovery—but not 'I am I'.

An important source of confusion in Nagel's thinking is his assumption that the word 'I' is used by each speaker, to *refer* to, to *designate*— *something*. But that is not how 'I' is used.[3] If it were, then 'I am I' might be false, because 'I' in these two occurrences had been used to refer to different things. Nagel's statement, 'I am TN', could also be false, not because the speaker was not TN, but because Nagel had mistakenly used 'I' to refer to the wrong thing. If Nagel had not assumed that 'I' is used, like a name, to designate something, he would not have had the notion that in each person there dwells an *I* or *Self* or *Subject*—which uses that person as its point of viewing.

3. Cf. the essay 'Whether "I" Is a Referring Expression', Chapter 2 in this volume.

10

Turning to Stone

1

In the *Philosophical Investigations* Wittgenstein says:

> Couldn't I conceive that I had fearful pains and, while they lasted, I turned to stone? Indeed, how do I know, if my eyes are closed, whether or not I have turned to stone?[1]

Also he raises the question as to whether a *chair* might be thinking to itself (*PI* 361).

I think that my turning to stone is an easier achievement of imagination than my turning into a chair. In order to visualize the latter I would have to imagine radical changes in my body. What would become of my head, eyes, ears, nose, tongue, throat, teeth? What of my chest, stomach, buttocks? If my two legs became chair legs, where would the other two chair legs come from? A major rearrangement of my bodily shape would be required. What resulted would no longer be *my* shape.

Turning to stone is easier to imagine. No rearrangement of my members and bodily parts would need to be visualized. Eyes, ears, tongue, throat, stomach, limbs, would all be there. None of my bodily parts would be diminished. The spatial order between them would be preserved. The stone figure would have the shape of my body.

1. Ludwig Wittgenstein, *Philosophical Investigations*, ed. G. E. M. Anscombe and Rush Rhees, trans. G. E. M. Anscombe (Oxford: Blackwell, 1967), 283. Hereafter cited as *PI*.

2

What is the point of Wittgenstein's fantasy of turning to stone? He comes back to it: 'I turn to stone and my pain goes on' (*PI* 288). Surely this is crazy! Isn't it even self-contradictory? If I have turned to stone I am no longer a living thing: but if I am in pain then I must be alive! The fantasy is not merely bizarre—it is contradictory.

I think the fantasy should be regarded as a challenge to the assumption that it is inconceivable, logically impossible, that a stone figure should have sensations and thoughts. It is being put forward by Wittgenstein as a challenge to his previous assertion that 'one can say only of a living human being, and of what is like it (behaves like it), that it has sensations; it sees; is blind; it hears; is deaf; is conscious, or unconscious' (*PI* 281). Is there anyone who wants to challenge this assertion? Certainly. There are scores of philosophers who deny, or doubt, that the concepts of consciousness, perception, sensation, thought, are tied so closely to the concept of 'a living human being'. Daily it is becoming more respectable to believe that machines might think and be conscious; perhaps not yet, but probably in the future. Machines are neither human beings nor living creatures.

Wittgenstein's assertion conflicts with a strong philosophical inclination to think that what we *mean* by the words 'sensation', 'consciousness', 'fear', 'anger', 'pain', is something 'inner'. The behavior that is 'associated' with fear, pain, consciousness, is something 'outer'—and therefore irrelevant to the *meaning* of these psychological terms.

There is another philosophical inclination, or 'intuition', which is opposed to the one just mentioned. This is the view of logical behaviorism, which regards psychological concepts as 'logical constructions' out of behavior. But I won't go into this view, because Wittgenstein is not dealing with *it* in his fantasy of turning to stone.

This fantasy does have considerable plausibility for anyone who does not dismiss it, but lets it get a grip on him. Surely it seems *possible* that, as I sat in this chair, I should suddenly turn to stone. Perhaps not an empirical possibility, as far as I know; but a *logical* possibility. If my eyes happened to be closed at the time, I would not see my fingers or arms taking on the appearance of stone. So I might not even be aware of having turned to stone.

If I had been feeling a pain in a knee before this happened, isn't it *possible* that I should go on feeling the same pain *after* it happened?

If another person were close by he might see that my limbs, face, posture, had become rigid. If he touched my body he would perceive that it had the hardness and coldness of stone. He would think that I had lost sensation and consciousness: but he would be wrong!

Having turned to stone I would be incapable of any of the behavior by which consciousness or pain is indicated. I would not be able to clutch my knee, or cry out, or move my leg, or clench my teeth. Nor could I say that I am in pain.

Wittgenstein's concern here is with the philosophical conception that the normal behavioral 'expressions' of sensation and consciousness are only frequent 'accompaniments' of sensation and consciousness; that there is no kind of 'logical' connection. We all know that sometimes people feel pain without showing it by any 'expression' of pain. This may have happened to ourselves more than once. Smoke is a normal accompaniment of fire; but fire without smoke is possible, and sometimes occurs. It makes sense to speak of pain occurring without any expression of pain, just as it makes sense to speak of fire without smoke.

I think that the fantasy of turning to stone while the pain continues is Wittgenstein's device for eliminating *in totality* any of the human behavior, either actual or potential, that is normally indicative of sensation or consciousness. This device prepares the way for conducting a thought-experiment to test the conception that the behavior of a living human being has nothing to do with the *meaning* of these psychological terms.

3

Before coming to the test itself, let us run over some of the ground that Wittgenstein had made familiar. Remember that what is at issue is the conception that the phenomena of mind and consciousness are essentially 'inner' phenomena, and that human behavior, being something 'outer', can play no part in fixing the meaning of our mental concepts, our psychological language.

A perplexing question immediately arises. If that is so, how could anyone *learn* the meaning of such terms as 'pain', 'anger', 'feeling cold'? How could you and I have been *taught* their meaning?

The answer would have to be: one is *not* 'taught' their meaning. How could it be done? My mental states, feelings, episodes of consciousness, are not perceptible to other persons. They are hidden in me. They are not open to view. No other person can observe a mental state of mine and inform me that the name of that state is 'anger'. Nothing that I did or failed to do could give another person any grounds for encouraging or discouraging my application of a mental term to myself.

The only possibility seems to be that each person, *by himself*, gives meaning to his psychological terms. This procedure is called 'inner ostensive definition'. It works in this way: you focus your attention on a particular item of consciousness and *give* it a *name*. You think to yourself: 'I will give this a name, so that I can refer to it in the future. I will name it "anger", and when it presents itself again I will know what to call it'. You have given yourself a simple rule for the use of a word.

But intolerable consequences flow from this supposed procedure of inner ostensive definition. For one thing, no other person could know to what my mental terms refer, and so could not understand the sentences in which I employ those terms. My first person psychological language will be 'private' in the harsh sense that only *I* can understand it. In using that language I could be talking only to myself. I could not *inform* another person of what is on my mind or how I feel. Nor of course could I understand the psychological language of another person. How could I, or anyone, know whether you and I are referring to the same phenomena when we use the words 'pain' or 'joy' or 'anger'? As Wittgenstein puts it: 'If I know it only from myself, then I know only what *I* call it, not what another person calls it' (*PI* 347).

Now a philosopher might reluctantly accept the conclusion, perhaps with a certain melancholy, that no one else, not even his wife, understands him. But the worst is yet to come: a result that not even a resolutely melancholy philosopher can accept.

An 'inner ostensive definition' is supposed to establish a firm connection between a word and a particular mental state or occurrence. But since the mental phenomena have been assumed to be known only to the person who has them, it follows that whether a person will in fact be holding to that *same* connection in his subsequent applications of the word will be decidable by *himself alone!* The consequence is that in this 'private' psychological language, there can be no distinction between *following* the rule that was supposedly laid down by the inner ostensive definition and being under *the impression* that one is following it.

The notion of 'privacy' that is involved here has nothing to do with the fact that some people invent secret codes in which they record their reflections exclusively for their own use; nor with the fact that all of us often have thoughts, feelings, sensations, which we do not disclose to other persons, either in words or in other behavior. The philosophical notion of the 'privacy' of sensation and consciousness and, derivatively, the 'privacy' of each person's psychological language—is something entirely different. It is based on the idea that one's sensations and feelings *cannot* be disclosed, because they are 'inner'—necessarily hidden from the view of others. If I do assign names to the items of consciousness that are presented to me inwardly, I cannot explain the reference of those names to anyone else. No other person is qualified to have an opinion as to whether I am following the rules that I supposedly established by my inner ostensive definitions.

In the *Investigations* the explicit examination of the supposed privacy of mental language does not begin until number 243. But forty-one numbers previously, in the course of reflections on the concept of following a rule, Wittgenstein says:

> To *believe* one is following a rule is not to follow a rule. And therefore one cannot follow a rule 'privately', because then believing one was following a rule would be the same thing as following it. (*PI* 202)

This remark is, in a sense, a truism: but it is also a deadly blow to the notion that a person could fix the meaning of his mental terms by inner ostensive definitions. The application of the remark of 202 to this latter topic becomes evident when Wittgenstein is discussing the attempt to make a sign *mean* a certain sensation by virtue of the process of writing or pronouncing the sign while concentrating one's attention on the sensation. This process is supposed to impress on oneself the connection between the sign and the sensation.

Wittgenstein's well-known criticism of this supposition, at *PI* 258, goes roughly as follows: Impressing on yourself the connection of the sign with the sensation is supposed to bring it about that in the future you *correctly* remember the connection. But since all of this takes place 'inwardly' and 'privately', there will be no basis for you, or anyone else, to distinguish between your remembering the connection correctly, and its *seeming* to you that you remember it correctly. 'Seeming right' and 'being right' will come to the same—which is absurd. 'Being *right*' will have lost its meaning.

The striking point of 202 about following rules *in general*, is applied in 258 to the special case of a rule that is supposed to have been established by inner ostensive definition. Whether a person is following a rule, or using a sign correctly, is not something that can be settled solely by that person's impression or belief. The possibility of misremembering the use of a word or sign, of employing it wrongly and being corrected by others—is an essential feature of language. When we see that 'the private language of inner experience' eliminates this feature, we realize that it is only masquerading as a language.

4

The road to our understanding the meaning of mental terms by way of inner ostensive definitions has turned out to be no way at all. Let us start over in order to see what went wrong. One movement of thought that may have misled us was the assumption that feeling, emotion, thought, sensation, are 'inner' and that behavior is 'outer'. To what extent is behavior 'outer'? Are there not *natural expressions* of fear, anger, pain, *in behavior*? A child, starting to run out the door to join his playmates, is seized and stopped by a parent—which is followed by the child's screaming, kicking, struggling, sobbing. The parent knows that to be an outburst of fury—not just by that behavior, but by that behavior in *that situation*. The circumstances were an *occasion* for fury. In different circumstances the screaming and struggling would have been a manifestation of something else—perhaps of an epileptic seizure.

The behavior that is a 'natural expression' of rage, desire, or fear is not 'isolated' behavior, but behavior in particular situations. In the case of a child who has not yet learned words, this expressive behavior is the only basis the grown-ups have for perceiving that the child wants something, or is angry or afraid. It is their sole criterion. The introduction of the word 'criterion' is meant to indicate that there is a connection of *meaning* between the natural expressions and what they are expressions of. If this is so, then the way has been opened for understanding how a child can be *taught* the meaning of mental terms.

5

'But wait a moment', someone might object. 'You are going too fast. I agree that there are "natural expressions" of fear, anger, pain, and so on. But these constellations of behavior have no connection with the *meaning* of those terms. The shrieking and struggling is not fury it-self—but only an external accompaniment of fury. A person can be furious without revealing it by any cry, movement, gesture, facial ex-pression. You have already admitted that. So there is no *necessary* con-nection between any feeling and any outwardly perceptible behavior. The connection, when there is one, is *purely contingent.* That there is ever any "natural expression" of sensation or feeling is, logically speaking, *accidental'.*

6

This forthright opinion has a momentous implication. It implies that, 'logically speaking', human beings *could* have all of their normal sensa-tions, desires, emotions, without ever displaying any of the behavior that is the natural expression of those 'inner' phenomena. A child with an aching tooth would not whimper or hold its jaw or show any sign of discomfort. A carpenter who had hit a finger with a hammer would not cry out in pain, or grit his teeth, or flinch when the finger was grasped; he might carry on with his work as if nothing had happened.

It might be thought human beings would then be *suppressing* their in-clinations to whimper, cry out, flinch, and so on. We do this sometimes; why not all the time? All of the tendencies toward behavioral expres-sions of pain would be checked, controlled. Pain would occur, but never any expression of pain.

But if there was never any normal pain-behavior, what would be the sense of attributing 'suppressed' pain-behavior? The latter is a concep-tion that has meaning only when it is the exception, not the rule. It is just the same as with *orders.* Sometimes orders are not carried out: but it has no sense to suppose that many orders are given—but none are ever carried out (*PI* 345).

7

Let us return to the fantasy of turning to stone. I suggested that this is a stratagem for eliminating any human behavior, actual or potential, that is normally indicative of sensations or consciousness. A figure of stone cannot writhe in pain. But neither does it make sense to suppose that a stone figure is 'suppressing' its inclination to writhe, or to cry out. The concept of 'pain-behavior', whether actual or possible, has no application to a figure of stone.

I think it is significant that Wittgenstein presents the fantasy in *the first person singular.* 'Couldn't I conceive that I had fearful pains and, while they continued, I turned to stone?'. This supposition would not be so attractive if it were about another person: 'Can't I conceive that this man I see lying here in frightful pain should turn to stone, and his pain continue?'. It would be difficult to take this supposition seriously. Why? Because we would realize that our normal criteria for attributing either pain or the absence of pain to another person would not be applicable to a stone figure. The face and limbs of a stone man cannot be twisted with spasms of pain; nor, on the other hand, can a stone man assure us that he is cheerful and well. In my own case, however, I do not determine whether *I* am feeling well, or am suffering, from my perception of my demeanor, or bodily movements, or responses to questions. The supposition that *I* could turn to stone and yet be in pain, cannot be dismissed on the ground that then the criteria that *I* employ for determining whether *I* am or am not suffering would not apply. For *I* don't employ any criteria in my own case.

The fantasy of turning to stone can get a solid grip on one's imagination only if it is presented in the first person singular. There seems to be no obvious absurdity in thinking: 'I can conceive of its happening to *me* that while I was in pain I turned to stone—and the pain continued'.

So here we have a supposition; something imaginable; seemingly a real possibility. It is a supposition that carries profound philosophical consequences. It supports the picture of mental phenomena as 'inner'; it offers comfort to the conviction that behavioral 'expressions' of sensation and consciousness are irrelevant to the *meaning* of the terms 'sensation' and 'consciousness'. We are at an impasse. What is to be done?

8

At this juncture Wittgenstein makes a surprising move. He says: 'Suppose I were in error and it was no longer *pain?*' (*PI* 288). That is an extraordinary question: it seems quite mad. One wants to exclaim: 'But I can't be in error here; it means nothing to be in doubt as to whether I am in pain!' (*ibid.*).

Wittgenstein accepts this objection as justified—that is, as justified in respect to *the ordinary use* of the word 'pain', which provides no place for this doubt. But we are not staying with the ordinary use of the word, the actual 'language-game'. We are trying to conceive of a use of the word in which the expressions of sensation in behavior would have nothing to do with the meaning of the word.

Wittgenstein concludes this passage about turning to stone with a remarkable paragraph:

> That expression of doubt does not belong to the language-game; but if the expression of sensation, human behaviour, is eliminated then it seems that I *ought* to be in doubt. My temptation to say here that one could take a sensation for something other than it is, arises from this: If I assume the abolition of the normal language-game with the expression of a sensation, I need a criterion of identity for the sensation; and then the possibility of error also exists. (*PI* 288)

This reasoning is highly compressed and I will try to unpack it. The fundamental problem is whether there is an essential connection between the meaning of the word 'pain' and the natural expression of pain in behavior. There is a strong inclination to answer in the negative; to hold that the behavior is irrelevant to the concept of pain. This inclination is nourished by the notion that I can identify my sensations all by myself, without any help from others, and without any regard to my behavior. Wittgenstein has pushed this idea to the limit with his suggestion that then it should be conceivable that I might be in pain even though I had turned to stone. 'Turning to stone' is not just a dramatic device. It actually captures the idea that the behavior of living human beings has nothing to do with the meaning of the word 'pain'.

If the behavioral expression of sensation is discarded as irrelevant then, says Wittgenstein, it would appear that I *ought* to be in doubt as to whether I have correctly identified my sensation. Why so? Here we have to remember the point of 258, which was that its *seeming to me* that I am identifying something correctly is not the same as: identifying it correctly. In order to provide for this necessary distinction between my *impression* that something is so and its *being so*, I would need to employ a *criterion*, i.e. some measure or standard against which my impression could be checked for accuracy. In order to identify a sensation I would need a criterion of identity for the sensation. Otherwise it would *make no sense* to speak of my being right or wrong. (What criterion of identity I could use if I had turned to stone, I cannot imagine. But we don't have to go into that: for the thrust of the argument is to show that my using *any* criterion for identifying my sensation leads to an unacceptable result).

The final step of Wittgenstein's reasoning is to say that if I use a criterion for identifying the sensation I have, 'then the possibility of error also exists'. This is an easy point to see. It is something that is involved in the use of a criterion for anything. For example, I want to find out the length of a rug and so I employ a yardstick, this being a criterion of length. But I could lay the yardstick on the rug incorrectly, or I could miscount the number of times I have laid it on—thus making an error about the length. The same would be true if I employed a criterion for identifying my sensation: I might mistake it for something other than it is.

9

The reasoning we have just reviewed seems to me to be a convincing proof that the meaning of the word 'pain' has an essential connection with the behavioral expression of pain. There are, and have to be, criteria *in the language* for the correct employment of the word 'pain'. A child just learning language may use this word incorrectly in saying it has a 'pain'. The parents can see that this word does not fit with the child's behavior and situation. This could also happen to an adult who had lost his grip on the use of the word. What fits or doesn't fit the use of the word belongs to its 'grammar'. If my use of the word does not conform to its grammar, then I am not talking about *pain*.

It is a striking fact about first-person singular psychological sentences that, for the most part, we do not employ them in accordance with criteria. As Wittgenstein remarks, 'Of course I do not identify my sensations by criteria' (*PI* 290). But this should not mislead us into thinking that there are *no* criteria governing what I can say about my sensations.

Wittgenstein puts the following question: 'Do I say that I am talking to myself, because I am behaving in such-and-such a way?'. His answer is: 'I do *not* say it from observation of my behaviour. *But it only makes sense because I do behave in this way*' (*PI* 357, my emphasis in the second sentence.) The same holds for my saying that I am afraid or in pain. I do not say it from observation of my behavior. But what I say makes sense only if my circumstances and behavior are of the right sort.

The criteria for the use of the psychological terms 'pain', 'anger', 'fear', are *in the language*. They govern the use of third-person psychological sentences. If my behavior or situation does not satisfy those criteria, other speakers can correct my application of those words to myself. The philosophical idea that behavior is irrelevant would have the consequence that there would be *no* criteria for the use of the psychological terms, and therefore there would be no right or wrong in anyone's application of them—which would make them meaningless.

If I tried to rescue the situation by devising criteria for my application of those terms *to myself*, then I could make a mistake in employing those criteria—and thus conclude, for example, that I am feeling pain when I am not. This result violates the grammar of the word 'pain': but also it is abhorrent to the philosophical idea that each of us 'knows from his own case' what the word 'pain' means.

10

Wittgenstein's argument has established that there is an essential connection between the meaning of first-person psychological language and the primitive expressions of fear, anger, pain, in human behavior. But how does this connection make its appearance in the teaching of the language? Wittgenstein puts the question like this: 'How does a human being learn the meaning of the names of sensations?—of the word "pain" for example' (*PI* 244). In a familiar passage he suggests what seems to be the only possibility:

> Words are connected with the primitive, the natural, expressions of the sensation and put in their place. A child has hurt himself and cries; and now the grown-ups talk to him and teach him exclamations and, later, sentences. They teach the child new pain-behaviour.
>
> 'So you are saying that the word "pain" really means crying?'. On the contrary; the verbal expression of pain replaces crying and does not describe it. (*PI* 244)

This suggestion does *not* mean that the adults get the child to *identify* a sensation of his as pain. This would only reintroduce the untenable notion of 'inner ostensive definition'. Nor does the suggestion mean that the word 'pain' *stands for* or *refers to* crying—which would be a form of behaviorism. What the suggestion says is that the adults coax the child into *replacing* his crying with words such as 'hurts' or 'pain'. The crying was a primitive expression of pain. The uttered words, by taking the place of the primitive expression, *become* an expression of pain. Uttering those words becomes, for the child, a new form of pain-behavior; and for others it serves as a criterion for the child's being in pain.

The same will occur in the case of other 'mental' terms, such as 'anger' or 'fear'. A child expresses fear or anger in primitive behavior. The adults encourage it to *replace* that behavior with words, such as 'angry' or 'afraid'—thereby turning the child's utterance of those words into an *expression* of anger or fear. Thus the child's new verbal behavior serves as a criterion (not for the child, but for others) of its being angry or afraid.

I have no doubt that a good many philosophers regard Wittgenstein's assertion, in 281, of the primary position of the behavior of living human beings in our psychological concepts—as an unsupported dogma. On the contrary, Wittgenstein provides a rigorous defense of the assertion; and in his argument the fantasy of turning to stone plays a crucial role.

Wittgenstein on
Language and Rules

1

A paradoxical situation exists in the study of Wittgenstein. There is a sharp disagreement in the interpretation of his thinking about the concept of following a rule. According to one group of philosophers Wittgenstein's position is that this concept presupposes a human community in which there is agreement as to whether doing such-and-such is or is not following a particular rule. A second group of philosophers hold that this interpretation of Wittgenstein is not merely wrong, but is even a caricature of Wittgenstein's thought: for when Wittgenstein says that following a rule is 'a practice' he does not mean a social practice, he does not invoke a community of rule-followers, but instead he emphasizes that following a rule presupposes a regularity, a repeated or recurring way of acting that might be exemplified in the life of a solitary person. On the first interpretation it would have no sense to suppose that a human being who had grown up in complete isolation from the rest of mankind could be following rules. On the second interpretation such isolation would be irrelevant.

This dispute goes back to the first publication of the *Philosophical Investigations*[1] in 1953. Thirty-five years later it has not abated, but has become more intense. The publication or availability of most of the

---

1. Ludwig Wittgenstein, *Philosophical Investigations*, 3d ed., trans. G. E. M. Anscombe (New York: Macmillan, 1971). Hereafter cited as *PI* with paragraph number or page number.

corpus of Wittgenstein's writings has, oddly enough, not made a difference to this disagreement, even though a substantial part of the corpus
is devoted to reflections on the concept of following a rule.

The leaders of the second interpretation are G. P. Baker and P. M. S.
Hacker. For a number of years they have been devoted to an ambitious
study of Wittgenstein's philosophical work. This includes the comple-
tion of two volumes of a line-by-line commentary on the *Investigations*,
which at present has reached to *PI* 242.[2] Their scholarship is of high
quality. They have command of the whole of Wittgenstein's writings,
both published and unpublished. They trace remarks in the *Investigations* to their provenance in earlier manuscripts, typescripts, notebooks.
In interpreting a particular remark they bring to bear an impressive
knowledge of similar or related remarks that appear elsewhere in the
corpus, or in the published notes of those who attended Wittgenstein's
lectures in Cambridge.

In addition to their careful scholarship, Baker and Hacker usually interpret Wittgenstein's thinking in a sensitive and sensible way. Only
rarely do I find myself in disagreement with their reading of Wittgenstein, or feel that something has gone wrong. In their treatment of
Wittgenstein's remarks about following a rule, many of their comments
are penetrating.

I am dissatisfied, however, with the lack of importance they assign to
the presence of a community of people who act in accordance with
rules, as a necessary condition for there being any rule-following at all.
In my book *Nothing Is Hidden*[3] there is a chapter entitled 'Following a
Rule', in which I say that 'for Wittgenstein the concept of a rule presupposes a community within which a common agreement in actions
fixes the meaning of a rule';[4] and that 'the idea of a rule is embedded
in an environment of teaching, testing, correcting—within a community where there is an agreement in acting in a way that is called following the rule'.[5] In a critical review[6] Peter Hacker treated my book with
great generosity. But in reference to my suggestion that when Wittgenstein says, in *PI* 202, that one cannot follow a rule 'privately', 'he means
that the actions of a single individual, whether these actions are private

2. A third volume has been published reaching to *PI* 427—Ed.
3. Norman Malcolm, *Nothing Is Hidden* (Oxford: Blackwell, 1986).
4. *Ibid.*, 175.
5. *Ibid.*, 178.
6. P. M. S. Hacker, 'Critical Notice', *Philosophical Investigations* 10 (April 1987).

or public, cannot *fix the meaning of a rule*,[7] and also in reference to my statement that, according to Wittgenstein, 'the concept of following a rule implies the concept of a *community* of rule-followers',[8] Hacker said:[9] 'I believe this to be a demonstrably mistaken interpretation of Wittgenstein, but having discussed and documented the matter elsewhere I shall pass over it'. Hacker thus gracefully spared me from an onslaught, and instead referred the reader to the 'elsewhere', which is the book by himself and Baker, entitled *Wittgenstein: Rules, Grammar, and Necessity*,[10] the second volume of their commentary on the *Investigations*.

In taking up this issue I will not be able to quote any of Wittgenstein's remarks that Baker and Hacker have overlooked. But I see some of those remarks in a different light, and sometimes I will criticize, as misleading or erroneous, the Baker and Hacker formulations of Wittgenstein's intent.

2

An 'internal' relation. Baker and Hacker give the following succinct statement of their understanding of what is central in Wittgenstein's thought about the concept of following a rule, and also of their disagreement with the 'community' conception:

> The pivotal point in Wittgenstein's remarks on following rules is that a rule is *internally* related to acts which accord with it. The rule and nothing but the rule determines what is correct. This idea is incompatible with defining 'correct' in terms of what is normal or standard practice in a community. To take the behaviour of the majority to be the criterion of correctness in applying rules is to abrogate the internal relation of a rule to acts in accord with it.[11]

> There is no possibility of building consensus in behaviour (or shared dispositions) into the explanation of what 'correct' means except at the price of abandoning the insight that a rule is internally related to acts in accord with it.[12]

7. *Nothing Is Hidden*, 156.
8. *Ibid.*
9. 'Critical Notice', 149.
10. G. P. Baker and P. M. S. Hacker, *Wittgenstein: Rules, Grammar, and Necessity* (Oxford: Blackwell, 1986). Hereafter cited as *B&H*.
11. *B&H* 171–72.
12. *B&H* 172.

I will comment on these statements in a series of remarks:

(1) Wittgenstein certainly does hold that the acts that are in accord with a rule are 'internally' related to the rule, *in the sense* that if you do not do *this* you are not following the rule. If you are told to start with 1000 and to follow the rule '+2', you are not following that rule unless you write 1002. Or if you multiply 25 by 25 and do not get 625, you multiplied incorrectly. As Wittgenstein puts it: 'In mathematics the result is itself a criterion of the correct calculation'.[13]

(2) It would be an error, however, to take the remark that acts in accord with a rule are 'internally' related to the rule, *in the sense* that those acts are somehow 'already contained' in the rule. I am not yet attributing this error to Baker and Hacker, but am only clearing the ground. Wittgenstein speaks of the mythology of thinking that 'the rule, once stamped with a particular meaning, traces the lines along which it is to be followed through the whole of space',[14] and of the idea that 'the steps are *really* already taken, even before I take them in writing or orally or in thought'.[15] It is the feeling that when you follow a rule the particular applications of the rule exist in advance of your arriving at them.

In opposition to this philosophical picture, Wittgenstein remarks that 'a rule is not an extension. To follow a rule means to form an extension according to a "general" expression'.[16] Which is to say that the applications of a rule (its 'extension'), are not given with the rule, but have to be *produced*; the extension has to be *constructed*. This point sets the stage for the hard question—what *decides* whether a particular step taken, a particular application made, is or is not in accordance with the rule? This question is not answered by the declaration that a rule is 'internally' related to the acts that accord with it.

(3) 'The rule and nothing but the rule determines what is correct.' This seems to be the response of Baker and Hacker to what I called 'the hard question'. Wittgenstein puts that question as follows: 'But what if the actions of different people in accordance with a rule, do not agree?

13. Wittgenstein, *Bemerkungen, über die Grundlagen der Mathematik*, rev. and expanded ed., ed. G. E. M. Anscombe, Rush Rhees, and G. H. von Wright (Frankfurt am Main: Suhrkamp Verlag, 1974), 393. Hereafter cited as *RFM* with page number. (Quotations are my translation.)

14. *PI* 219.

15. *PI* 188.

16. Wittgenstein, MS 165, ca. 1941–44; unfortunately not published, 78. (Quotations are by page number and are my translation.)

Who is right, who is wrong?'[17] He then imagines cases where the disagreement might be due to a misunderstanding that could easily be
cleared up, or where a person who persisted in acting differently might
be regarded as mentally deficient. Wittgenstein goes on to say:

> But what if the lack of agreement was not the exception but the
> rule?—How should we think of that?
>
> Well, a rule can lead me to an action only in the same sense as can
> any direction in words, for example, an order. And if people did not
> agree in their actions according to rules, and could not come to
> terms with one another, that would be as if they could not come to-
> gether about the sense of orders or descriptions. It would be a 'con-
> fusion of tongues', and one could say that although all of them
> accompanied their actions with the uttering of sounds, nevertheless
> there was no language.[18]

This is one of the many examples of Wittgenstein's insistence that there
can be rules only within a framework of overwhelming agreement. He
says:

> It is of the greatest importance that hardly ever does a quarrel arise
> between human beings, over whether the colour of this object is the
> same as the colour of that one, the length of this stick the same as the
> length of that one, etc. This quiet agreement is the characteristic sur-
> rounding of the use of the word 'same'.
>
> And one must say the analogous thing of proceeding according to
> a rule.
>
> No row breaks out over whether a rule was complied with or not.
> People don't come to blows, for example. That belongs to the frame-
> work in which our language works (for example, in giving a descrip-
> tion).[19]

In asserting that 'the rule and nothing but the rule determines what is
correct', Baker and Hacker do not seem to give sufficient recognition
to Wittgenstein's insight that a rule does not determine anything *except*
within a setting of quiet agreement. If you imagine *that* no longer existing, you become aware of the *nakedness* of the rule. The words that ex-

17. MS 165, 91.
18. MS 165, 93–94.
19. *RFM* 323.

press the rule would be without weight, without life. A signpost would not *be* a signpost. A rule, *by itself,* determines nothing. The assertion that 'nothing but the rule determines what is correct', is a seriously misleading account of Wittgenstein's thinking about rules.

Wittgenstein attempted to clarify for himself the concept of a rule, by approaching it from different directions. He asked himself, for example, *what kind of fact* it is that a rule *requires* a particular step to be taken:

> That a rule *requires* this step, can be a psychological fact. Namely, that we proceed in *this* way, without reflection or doubt.
> But it can also lie in this, that we can agree with one another, and that all of us proceed in *this same way.*[20]

What is here called the 'psychological' fact of the rule's *requiring this* step, namely, the fact that we take this step without looking for a reason, or considering other possibilities, or having any doubt whatever—might be what leads Baker and Hacker to assert that 'the rule and nothing but the rule determines what is correct'. The *second* fact that Wittgenstein mentions is, by implication, *not* 'psychological'. It could perhaps be called the 'logical fact' of the rule's *requiring* this step, namely, the fact that *all* of us, in agreement with one another, proceed in *this* way.

Further on in MS 165, Wittgenstein returns to the ambiguity of the notion that a rule *requires* a certain step:

> Often one can say: this pattern, *looked at* so, must have this continuation.
> I want, however, to stipulate an 'interpretation' ['*Auffassung*'], (something like the old 'Proposition'), which determines the series like an infallible machine through which a conveyor belt runs. So that only this continuation fits this interpretation.
> In reality, however, there are not two things that here fit together.
> But one can say: You are, by your training, so adjusted [*eingestellt*], that always, without reflection, you declare some definite thing to be that which fits. Something that agrees with what others declare to be what fits.[21]

This picture of the interpreted rule as determining a series like an infallible conveyor belt is replaced by a picture of what is down to earth,

20. MS 165, 75–76.
21. MS 165, 86–87.

and human: i.e., the picture of a person who, having been given a certain training, then goes on to determine, without reflection, that the rule requires *this* step, a step that others (having had the same training) will agree to be what the rule demands.

Wittgenstein insists that it is of 'the greatest importance' that there is agreement in the application of words, and about whether doing *that* is in accord with *this* rule. He is saying that this agreement is necessary for the existence of *language*.

> The phenomenon of language rests on regularity, on agreement in acting.
>
> Here it is of the greatest importance that all of us, or the overwhelming number, agree on certain things. For example, I can be sure that the colour of this object will be called 'green' by most people who see it.[22]

In the passages that I have cited from MS 165 and *RFM*, Wittgenstein is saying, clearly enough, that *without* general agreement as to what is 'the same', as to whether going on *thus* fits *this* rule—there would not be rules, descriptions, or language, but at most 'a confusion of tongues'. Baker and Hacker are fully aware of such passages, but in their zeal to combat the notion of 'community agreement', the thrust of Wittgenstein's remarks seems to slide by without making an impact. I suspect that in part this may be due to their being confused by their formulation, 'The rule and nothing but the rule determines what is correct'. This might be understood as merely a repetition, in different words, of their immediately preceding statement that 'a rule is *internally* related to acts which accord with it'[23]—which *can* be read as a correct interpretation of Wittgenstein. But Baker and Hacker also give to their phrase, 'nothing but the rule determines what is correct', a meaning that would isolate rules from their dependence on human agreement. They say:

> It would be absurd to hold that a condition of *this* act . . . being in accord with *this* rule . . . is that people in general agree on the application of rules or that people agree that writing *this* accords with *this*. Of course, if there were no agreement, there would be no common con-

22. *RFM* 342.
23. *B&H* 171–72.

cept of addition, of adding 2, of the series of even integers. But it is an error to insert a community agreement between a rule and what accords with it. For if the rule is given, then so is its 'extension'.[24]

In this last sentence, Baker and Hacker *seem* to be going against Wittgenstein's comment that 'A rule is not an extension'.[25] For how can it be true that 'if a rule is given then so is its extension'—*if* the rule is *not* its extension? Or do Baker and Hacker, after all, think that although a rule is not its extension, the rule *contains* its extension? If a rule neither is, nor contains, its extension, there is no sense left for the assertion that if a rule is given then so is its extension. Furthermore, this assertion may help to explain why Baker and Hacker do not find the nearly universal agreement in applying a rule as striking and important a phenomenon as did Wittgenstein. For how could people *fail* to agree in applying a rule, *if* when a rule is given so is its extension?

The troubling philosophical problem is precisely that when a rule is given its extension is *not* given. As Wittgenstein says, 'To follow a rule means to *form* [*bilden*] an extension according to a "general" expression'.[26] It would seem that different people, with similar training and equal intelligence, *could* form *different* extensions in accordance with the same general expression. They could go on differently. Indeed, that *could* happen—and sometimes does happen. But if such divergence became frequent, then the understanding of what rules are, and what following a rule is, would have disappeared. The fact that almost everyone does go on in the same way, is a great example of a 'form of life', and also an example of something that is normally hidden from us because of its 'simplicity and familiarity'.[27]

In the passage just quoted from Baker and Hacker, they say that 'it is an error to insert a community agreement between a rule and what accords with it'.[28] Certainly one does not take a vote before following a rule—*if* that is what is meant by 'inserting a community agreement'. I will discuss this matter in Section 3.

In the same passage Baker and Hacker allow a *limited* importance to 'agreement', when they say that 'if there were no agreement, there

24. *B&H* 243.
25. MS 165, 78.
26. *Ibid.*, my emphasis.
27. *PI* 129.
28. *B&H* 243.

would be no common concept of addition'.[29] An unwary reader might think they were interpreting Wittgenstein as I do. But the emphasis here should be on 'common'. Baker and Hacker think that without agreement there could be concepts but not *common* concepts, rules but not *shared* rules, language but not *shared* language. This is their gloss on Wittgenstein.

But Wittgenstein himself does not employ these qualifications of his theme. He says, for example, that 'if there was no agreement in what we call "red", etc., etc., language would come to an end'[30]—*language*, not 'shared' language. Quiet agreement 'belongs to the framework in which our language works'[31]—*our language*, not our 'shared' language. 'The phenomenon of language rests on regularity, on agreement in action'[32]—no 'shared' here. 'The phenomena of agreement and of acting according to a rule, are inter-connected'[33]—*rule*, not 'shared' rule.

Wittgenstein likens following a rule to obeying an order; and he asks 'How is what I do, connected with these words?' His answer is, 'only through a general practice'.[34] His point is that following a rule is something that can occur only within the framework of a *general* practice. Here he speaks of 'following a rule', *not* of following a 'shared' rule. Referring to the imagined case in which people no longer agreed in their actions according to a rule, and could not come to terms with one another, he says that the upshot would be that there would be 'no language'[35]—*not* 'no "shared" language'.

Baker and Hacker have a formidable knowledge of Wittgenstein's writings; yet they put a strained interpretation on what he says about 'general practice' and 'agreement in acting'. Why do they not read him as saying straightforwardly that without the framework of general practices and large agreement there would be neither rules nor language? Why this resistance to Wittgenstein's plain words? I will speculate about this in Section 5. At present let us note how Baker and Hacker, in their own thinking, reject the idea that the existence of rules requires general agreement. They say:

29. *Ibid.*
30. *RFM* 196.
31. *RFM* 323.
32. *RFM* 342.
33. *RFM* 344.
34. MS 165, 79.
35. MS 165, 94.

Is it then to be argued that a condition for there *being any rules* is that there be general agreement on what acts accord with what rules? This is multiply confused. First, . . . there is nothing conceptually awry about solitary rule-followers or unshared rules. Secondly, the very form of the question presupposes that rules and what accords with them, as well as understanding a rule and knowing what accords with it, are externally related.[36]

According to Baker and Hacker, to hold that 'general agreement on what acts accord with what rules' is 'a condition for there being any rules', implies that there cannot be 'solitary rule-followers or unshared rules'. I will take up this issue in Section 4. But their claim that 'the very form of the question presupposes that rules and what accords with them . . . are externally related', I will consider now.

3

A consensus of action. Baker and Hacker say that rules and what accords with them are related 'internally', not 'externally'. This is ambiguous. It could come to the same as their puzzling assertion that 'if a rule is given then its extension is given', which I have already criticized. But it could also be taken to mean that to conceive of general agreement as a condition for rule-following would be, as they put it, 'to insert a community agreement between a rule and what accords with it'.[37] Now if 'to insert a community agreement' would mean, for example, that when I am driving on a road and come to a signpost, I stop other motorists in order to collect their opinions as to which direction is indicated by the signpost—then it is obvious that agreement does not enter the scene in that way. Normally it does not 'enter the scene' at all, but remains quietly in the background. Wittgenstein makes this distinction clearly, in remarks that are well known to Baker and Hacker: '*Colour-words* are taught like *this*: "That's red", e.g.—Our language-game only works, of course, when a certain agreement prevails, but the concept of agreement does not enter into the language-game'.[38] You can

---

36. *B&H* 243.
37. *Ibid.*
38. Wittgenstein, *Zettel*, ed. G. E. M. Anscombe and G. H. von Wright, trans. G. E. M. Anscombe (Oxford: Blackwell, 1967), para. 430. Hereafter cited as *Z* followed by paragraph number.

picture the chaos that would occur at a busy London intersection if drivers did *not* agree as to which direction to turn in following a sign. If they were not in agreement the signposts could be removed, since they would have ceased to function as signposts. On the other hand, a driver does not usually seek the opinions of others before making a turn. Wittgenstein explains what he means by the remark that 'the concept of agreement does not enter into the language-game':

> You say '*That* is red', but how is it decided if you are right? Doesn't human agreement decide?—But do I appeal to this agreement in my judgments of colour? Then is what goes on like *this*: I get a number of people to look at an object; to each of them there occurs one of a certain group of words (the so-called colour-words); if the word 'red' occurred to the majority of the spectators (I myself need not belong to this majority), the predicate 'red' rightly belongs to the object.[39]

> Does human agreement *decide* what is red? Is it decided by appeal to the majority? Were we taught to determine colour in *that* way?[40]

If I am in doubt (as sometimes happens) whether the color of some object is blue or green, I may ask another person, 'What would you call this color?'. But in the vast number of cases I apply color-predicates without consultation. This is true of nearly everyone. Usually we do not have 'opinions' about colors, and we make no appeal to the majority. Nevertheless, we 'agree in the language' we use.[41] For the most part, each one of us does apply color-words unhesitatingly, *on his own*—yet we *agree*! Nothing could be more astonishing! But if it were not for this astonishing fact, our 'color-words' would *not be* color words.[42]

And of course the same thing holds for arithmetical calculations. In lectures Wittgenstein gave the following illustration:

> Suppose that we make enormous multiplications—numerals with a thousand digits. Suppose that after a certain point, the results people get deviate from each other. There is no way of preventing this deviation: even when we check their results, the results still deviate. What would be the right result? Would anyone have found it?

39. *Z* 429.
40. *Z* 431.
41. *PI* 241.
42. See *PI* 226.

Would there be a right result?—I should say, 'This has ceased to be a calculation'.[43]

The point is clear. If there were widespread and irremovable differences in the results obtained by different persons, then what they were doing would no longer be called 'multiplication'. Multiplication requires *consensus*. But what sort of consensus is this? Is it a consensus of *opinions*? Wittgenstein's response to this question would be the same one that he made to the suggestion that perhaps he was saying that 'the truths of logic are determined by a consensus of opinions':

> Is this what I am saying? No. There is no *opinion* at all; it is not a question of opinion. They are determined by a consensus of *action*: a consensus of doing the same thing, reacting in the same way. There is a consensus but it is not a consensus of opinion.[44]

Without a consensus of action and reaction, there would not be concepts, language, rules. It is irrelevant whether one calls this consensus a 'presupposition', a 'condition', or part of the 'framework' of language.

As I suggested previously, it may be that the failure of Baker and Hacker to appreciate the full significance of human agreement is due to their idea that 'the rule and nothing but the rule determines what is correct'—and perhaps also due to their declaration that 'if the rule is given then so is its extension'. These formulations *conceal the possibility* of widespread disagreement in the application of rules, and thereby *diminish* the significance of agreement for the concept of a rule.

When Baker and Hacker ask the question, 'Is it then to be argued that a condition for there *being any rules* is that there be general agreement on what acts accord with what rules?', and then go on to declare that 'the very form of the question presupposes that rules and what accords with them . . . are externally related'[45]—they are misinterpreting Wittgenstein. For he certainly does hold that without general agreement there would be neither rules nor language—as is clear from the remarks I quoted in Section 2 (i.e., *RFM* 196, 323, 342, 344; MS 165, 75–76, 79, 86–87, 94; *PI* 240; *Z* 430). This view, as it was meant by

---

43. *Wittgenstein's Lectures on the Foundations of Mathematics*, Lecture notes taken by four people, ed. Cora Diamond (Ithaca: Cornell University Press, 1976), 101. Hereafter cited as *LFM*.
44. *LFM* 183–84.
45. *B&H* 243.

Wittgenstein, does *not* presuppose that rules and what accords with them are 'externally related'. For if 'externally related' means that a general agreement is 'inserted between a rule and what accords with it', or means that one determines whether *this* action accords with *that* rule, by canvasing the opinions of people—then of course Wittgenstein does not hold that a rule and what accords with it are 'externally related'. His position is stated concisely in *Z* 430: our language-games of following rules in arithmetic, of color judgments, of measuring, and so on, would not work *except* in the framework of general agreement—*but* a canvasing and testing of agreement does not enter into the actual *operation* of the language-games.

4

Solitary rule-followers. As previously noted, Baker and Hacker allow a restricted significance to general agreement. They remark that 'in a certain sense we can say that following a rule is "founded on agreement" '.[46] They say: 'A framework of agreement *in behaviour* is presupposed by each of our shared language-games . . . agreement in the results of calculating is of the essence of a shared technique of calculating'.[47] And they say: 'For there to be an agreed (shared) rule is for there to be agreement in its application'.[48]

The appearance of the word 'shared' in these comments is their compromise with Wittgenstein. According to them, not language-games, techniques of calculating, rules, *simpliciter*, are founded on agreement, but only 'shared' ones. Commenting on *PI* 199, Baker and Hacker say:

> Note that W's emphasis here is not on the need for *joint* activity, but on recurrent activity. The concept of following a rule is here linked with the concept of regularity, not with the concept of a community of rule-followers.[49]

In reference to Wittgenstein's remark in *PI* 202, that 'following a rule is a practice', they say:

46. *B&H* 248.
47. *Ibid.*
48. *B&H* 249.
49. *B&H* 140.

But it is not part of the general concept of a practice (or of Wittgenstein's concept) that it *must* be shared, but only that it must be
sharable. It must be possible to teach a technique of applying a rule to
others, and for others, by grasping the criteria of correctness, to determine whether a given act is a correct application of the rule. It
must be *intelligible* that others can qualify as masters of any genuine
technique.[50]

In their book *Scepticism, Rules, and Language*, they comment on the appearance of the term '*Praxis*' in *PI* 202, as follows:

It is a misinterpretation to take '*Praxis*' here to signify a social practice. . . . The point is *not* to establish that language necessarily involves a community . . . nothing in this discussion involves any
commitment to a multiplicity of *agents*. All the emphasis is on the regularity, the multiple *occasions* of action.[51]

And they say: 'Whether a person is following a rule, or only thinks incorrectly that he is following a rule, does not depend on what others
are or might be doing.[52] Let us return to their detailed commentary
on the *Investigations*. In their comment on *PI* 198, where Wittgenstein
says that a person 'directs himself by a signpost only insofar as there
exists a regular use of signposts, a custom', Baker and Hacker say the
following: 'By offering this as part of the clarification of the concept
of going by a signpost, Wittgenstein *seems* to have built into this concept the existence of a *shared* pattern of behaviour'.[53] But they claim
that to believe this is so is a serious misinterpretation of Wittgenstein;
for he never intended to deny the possibility of there being solitary
rule-followers:

He was aware of the danger that his remarks about agreement might
be misinterpreted in this way. He quite explicitly took care *not* to exclude the possibility that a solitary individual could follow a rule or
speak a language to himself.[54]

50. *B&H* 164.
51. G. P. Baker and P. M. S. Hacker, *Scepticism, Rules, and Language* (Oxford: Blackwell,
1984), 20. Hereafter cited as *SRL*.
52. *SRL* 76.
53. *B&H* 170.
54. *B&H* 172.

It is far from clear what the issue is here. Can a 'solitary individual' follow a rule? Most of us follow rules when we are alone. I calculate my income tax alone. I write letters, read, think, when I am alone. I was brought up in the English language and carry it with me wherever I go. If I were shipwrecked, like Robinson Crusoe, on an uninhabited island, I would retain (for a time at least) my knowledge of English and of counting and arithmetic. It is normal for people to do calculations, carry out instructions, prepare plans, in private. In this sense, all of us are 'solitary individuals' much of the time.

Of course all of us have spent many years in being taught to speak, write, calculate. We grew up in communities of language-users and rule-followers. The *philosophical* problem about 'solitary rule-followers' should be the question of whether someone who grew up in total isolation from other human beings could create a language for his own use. Could there be a Crusoe who (unlike Defoe's Crusoe) was never a member of a human society, yet invented a language that he employed in his daily activities? And does Wittgenstein concede such a possibility? Baker and Hacker contend that he does:

> Ruminations about desert islanders seem to be attempts to raise the philosophical question of under what conditions we can intelligibly apply the concept of speaking a language. Wittgenstein argued that the solitariness or isolation of an individual is irrelevant to the question of his speaking a language. What is crucial is the *possibility* of another's mastering the 'language' that the solitary person 'speaks'. It is certainly conceivable, Wittgenstein claimed, that each person spoke only to himself, that he was acquainted only with language-games he played with himself (giving himself orders or exhortations, asking himself questions, etc.), and even that the language of such speakers had an extensive vocabulary. An explorer who studied these monologuists could grasp the thoughts they expressed and arrive at a probable translation into his own language by observing how their activities were correlated with their articulate speech. By learning their language he would be in a position to predict what they would do in so far as what they say includes predictions or decisions.[55]

It is astonishing to find Baker and Hacker declaring that Wittgenstein *claimed* that it is conceivable that 'each person spoke only to him-

55. *B&H* 175–76.

self'. Would this alleged claim mean that it is conceivable that every person in the world might have spoken only to himself? Where do Baker and Hacker think they find such an extraordinary assertion by Wittgenstein? They make a similar claim in the *Scepticism, Rules, and Language*. They say that, according to Wittgenstein, 'There could be men who know only language-games that one plays by oneself, etc.'.[56] Baker and Hacker refer here to a passage in MS 124, which is an early version of the first paragraph of *PI* 243. This version of 243 reads as follows:

> A human being can encourage himself, give himself orders, obey, blame and punish himself; he can ask himself a question and answer it. We could even conceive of human beings who spoke only in mono-logue; who accompanied their activities by talking to themselves.— An explorer who observed them and listened to their talk might succeed in translating their language into ours. (This would enable him to predict these people's actions correctly, for he also hears them making resolutions and decisions.)

Where in this passage is there any ground for attributing to Wittgenstein the declaration that it is conceivable that 'each person spoke only to himself'? Are Baker and Hacker making an illegitimate use of the proposition 'What *sometimes* happens might *always* happen', which Wittgenstein warns against in *PI* 345?

In *PI* 243 Wittgenstein immediately moves on from the opening paragraph, to introduce an entirely different topic—namely, the notion of a language that is 'private' in the sense that the words of this lan-guage 'are to refer to what can be known only to the person speaking'. Wittgenstein does not stop to fill in a possible background for those imagined people who speak only in monologue. He leaves that to the reader. It is easy to supply a background that does not imply that those people had spoken only in monologue for their entire lives. For exam-ple, after a normal upbringing, they might have become members of a monastic order that forbade its members to speak to one another. Or, as H. O. Mounce suggests, 'suppose that some terrible affliction has fallen on a whole population, so that people speak only to themselves, having lost all interest in one another'.[57]

---

56. *SRL* 41.
57. H. O. Mounce, 'Following a Rule', *Philosophical Investigations* 9 (July 1986), 198.

Nothing in *PI* 243 warrants the reading that Wittgenstein was saying that it is conceivable 'that each person spoke only to himself'. Baker and Hacker seem to take this to be a claim by Wittgenstein that there could be people who during their *entire* lives never spoke to anyone, nor were ever spoken to, yet each of whom developed a spoken language, by himself, and that (miraculously) they developed the *same* language!

In the revised and expanded edition of *Remarks on the Foundations of Mathematics*, Part VI is wholly new. It consists of MS 164, probably written in the period 1941–44. According to the editors, it is 'perhaps the most satisfactory presentation of Wittgenstein's thoughts about the problem of following a rule'.[58] Let us look at some of the passages in Part VI:

> If one of two chimpanzees one time scratches the figure /– –/ in the earth, and thereupon the other one scratches the series /– –/ /– –/, etc., the first one would not have given a rule and the other one be following it, no matter what else went on at that time in the minds of the two of them. But if one observed, e.g., the phenomenon of a kind of instruction, of showing how and imitation, of successful and un-successful attempts, of reward and punishment, and the like; if at length the one who had been so trained, put figures which he had never seen before, one after the other as in the first example, then we should indeed say that the one chimpanzee writes down rules and the other follows them.[59]

Baker and Hacker refer to this passage, but seem not to catch its significance. They say, rightly, that it is 'the *circumstances* surrounding the particular act that makes the difference between following a rule and not following the rule'.[60] Yet in a summary of their interpretation, they say: 'Wittgenstein's verdict is clear: a solitary individual can follow a rule'.[61] But the striking *difference* in circumstances, in Wittgenstein's example, is that in the second case there is instruction, demonstration, correction, reward, punishment—and thus the establishing and enforcing of *the right way* of going on. If you conceive of an individual who has been in solitude his whole life long, then you have cut away the background of

58. *RFM* 29.
59. *RFM* 345.
60. *B&H* 177.
61. *Ibid.*

instruction, correction, acceptance—in short, the circumstances in which a rule is given, enforced, and followed.

As previously noted, in expounding *PI* 199 (where it is said that 'to understand a language means to master a technique', and that 'to follow a rule, make a report, give an order, play a game of chess, are *customs* (uses, institutions)')—Baker and Hacker say that Wittgenstein's emphasis there is on *recurrent* activity, not on *joint* activity:

> The concept of following a rule is here linked with the concept of regularity, not with the concept of a community of rule-followers.[62]

> Mastery of a technique is manifest in its exercise on a multiplicity of *occasions*.[63]

Baker and Hacker are interpreting Wittgenstein in a way that will *not* have him meaning that following a rule requires a framework of agreement—but only as meaning that it requires 'regularity' in the sense of 'recurrent' action, repetition, a multiplicity of occasions. They are right to this extent: Wittgenstein did hold that the concept of following a rule has application only when there is a 'multiplicity of occasions'. In *PI* 199 he says, 'It is impossible that there should have been only a single time that someone followed a rule'. In *RFM* he says: 'In order to describe the phenomenon of language one has to describe a practice, not a one-time occurrence, *whatever it might be*'.[64] He asks himself, 'But how often must a rule be actually applied, in order for one to have the right to speak of a rule?'[65] He doesn't answer the question—because it cannot be answered. But clearly there must be some *regularity* in acting. This is *one* dimension of the concept of following a rule.

But regularity is not enough. Another dimension of the concept of following a rule is *agreement* between different people, in applying a rule. Here is a longish passage from *RFM*:

> The word 'agreement' and the word 'rule' are *related* to one another; they are *cousins*. The phenomena of agreement and of acting according to a rule are interdependent. To be sure, there could be a caveman who produced for himself a *regular* sequence of figures.

62. *B&H* 140.
63. *Ibid.*
64. *RFM* 335.
65. *RFM* 334.

He amuses himself, for example, by drawing on the wall of the cave

—·— —·— —·— —·

or —·—·—·—··—·—··—·—

But he does not follow the general expressions of a rule. And we do not say he is acting according to a rule, just because we can form such an expression.

What if in addition he developed π! (I mean, without a general expression of a rule.)

Only in the practice of a language can a word have meaning. Certainly, I can give myself a rule and then follow it. But isn't it only a rule, because it is analogous to that, which in the dealings of human beings, is called a 'rule'?

If a thrush in its singing constantly repeats for some time the same phrase, do we say perhaps it gives itself each time a rule, which it then follows?[66]

Both caveman and thrush produce regular sequences—but they are not following rules, and their marks and sounds have no meaning in the sense that words have meaning. A rule can exist only in a human practice, or in what is analogous to it. And what a rule requires and what following it is presupposes the background of a social setting in which there is quiet agreement as to what 'going on in the same way' is. This is an agreement in *acting*, not in opinions: 'The agreement of human beings, which is a presupposition of logic, is not an agreement in *opinions*, let alone opinions about questions of logic'.[67] Agreement is a presupposition of *logic*, not just of 'shared' logic. Baker and Hacker want to interpret Wittgenstein as conceding that someone who lived a totally solitary life, from birth to death, might have the mastery of an unshared logic and language, and presumably of an unshared arithmetic. In this connection, Wittgenstein asks some interesting questions:

Could there be an arithmetic without agreement between those who calculate?

Could a solitary person calculate? Could a solitary person follow a rule?

Are these questions perhaps like this one: 'Can a solitary person carry on a trade?'.[68]

66. *RFM* 344–45.
67. *RFM* 353.
68. *RFM* 349.

Baker and Hacker refer to this last question (which Wittgenstein does not answer). They say: 'Clearly the answer is negative'.[69] This response to Wittgenstein's question is surprising. They intend to be expounding Wittgenstein, and here they assume that his answer, not just their own answer, would be in the negative. I think the opposite.

Consider Wittgenstein's frequent remarks of the following sort: 'The phenomenon of language rests on regularity, on agreement in acting'.[70] 'The agreement of human beings . . . is a presupposition of logic'.[71] 'Our language-game only works, of course, when a certain agreement prevails'.[72] 'The phenomena of agreement and of acting according to a rule are interdependent'.[73] Reflection on such comments convinces me that Wittgenstein's own answer to the question he posed would be affirmative. The supposition that a forever-solitary being could have a language, or an arithmetic, or follow a rule, *would* be like the comical supposition that a being so placed could 'carry on a trade'.

To speak a language is to participate in a way of living in which many people are engaged. The language I speak gets its meaning from the common ways of acting and responding of many people. I *take part* in a language in the sense in which I *take part* in a game—which is surely one reason why Wittgenstein compared languages to games. Another reason for this comparison is that in both languages and games there are *rules*. To follow the rules for the use of an expression is nothing other than to use the expression as it is ordinarily used—which is to say, as it is used by those many people who take part in the activities in which the expression is embedded. Thus the meaning of the expression is *independent* of me, or of any particular person; and this is why I can use the expression correctly or incorrectly. It has a meaning independent of *my* use of it. And this is why there is no sense in the supposition that a forever-solitary person could know a language, any more than he could buy and sell.

This point can be applied to the assertion of Baker and Hacker that 'it is not part of the general concept of a practice (or of Wittgenstein's concept) that it *must* be shared, but only that it must be *sharable*'.[74] They

69. *B&H* 140.
70. *RFM* 342.
71. *RFM* 353.
72. *Z* 430.
73. *RFM* 344.
74. *B&H* 164.

are right in half of what they say: a practice must be sharable. But something is sharable only if there is something to be shared. The forever-solitary person could make sounds and marks. This would be only what *he* does. The sounds and marks would not have a meaning *independent* of his production of them—which comes to saying that they would *not have meaning* in the sense that words have meaning.

Wittgenstein says that 'to imagine a language means, to imagine a form of life'.[75] The expression 'a form of life' suggests some typical or characteristic behavior of a species, a tribe, a clan, a society, a people, a culture. Describing the form of life of a species would be describing its natural history. One species of animals dwells in trees, another in caves. One human tribe obtains food by hunting, another by tending crops. These would be differences in forms of life.

When Wittgenstein connects a language with a human form of life, he is seeing a language as embedded in some characteristic way of acting of many people, not in the behavior of a single individual. He says that he is providing 'remarks on the natural history of human beings'.[76] His term 'language-game' is meant to emphasize that a use of language reflects a form of life. The daily exchange of greetings is an example of a form of life and of a use of language that is characteristic of many human societies. The exchange of greetings can be called a *practice*, a *custom*, an *institution*. There is no difficulty about this example.

What is harder to grasp is Wittgenstein's conception that *following a rule*, just as much as the exchange of greetings, is a *practice*,[77] a *custom, an institution.*[78] It is *a form of life*, a feature of *the natural history* of human beings. Baker and Hacker declare that when Wittgenstein says that following a rule is 'a practice', he cannot mean 'to differentiate something essentially social from something individual which may be done in privacy'.[79] It seems clear to me, however, that Wittgenstein *is* saying that the concept of following a rule is 'essentially social'—in the sense that it can have its roots only in a setting where there is *a people*, with common life and a common language. Which is to say that it would make no sense to suppose that an individual who had lived in

75. *PI* 19.
76. *PI* 415.
77. *PI* 202.
78. *PI* 199.
79. *B&H* 177–78.

complete isolation, from start to finish, could have been following rules. Undoubtedly this conception provokes great philosophical resistance—but this should not prevent us from seeing that it truly is Wittgenstein's conception.

Baker and Hacker go so far as to claim that Wittgenstein took *precautions* to ensure that his thinking about his concept of following a rule was not to be understood as eliminating the possibility of a forever-solitary rule-follower;

> Wittgenstein's reaction to the suggestion that the practice of following a rule is essentially social is not a mere matter of speculation and conjecture. He was aware of the danger that his remarks about agreement might be misinterpreted in this way. He quite explicitly took care *not* to exclude the possibility that a solitary individual could follow a rule or speak a language to himself.[80]

This statement by Baker and Hacker conflates two different things. Whether the concept of following a rule is the concept of something 'essentially social' is an important philosophical issue. Whether 'a solitary individual' can follow a rule or speak to himself is no issue at all, since most of us are solitary a good part of the time.

Baker and Hacker say: 'It is noteworthy that Wittgenstein explicitly discussed Robinson Crusoe'.[81] This would be noteworthy only if Wittgenstein had conceived of a 'Robinson Crusoe' who (unlike Defoe's invention) had *never* encountered other people, yet in his lifelong isolation had created a language. But of course Wittgenstein did not conceive of *such* a Crusoe. He imagines a Crusoe who talks to himself,[82] but there is no indication that he is conceiving of anyone other than Defoe's Crusoe.

More interesting is a reference he makes to a Crusoe, in connection with the concept of giving an order:

> Ordering is a technique of our language.
>   If someone came into a foreign country, whose language he did not understand, it would not in general be difficult for him to find out when an order was given.

---

80. *B&H* 172.
81. *B&H* 173.
82. MS 165, 103.

But one can also order oneself to do something. If, however, we observed a Robinson, who gave himself an order in a language unfamiliar to us, this would be much more difficult to recognize.[83]

Wittgenstein is saying that giving orders and obeying orders is a pattern of action and reaction which could fairly easily be discerned by us, even if the language was foreign—whereas such a pattern would be more difficult to perceive in the case of an isolated individual. But there is no hint that this 'Robinson' had been isolated for his entire life.

Still more interesting is the following:

> What if the human being (perhaps a caveman) always spoke only to himself. Think of a case in which we could say: 'Now he is considering whether he should do so-and-so. Now he has made a decision. Now he orders himself to act'. It is possible to imagine something of that sort, if he perhaps makes use of simple drawings, which we can interpret.[84]

There is no suggestion that this caveman had lived in complete separation from other human beings for his whole life, any more than it is suggested in *PI* 243 that the people who spoke 'only in monologue', had *never* taken part in a common language. Wittgenstein's main point here is that we can often perceive what a person is thinking and deciding, from his circumstances, together with his gestures, movements, facial expressions, even if we do not hear his words, or do not understand them. (In the case of the caveman, his drawings of familiar objects might make this easier for us.) Wittgenstein always puts emphasis on the fact that the words of language have meaning only because they are enmeshed in common patterns of human life. Even familiar words, when separated from these patterns, cease to be language:

> If we conceive of a being who, as we would say, performed actions totally without rhyme or reason, and accompanied these actions with sounds, perhaps with sentences of the German language, still this being would have no language.[85]

According to Baker and Hacker, 'Wittgenstein argued that the solitariness or isolation of an individual is irrelevant to the question of

83. MS 165, 108.
84. MS 165, 116–17.
85. MS 165, 96.

his speaking a language'.[86] This is an extraordinary assertion. Here, as before, the words 'isolation' and 'solitariness', are ambiguous. Wittgenstein did not and had no need to 'argue' that an individual who grew up in a linguistic community, in the normal way, could later live along and continue to think, write, and talk to himself. This was never an issue. On the other hand, it is not true that Wittgenstein *argued* for the view that a being who had *always* lived in solitude *could* have the mastery of a language. If he argued for anything, it was for just the opposite.

There is a passage in MS 165 that Baker and Hacker cite in support of their interpretation: 'One can indeed imagine a human being who lives by himself and draws pictures of the objects around him (perhaps on the walls of his cave), and such a picture-language could be readily understood'.[87] Let us *arbitrarily assume* that Wittgenstein was imagining someone who had *always* lived alone, and who was employing a picture-language (*Bildersprache*). Would Wittgenstein be implying that there could be a forever-solitary person with a language? Baker and Hacker construe the example in that way. Their comment is:

> Provided that his symbolism resembles paradigmatic languages closely enough . . . then we can discover that he is master of a language. And parallel possibilities hold for determining whether he follows other rules and applies various techniques.[88]

Is there any ground for assuming that the drawings of this solitary being are done in accordance with rules? One of our small children, before it knew any words, might draw something that we could recognize as a picture of a house. But this does not mean that the child is employing a 'symbolism'. A linguistic symbol is a sign or mark, the use of which is governed by rules, and thus can be employed correctly or incorrectly. In this sense, there is no 'mastery of a language' exhibited by the child or the caveman. It is probably natural enough to call the cave drawings a '*Bildersprache*', since they are recognizably pictures of surrounding objects. But they are not language, any more than are the tunes that birds whistle.

86. *B&H* 175.
87. MS 165, 105.
88. *B&H* 175.

In another example (to which I previously referred), a caveman is imagined to be drawing regular patterns on the cave wall. But, says Wittgenstein, he is not following the general expression of a rule—and so he is not acting according to a rule.[89] For Wittgenstein, following a rule is fundamental to language.[90] If so, then the cave pictures and patterns are not *close enough* to what Baker and Hacker call 'paradigmatic languages'.

They concede that 'Wittgenstein stressed the importance of regularity and agreement for the application of the concept of following a rule'.[91] They go on to say the following:

> To interpret his observations as parts of a proposal to *define* 'accord with a rule' in terms of agreement is unsupported by sound textual evidence, and it conflicts with his *Grundgedanke* that accord is an internal relation of an act to a rule.[92]

Now of course Wittgenstein did not attempt to *define* 'accord with a rule', any more than he tried to define 'language' or 'game'. He did not think that definitions of such concepts were of any value. But he did hold that in the absence of a consensus in action, there would be no *concept* of a *rule*. This interpretation is supported by 'sound textual evidence', as I have tried to show. As to whether Wittgenstein's alleged '*Grundgedanke*' is that 'accord is an internal relation of an act to a rule'—I have said enough about that in Section 2.

Baker and Hacker declare that they have given the notion of agreement 'a major role' in their exposition of Wittgenstein's ideas.[93] They direct the reader to their essay, 'Agreement', which begins at p. 243 of their commentary. But I have already pointed out, also in Section 2, that they there interpret agreement to be important only for *shared* language, *shared* rules, *common* concepts. This is an unwitting reduction of Wittgenstein's originality. That human agreement is necessary for 'shared' language is not so striking a thought as that it is essential for language *simpliciter*.

89. *RFM* 344.
90. *RFM* 330.
91. *B&H* 179.
92. *B&H* 179–80.
93. *B&H* 179.

5

A conjecture. For a good many years, Baker and Hacker have been
pursuing an assiduous study of Wittgenstein's writings. It is clear that
they revere Wittgenstein: their admiration of his work is manifest
throughout their commentaries. When I ask myself how they could
adopt and wholeheartedly expound what seems to be a plainly mistaken interpretation of Wittgenstein's thought, the only answer that
seems plausible to me is the following: Baker and Hacker, in their own
philosophical thinking, consider it to be *obvious* that an individual human being *could*, logically speaking, have a language, *could* follow a rule,
could know the meaning of a word, even if he was and forever had been
isolated from human company. Is it likely that so great a philosopher as
Wittgenstein should have fallen into the misguided confusion of believing that language and rule-following *necessarily* require a community
of speakers? No indeed! It is, therefore, a valuable service to Wittgenstein to defend him at every turn from such a discreditable reading.

I have quite a lot of sympathy for this attitude. I know, both from my
own inclinations, and from what I have observed of the reactions of many
students and colleagues, that it is a thoroughly natural tendency of philosophical thinking to regard it as *self-evident* that a person who had never
been a member of a human society could give a name to something and
then go on to employ that name in that 'same' meaning, and could make
a signpost for his own use and thereafter take his direction from it.

Colin McGinn, in his book *Wittgenstein on Meaning*, provides a nice expression of this tendency. He defends what he calls 'the natural idea that
which concepts a person possesses depends simply on *facts about him*'.[94]
He goes on to say: 'we can thus form a conception of someone possessing
concepts and following rules without introducing *other* persons into our
thought'.[95] McGinn distinguishes between what he calls 'the individualistic conception' and 'the community conception' of rules and rule-following. He subscribes to the individualistic conception, holding that 'the
existence of others is *not* logically necessary for the possession of concepts,
language and rules'.[96] It seems to him to be possible 'that God could have
created a single rule-follower alone in the universe for all time'.[97]

94. Colin McGinn, *Wittgenstein on Meaning* (Oxford: Blackwell, 1984), 191.
95. *Ibid.*
96. *Ibid.*
97. *Ibid.*

This natural bent in philosophy was explored and criticized by Wittgenstein with remarkable energy and tenacity in his post-*Tractatus* writings. A consideration of absolutely fundamental importance, which he brings out in *PI* 202, is the necessary distinction between one's following a rule, and one's *thinking* one is following a rule. If you try to imagine someone who had never participated in human society, inventing a rule for himself and undertaking to follow it, you will realize that there would be no foothold there for that necessary distinction.

A considerable number of philosophers have grasped the significance of this point. Benjamin Armstrong is one of them. Applying the point to signs and words, he says:

> Words, if they are to be words, cannot mean whatever an individual happens to 'think they mean'; a correct use cannot be whatever an individual happens to do with a sign. It must be possible for an individual to use a sign incorrectly, if it is to be a word; i.e., if it is to *mean one thing rather than another*.[98]

There must be a use of a sign that is *independent* of what an individual speaker does with it, in order for the latter's use of the sign to be correct or incorrect. As Armstrong says: 'The independent "way of using a sign" that is required for the satisfaction of the conditions on a correct use cannot be provided by a single individual'.[99] This independence-condition can be satisfied only if there is a community of speakers who use the sign in a customary way.

In his 1939 lectures in Cambridge, Wittgenstein expressed this point in a concisely memorable way. He was talking about the notion of 'knowing the meaning' of a word. What he said was: 'To know its meaning is to use it *in the same way* as other people do'.[100]

98. Benjamin F. Armstrong, Jr., 'Wittgenstein on Private Languages', *Philosophical Investigations* 7 (January 1984), 54.
99. *Ibid.*, 61.
100. *LFM* 183.

12

Language Game (2)

1

In his essay 'Wittgenstein's Builders'[1] Rush Rhees presents a deeply thoughtful criticism of some of Wittgenstein's statements about Language Game (2) of the *Philosophical Investigations*. This 'language game' or 'language' is described by Wittgenstein as follows:

> The language is meant to serve for communication between a builder A and an assistant B. A is building with building-stones: there are blocks, pillars, slabs and beams. B has to pass the stones, and that in the order in which A needs them. For this purpose they use a language consisting of the words 'block', 'pillar', 'slab', 'beam'. A calls them out;—B brings the stone which he has learnt to bring at such-and-such a call.[2]

Wittgenstein adds: 'Conceive this as a complete primitive language'. Further on he says: 'We could imagine that the language of (2) was the *whole* language of A and B; even the whole language of a tribe' (*PI* 6). In *The Brown Book* he describes the same language game and says: 'Let us

---

1. Rush Rhees, 'Wittgenstein's Builders', in *Discussions of Wittgenstein* (London: Routledge and Kegan Paul, 1970), p. 76.
2. Ludwig Wittgenstein, *Philosophical Investigations*, ed. G. E. M. Anscombe and Rush Rhees, trans. G. E. M. Anscombe (Oxford: Basil Blackwell, 1958), 2. Hereafter cited as *PI*.

imagine a society in which this is the only system of language'.[3] A few pages later he says of (2) and other simple language games:

> We are not . . . regarding the language games which we describe as incomplete parts of a language, but as languages complete in themselves, as complete systems of human communication. To keep this point of view in mind, it very often is useful to imagine such a simple language to be the entire system of communication of a tribe in a primitive state of society. (*BB*, p. 81)

Wittgenstein does go on to say that the words of this tiny vocabulary will be spoken in a context other than the activity of building, namely, in the *teaching* of the language. 'The children are brought up to perform *these* actions, to use *these* words as they do so, and to react in *this* way to the words of others' (*PI* 6). An 'important part' of this training will be the 'ostensive teaching of words' which 'will consist in the teacher's pointing to the objects, directing the child's attention to them and at the same time uttering a word; for instance, the word "slab" as he points to that shape' (*ibid.*). In addition to the ostensive teaching there will be these other phases of the training:

> In instruction in the language the following process will occur: the learner *names* the objects; that is, he utters the word when the teacher points to the stone—And there will be this still simpler exercise: the pupil repeats the words after the teacher. (*PI* 7)

Wittgenstein mentions these different phases of the training because of their similarity to the ways in which our own children learn words. For example, of the ostensive teaching he remarks: 'I say that it will form an important part of the training because it is so with human beings' (*PI* 6). Wittgenstein is making it explicit that the words will be uttered and responded to *outside* of the activity of building—although in preparation for it.

2

We come now to Rhees's criticism. He objects seriously to the idea that Language Game (2) might be the entire language of a tribe. He says:

---

3. Wittgenstein, *The Brown Book* (Oxford: Basil Blackwell, 1958), p. 77. Hereafter cited as *BB*.

The trouble is not to imagine a people with a language of such limited vocabulary. The trouble is to imagine that they spoke the language only to give these special orders on this job and otherwise
never spoke at all. I do not think it would be speaking a language.[4]

As we have noted, this is not a strictly exact account of the matter. The
words are not used *only* on the job; they are also used in *teaching* the language. Rhees refers to this point. He says:

When Wittgenstein suggests that in this tribe the children might be
taught these shouts and how to react to them, I suppose this means
that the adults would be using the expressions in giving the instruction, and this would be different from using them on the actual job.
If they belong to a language, this is natural enough, just as it would be
natural for the builders to use them in referring to the job when they
had gone home. But then using the expressions and understanding
the expressions would not be simply part of the building technique.
Understanding 'slab' would not be just reacting correctly on the job.
(*WB*, p. 77)

But in Wittgenstein's account, which brings in teaching, understanding
'slab' would indeed *not* be just reacting correctly on the job. Both adults
and children would employ the expressions outside of the context of
actual building.

Still, the use of the expressions is severely limited. Certainly there is
no provision for the workers to talk about the job when they go home.
Nor are there any words for referring to things so important to human
life as food or sleep or illness or death.

What worries Rhees, however, is not that the language has so poor a
vocabulary, but rather that the words are used (apart from the teaching) only in the bare routine of orders and reactions on the building
sites. One apparent difficulty with this conception of a 'language' is put
admirably by Rhees:

If it is an actual building job, it will not always go according to plan;
there will be snags. But when these builders come on a snag which
holds up the work and baffles them, then although they have been

4. Rhees, 'Wittgenstein's Builders', p. 76. Hereafter cited as *WB*.

speaking to one another in the course of their routine, they do not speak while they are trying to find what the trouble is. What they have learned are *signals* which cannot be used in any other way.

But this will not do what Wittgenstein wanted. It does not show how speaking is related to the lives which people lead. (*WB*, p. 77)

But Rhees says that his 'chief difficulty' is the following. If those people 'had learned only those shouts and reactions there would not be any distinction of sense and nonsense' (*WB*, p. 77).

> Unless there were a difference between learning to move stones in the ways people always do, and learning what makes sense, then I do not think we could say they were learning to speak.
>
> In our language as we speak it there are standards of what is correct or incorrect, and these come in when we say someone has misunderstood. But I do not see how there can be any such standard in the game Wittgenstein has described. (*WB*, p. 78)

Rhees is stressing the idea that uttering certain words within a particular routine is not *speaking* unless those words are used elsewhere.

> It is the way in which we have come to know them in other connections that decides whether it makes sense to put them together here, for instance: whether one can be substituted for another, whether they are incompatible and so forth. The meaning that they have within this game is not to be seen simply in what we do with them or how we react to them in this game. (*WB*, p. 79)

If the builders 'speak to one another, the meaning of the expressions they use cannot lie wholly in the use or the reaction that it receives in this job' (*WB*, p. 79).

> If people are speaking together, . . . the remarks they make have something to do with one another, otherwise they are not talking at all, even though they may be uttering sentences. And their remarks could have no bearing on one another unless the expressions they used were used in other connections as well.
>
> If someone learns to speak, he does not just learn to make sentences and utter them. Nor can he merely have learned to react to others. If that were all he ever did, I should not imagine that he could

speak, and I should never ask him anything. When he learns to speak, he learns to tell you something; and he tries to.

In learning to speak he learns what can be said; he learns, however fumblingly, what it makes sense to say. He comes to have some sense of how different remarks have something to do with one another. (*WB*, p. 79)

Learning what pieces to call slabs and what to call beams is not enough for learning to speak. 'It has more to do with what it makes sense to answer or what it makes sense to ask, or what sense one remark may have in connection with another' (*WB*, p. 80).

> If I know you can speak, then it makes sense for me to ask you what you mean, to try to get you to say more clearly what you want, and to ask you questions about it: just as truly as it makes sense for me to answer you. The example of the builders does not seem to allow for any of these. (*WB*, p. 81)

In these remarks about speech and language Rhees is stressing the importance of *conversation*. He says:

> Not all speech is conversation, of course, but I do not think there would be speech or language without it. If there were someone who could not carry on a conversation, who had no idea of asking questions or making any comment, then I do not think we should say he could speak. (*WB*, p. 81)

The bare description of Language Game (2) does not provide for conversation; yet Wittgenstein is supposing that it might be the *whole* language of the tribe. If conversation is essential for speech or language, then Game (2) is not a language, and when a builder calls out the words for building stones he is not speaking.

Referring to Wittgenstein's remark, 'To imagine a language means to imagine a form of life' (*PI* 19), Rhees says:

> The activity of the builders does not give you an idea of a people with a definite form of life. . . . The description of them on the building site, if you add 'this may be all', makes them look like marionettes. (*WB*, p. 83)

3

Rhees's criticism is acute, and I agree with it *insofar* as it is based solely on Wittgenstein's *explicit* description of Language Game (2). I will suggest, however, that there is something *in the background* of Language Game (2) which, when brought to the fore, makes it possible to view the builders and their helpers in a different light from that in which Rhees sees them. I begin by quoting a paragraph from *Zettel*, which is a comment about Game (2).

> (On language game no. 2) 'You are just tacitly assuming that these people *think*; that they are like people as we know them in *that* respect; that they do not carry on that language game merely mechanically. For if you imagined them doing that, you yourself would not call it the use of a rudimentary language.'
> What am I to reply to this? Of course it is true that the life of those human beings must be like ours in many respects, and I said nothing about this similarity. But the important thing is that their language, and their thinking too, may be rudimentary, that there is such a thing as 'primitive thinking' which is to be described via primitive *behaviour.* The surroundings are not the 'thinking accompaniment' of speech.[5]

Here Wittgenstein is typically voicing an imagined criticism. What motivates the criticism is the inclination to feel that, if one conceives of Game (2) as the entire language of a people, one will have the impression that those people carry on that game 'merely mechanically'. This reminds us of Rhees's comment: 'The description of them on the building site, if you add "this may be all", makes them look like marionettes'. Acting *merely mechanically*; looking like *marionettes*: these are the same objection.

Wittgenstein's reply is highly interesting. Of course he does *not* admit that he was making the unspoken 'assumption' that those people *think*, in the sense of there being thinking concealed behind the outward behavior. But what he does say has a bearing on the relevance of Rhees's criticism. He says: 'the life of those human beings must be like ours in many respects, and I said nothing about this similarity'. I will dwell on this remark.

5. Wittgenstein, *Zettel,* ed. G. E. M. Anscombe and G. H. von Wright, trans. G. E. M. Anscombe (Oxford: Blackwell, 1967), 99. Hereafter cited as Z

If the life of those people is like our life in many ways, then we are assured not only that they are human beings, but also that in their natural,
unlearned, behavior they will express desire, hunger, fear, anger, surprise, disappointment, satisfaction, joy, and so on—just as we do. In the
description of Language Game (2) there is nothing that *excludes* the possibility that those people will sometimes whistle or hum while they work,
or nod at one another in good humor, or occasionally make cheerful
dancing movements as they come and go. That their few words occur
only in the work of building, and in teaching the words, does not in itself
require that we picture them as behaving stolidly or mechanically.

In teaching the words to the children there will be plenty of occasions for behavioral expressions, on the part of the adults, of urging, ap-
proval, impatience, disapproval. There will be smiles, frowns, gestures
of encouragement or of acceptance or rejection. The children too will
sometimes look puzzled, or dejected, or triumphant.

In the work on the building sites there will of course be 'snags' and
accidents. A stone will slip from a worker's hands and strike his foot,
and he will cry out with pain. Perhaps other workers will show their concern and sympathy in instinctive sounds and actions. In *Zettel* Wittgenstein remarks that 'it is a primitive reaction to tend, to treat, the part
that hurts when someone else is in pain; and not merely when oneself
is' (*Z* 540). He asks himself what the word 'primitive' means here, and
replies: 'Surely that this sort of behaviour is *pre-linguistic*: that a language
game is based *on it*, that it is the prototype of a way of thinking and not
the result of thinking' (*Z* 541). He further says:

> Being sure that someone is in pain, doubting whether he is, and so
> on, are so many natural, instinctive kinds of behaviour towards other
> human beings, and our language is merely an auxiliary to, and fur-
> ther extension of this behaviour. Our language game is an extension
> of primitive behaviour. (*Z* 545)

We are surely entitled to attribute to the people of Language Game (2)
these kinds of primitive reactions to the injuries of their fellow workers.
And we can imagine that if a worker was trying to lift a stone that was
too heavy for him another might hasten to help him.

In *Zettel* 103 Wittgenstein refers to the distinction between working
'mechanically' and making 'trials and comparisons' as one works. This
latter could be exemplified in the behavior of a worker in Game (2).

Suppose a builder is trying to fit a slab between two other slabs, but it will not go. He expresses frustration in sounds and gestures. After viewing the situation for a while, he proceeds to chip from one end of the slab until it finally fits—whereupon he laughs and claps his hands in satisfaction. Wittgenstein says:

> Were we to see beings at work whose *rhythm* of work, play of expression, etc., was like our own, except for their not speaking, perhaps we would say that they thought, considered, made decisions. For there would be a *great deal* there corresponding to the action of ordinary human beings. (Z 102)

From the cue that the life of the builders 'must be like ours in many respects', and that there will be 'a great deal there corresponding to the action of ordinary human beings', I think we can fairly conclude that there is no justification for supposing that the workers of Game (2) will always work 'mechanically' or that on the building sites they will 'look like marionettes'.

I turn now to Rhees's 'chief difficulty', which is that if the people of Game (2) had 'learned only those shouts and reactions there would not be any distinction of sense and nonsense' (*WB*, p. 77). Let us suppose that a worker is building a wall. Only slabs are used in walls: beams are used only in roofs. We may even suppose that beams physically *cannot* be used in walls because of their shape. Now this builder, at work on a wall, calls out to his helper 'Beam'. The helper looks at him in astonishment—then bursts into laughter. The startled builder looks at the helper, then at the wall, then back at the helper with a grin of embarrassment. He slaps himself on the head, and then calls out 'Slab'. The chuckling helper brings him a slab.

Cannot we say that the builder's original call, 'Beam', was, in that situation, *nonsense*; and that first the helper and then the builder perceived that it was nonsense? The utterance 'Beam' was 'incompatible' with the situation. When the builder realized this he made a correction.

It is true that those people do not have *conversation*. But this exchange was *similar* to conversation. The astonishment and laughter of the helper was a 'criticism' of the builder's utterance. The latter's response was an acceptance of the criticism. Rudimentary thinking occurred on both sides, thinking that was exhibited in the rudimentary behavior. I do not see that full-blown conversation is essential for speech and language, or for a distinction between sense and non-sense.

The vocabulary of this people consists of only four words. But the *uttering* of those words could have different functions in different circumstances. If a builder says 'Block' when a helper expected 'Slab', the helper might say 'Block?' with an expression of uncertainty. And the builder might repeat 'Block!' with emphasis. Here would be something resembling question and reply. The helper would be asking the builder whether he *meant* 'Block', and the builder would be saying that he did mean that. Rhees says:

> If I know you can speak, then it makes sense for me to ask you what you mean, to try to get you to say more clearly what you want, and to ask you questions about it: just as truly as it makes sense for me to answer you. The example of the builders does not seem to allow for any of these. (*WB*, p. 81)

It is true that in Wittgenstein's bare description of Language Game (2) the only mentioned function of a builder's utterances is that they are *orders*; and no linguistic reply is assigned to a helper. But if the life of those people 'must be like ours in many respects', then it would be natural enough that a helper should sometimes question the meaning of an order, and that a builder should answer the question. This enriching of their utterances would not require an expansion of their vocabulary.

What we may find most implausible about the people of Language Game (2) is that they have words *only* for building stones—but none for food or danger, day or night, sleeping or waking, illness or death, or changes of weather. The people do not have names, nor are there words for parents or children. They do not even have a word for the activity of building, nor one for the purpose of it.

To make this intelligible would require a more imaginative description of their environment and their life than I am capable of providing. But here are some feeble suggestions: they do not have a word for food because nature supplies them with food in abundance, ready to hand; no planning or preparation is needed. When one of them is ill those who perceive it express concern in instinctive sounds and helpful actions. When they bury their dead they bow their heads, and there is some weeping; but there is no other ceremony, nor is there prolonged grieving. Bad weather does not disturb them; when it rains they easily take shelter under the trees. When night falls they go to sleep; when it grows light they wake up. They do not warn against dangers; but if one of them is attacked by a savage animal the others come to his aid.

Why is the activity of building so important for them that their only words are the names of building stones? And what is the purpose of the buildings? Well, let us think of the adults of the tribe as like our small children, who delight in creating structures out of sand or from little blocks of wood—but for no purpose other than the activity itself. The people of the tribe do not use the buildings, but sometimes they like to look at them.

The four types of building stones are amply provided by nature. The adult who arrives first in the day at a building site takes over as the builder for that day; those who arrive later are his helpers. This arrangement is not decided upon in any previous agreement; it is just what they do spontaneously. There are no assignments or roll calls or reports on the work; so there is no need for names of individuals. They have no leaders or votes. The children of the tribe are fed and looked after by whichever adults are at hand; there are no families. These are simple people leading a simple life. Their only form of social organization is in their building activity, which for them is endlessly absorbing.

Perhaps by thinking along such lines we can make plausible the conception that Language Game (2) might be the *whole* language of a tribe.

13

The Mystery of Thought

If someone asked me where Napoleon was born I could answer, 'Napoleon was born in Corsica'. In daily life it would not be felt that there was anything mysterious or paradoxical in this remark. Yet to philosophical reflection it can easily seem so. For consider this: Napoleon is dead; he no longer exists. The philosophical perplexity is: how can I think of someone or something that does not exist? How was it possible for me to refer to, to mean, Napoleon *himself?*

In his writings after the early 1930s Wittgenstein pays a lot of attention to the philosophical impression that thought and thinking are mysterious. In the *Philosophical Investigations*[1] he says:

> 'This strange thing, thought'—but it does not strike us as strange when we are thinking. Thought does not strike us as mysterious while we are thinking, but only when we say, as it were in retrospect: 'How was that possible?'. How was it possible for thought to deal with the very object *itself?* It seems to us as if we had captured reality with our thought. (428)

Intending something, planning something, wishing for something, remembering something, expecting something, understanding something—all of these are forms of thought. In each there is an object—that which is intended, planned, wished for, expected, remembered,

---

1. Ludwig Wittgenstein, *Philosophical Investigations*, ed. G. E. M. Anscombe and Rush Rhees, trans. G. E. M. Anscombe (Oxford: Blackwell, 1967). Hereafter cited as *PI.*

understood. If I *intend* to construct a garden, then the garden does not yet exist; so how can *it* be the object of my intention? If I *remember* an event that occurred a month ago, that event no longer exists; so how can *it* be the thing I remember?

An answer to which philosophers have felt driven is to say that the 'ostensible' object cannot be the 'immediate' object of thought: there must instead be some substitute or replacement for it in the present thought. In his *Philosophische Bemerkungen*,[2] the first book that Wittgenstein wrote after his return to philosophical research, it would seem that he was tempted by this position. For he says: 'If I wish that *p* were the case, then of course *p* is not the case, and there must be a substitute for *p* in the state of wishing, as indeed in the expression of the wish' (p. 66). Consider an example: If I wish it would stop raining, then the rain has not stopped; therefore, the situation of the rain's having stopped cannot be in my 'state of wishing', but only some *substitute* for it. Would this mean that I do not actually wish for the rain to stop, but instead for something else?

One cannot extract much from this brief remark in the *Bemerkungen*. If Wittgenstein did have this temptation, I think it was momentary; for on the next page he says: 'If one were to ask: Do I expect the future itself or only something similar to the future?, that would be nonsense' (p. 67). If I say, 'I expect snow tomorrow', that sentence is an expression of an expectation and of a thought. The object of expectation and of thought is spelled out in the words, 'snow tomorrow'. If I cannot expect snow tomorrow but only something 'similar' to it, what might *that* be? Would it be rain or mist tomorrow? But that would be a different expectation.

It is indeed nonsense to say that you cannot expect the future but only something 'similar'. This has an implication for wishing too. My wish that the rain would stop is focused on *the rain's stopping*, not on something similar.

In philosophical thinking about *memory* there has always been a tendency to conclude that past events and situations cannot be the immediate objects of memory. It has seemed that what is present in memory, or to memory, cannot be the past event that we *say* we remember, but only a *representation* of it. In *The Analysis of Mind*[3] Russell said that

2. Wittgenstein, *Philosophische Bemerkungen*, ed. Rush Rhees (Frankfurt: Suhrkamp, 1964).

3. Bertrand Russell, *The Analysis of Mind* (London: Allen and Unwin, 1949).

> the past event which we are said to be remembering, is unpleasantly remote from the 'content', i.e. the present mental occurrence in remembering. (P. 164)

> Remembering has to be a present occurrence in some way resembling, or related to, what is remembered. (P. 163)

The most popular candidate for the required representation is an *image*. 'Memory demands an image', Russell said (p. 186). Memory images are supposed to be 'copies', more or less accurate, of past events. They are supposed to bridge the gap between the present occurrence of remembering and the no-longer-existing past event. They are the substitutes, surrogates, representatives, for the past events that, it seems, *cannot* be present to thought.

But can any view that replaces the ostensible object of thought with a representation be satisfactory? Surely not. Let us go back to the example of Napoleon. I said to someone, 'Napoleon was born in Corsica'. It was argued that Napoleon *himself* could not be the object of my thought, but that the actual object present in or to my thought was a representation of Napoleon. If that were so, would I be saying that my 'representation' of Napoleon was born in Corsica? Perhaps for Corsica also I would need a representation: for although Corsica presently exists, it is a very large island, consisting of many forests, cliffs, huge boulders. How could all, or any, of that be in my mind? So if my thought contains representations for both Napoleon and Corsica, is what I am saying this: a representation of Napoleon was born in a representation of Corsica? This would not be the end of the substitutions that would need to be made. The outcome would be that the original simple statement was turned into a complex and nonsensical mixture of representations.

An expression of expectation is the expression of a thought. Suppose you see someone pointing a gun: you say, 'I expect a bang'. The gun is fired, the bang occurs. Wittgenstein asks: 'Was that bang somehow already in your expectation?' (*PI* 442).

The question is embarrassing. You expected the sound of a gun. It seems that either this sound was there in your expectation, or it was not. But then we are caught on the horns of a dilemma. If we say that the sound of the shot was there in your expectation, then it seems that this sound occurred *before* the gun was fired—which is ridiculous. If we say that the bang of the gun was *not* in your expectation, then it seems that the bang that occurred when the gun was fired could not have fulfilled your expectation.

Furthermore, suppose you said, 'The report was not so loud as I had expected'. Wittgenstein asks: 'Then was there a louder bang in your expectation?' (*PI* 442). The question is comical, yet is presented with serious intent. It confronts us with the absurdity of the suggestion that there were *two* bangs, one louder than the other. It makes us aware of our confusion about the concept of expectation.

What is it that draws us into this confusion, not just about expectation, but more generally about the concept of an object of thought? Wittgenstein provides a clue in the next remark in the *Investigations*. He asks us to consider the two sentences, 'Here is a red patch', and 'There is no red patch here'. He then remarks that 'the word "red" occurs in both; so this word cannot signify (*anzeigen*) the presence (*Vorhandensein*) of something red' (443). I think this remark is the key to our problem about the object of thought. We are strongly attracted by the assumption that the *meaning* of a word is something that 'corresponds' to the word. For example, we are inclined to think that the meaning of the word 'red' is something red. But this cannot be so when the word 'red' occurs in the sentence 'There is nothing red here'. We cannot even say that the meaning of 'red' is the existence of red color. For if a radical change in the atmosphere had the effect that the color red no longer existed, the word 'red' would not thereby lose its meaning. It would make sense to say, 'There used to be red color, but not now'. Similarly, in the sentence 'I expect the sound of a shot', the meaning of the phrase 'the sound of a shot' cannot be the occurrence of the sound of a shot—since this same phrase occurs in the sentence, 'I do not expect the sound of a shot'.

Wittgenstein criticized this assumption early in the *Investigations*. He said that 'the word "meaning" is used incorrectly if one designates by it the thing that "corresponds" to the word' (40). He went on to say: 'This is to confuse the meaning of a name with the *bearer* of the name' (40). Napoleon bore the name 'Napoleon', but he was not the meaning of the name, for when he died his name did not lose its meaning. In the just quoted remarks Wittgenstein was referring primarily to proper names. But the remarks have a wider application—to general names such as 'red' or 'pain'; to phrases such as 'the sound of a gun'; and even to full sentences ('It is raining', 'The phone rang')—sentences that are used to describe states of affairs.

I am suggesting that when we think philosophically about the meaning of proper names, general names, phrases, sentences ('expressions', for short)—our foremost inclination is to suppose that the *meaning* of an expression is some thing, event, situation, or state of affairs; something that exists. But various considerations make us realize that this initial conception cannot be right. Some of these considerations are the following:

(1) Mistaken assertions, false judgments—e.g., you said 'It is raining' but you were wrong. So what existing state of affairs could be the meaning of your statement?

(2) Wishing, hoping, planning, intending, expecting, predicting—the thing or situation hoped for, intended, expected, etc., typically does not yet exist; therefore the meaning of the expressions we use to refer to those objects of thought cannot lie in something presently existing.

(3) Memory and thought about the past—when the past things or situations no longer exist, it would seem that our thought cannot be dealing with those things themselves.

(4) Negation and denial—e.g., you say 'p is false', or 'It is not the case that p'. The sentence 'p' is contained in your total assertion: but if the meaning of 'p' is the state of affairs p, then it seems that your whole assertion is a contradiction. Negation appears to be an incoherent concept.

If, despite these difficulties, we cling to the assumption that the object of thought must be something that coexists with the thought and is present in the thought, then we have to devise some substitute, some surrogate, for what we originally took to be the object of thought. The surrogate has to have two properties: (1) it must presently exist; (2) it must resemble, be similar to, that which was originally conceived to be the object of thought. This is why, in philosophical thinking about memory, it has so frequently been supposed that remembering 'demands' a memory-image. When we remember we do *sometimes* have memory-images. This fact perhaps helps us to swallow the assumption that 'genuine' remembering *requires* an image. The postulated image must have the two necessary properties of being (1) something that exists when we remember, and (2) something that more or less resembles the past thing or event, which we assumed was the immediate object of memory, before we ran into difficulty.

Wittgenstein illustrates our temptations in these areas with many examples. He says:

Perhaps one has the feeling that in the sentence 'I expect he is coming' one is using the words 'he is coming' in a different meaning than
in the assertion 'He is coming'. But if it were so how could I say that
my expectation had been fulfilled? (*PI* 444)

Why does this feeling exist? It arises from the assumption that the
meaning of the words 'He is coming' is the actual occurrence of his
coming. And so we conclude that those words cannot mean the same
in the expression of expectation, since I can expect his coming even if
he doesn't come. If we had not made that assumption about the meaning of the words 'He is coming', we would not have had the inclination
to think that they mean something different in the expression of expectation.

In a remark about negation Wittgenstein says: 'The feeling is as if the
negation of a proposition had first to make it true in a certain sense, in
order to negate it' (*PI* 447). Why do we have this temptation? Because
the assertion 'It is not true that it is snowing' contains the words 'it is
snowing', and we have the inclination to think that the *meaning* of these
words is the occurrence of snow. We realize, however, that it is too absurd to suppose that a negation really contradicts itself. So what we
vaguely assume is that the meaning of the words 'it is snowing', as they
occur in the negation, is not actual snowing but something 'resembling' it—perhaps a mental image of snowing.

Here are other examples provided by Wittgenstein:

'If I say I did *not* dream last night, still I must know where to look for
a dream; that is, the sentence "I dreamt", applied to the actual situation, may be false but must not be senseless'.—Does that mean that
you did after all feel something, as it were the suggestion of a dream,
which made you aware of the place which a dream would have occupied?
    Or: if I say 'I have no pain in my arm', does that mean that I have
a shadow of a feeling of pain, which as it were suggests the place
where pain could have entered? (*PI* 448)

This questioning is brilliant. Must I feel a shadow of pain, perhaps a
very slight pain, in order to acknowledge that I am *not* in pain? These
examples (the 'suggestion' of a dream, the 'shadow' of a pain) are like
the 'image' of a past situation in remembering it, and the 'mental representation' of Napoleon when he is the subject of our conversation.

We seem to be under the influence of the following conception: When we speak, and when we take in the words of another speaker, we are understanding *something*; and that something must be *there*, present to our understanding, simultaneous with our hearing or uttering the words. Each word has a meaning: so we grasp the meaning of each word as the sentence flows past.

In *Zettel*[4] Wittgenstein says of this conception: 'We don't get away from the idea that the sense of a sentence accompanies the sentence; is there alongside of it' (139). In the *Investigations* he says: 'We don't escape from the notion that using a sentence consists in our thinking (*vorstellen*) of something with each word' (449).

These ideas to which Wittgenstein refers are a misrepresentation of actual discourse in language. If someone says to me, 'Please open the window', I will respond without considering the meaning of each word. As Wittgenstein remarks: 'When I think in language, "meanings" don't go through my mind alongside the verbal expressions; but the language itself is the vehicle of thinking' (*PI* 329). The point is that in our normal discourse, when we speak and respond to the words of others, this exchange does not have to be supplemented by something 'mental'— neither by images of the things that are the subjects of the discourse, nor by silent thoughts about the meanings of the words employed in the discourse.

Sometimes images do occur, and sometimes they assist understanding. If someone is trying to tell me how to get to a certain street in London, it may help me if I visualize the layout of the streets. Also it sometimes happens in conversation that an unfamiliar word is used, and I struggle to think of its meaning. But the mention of such incidents merely emphasizes how *infrequent* they are in proportion to the number of situations in which communication in language takes place with no reliance on imagery and with no thought of the meanings of the words. If a friend said to me 'My head still aches', I might reply 'You had better take some more aspirin'—*without* the intervention of an image of aspirin, or of a shadow of pain, or of any silent thinking about the meanings of his or my words. My reply, the words I spoke, showed my understanding of what he said. He uttered some words; I responded with some words; that may be *all* that took place.

4. Wittgenstein, *Zettel*, ed. G. E. M. Anscombe and G. H. von Wright, trans. G. E. M. Anscombe (Oxford: Blackwell, 1967).

In this connection Wittgenstein makes some remarks that are amusing in their slyness:

> If I give someone an order, it is for me *quite enough* to give him signs. And I would never say: This is only words, and I must get behind the words. Equally, when I have asked someone something and he gives me an answer (that is, a sign) I am satisfied—that was what I expected—and I don't object: That's a mere answer. (*PI* 503)

This conception is difficult to accept. It may seem that Wittgenstein, and I in agreement with him, are holding that people in conversation are merely uttering sounds and not meaning anything by them. But of course this isn't so. The friend who said that his head still aches meant what he said; and when I replied that he should take more aspirin I meant what I said. The point is, however, that this *meaning* what was said was *not* something that was present alongside of, or in addition to, the uttering of the words.

The objection one feels can be put by saying that the uttered sounds are, *in themselves*, 'dead'; by themselves they do not *say* anything. Wittgenstein agrees with this. In the *Investigations* he draws a horizontal arrow; and he asks, 'How does it come about that this arrow *points?*'. The objector replies that 'the dead line' does *not* point: 'only the psychical, the meaning, can do that'. Wittgenstein replies: 'That is both true and false. The arrow points only in the use that a living being makes of it. This pointing is *not* a hocus-pocus which only the mind can perform' (*PI* 454). Wittgenstein says here that the objector's contention is both true and false. What is *true* is that if the arrow were isolated from human conventions and practices, it would not *point*. What is *false* is that there must be something mental, 'psychical', an act of meaning, added to the drawn arrow.

If you were following a trail marked by arrows painted on trees and rocks, when you came upon an arrow there would be no act of interpretation or of thinking to yourself, 'I am supposed to go *that* way'. You would *just go* that way. Early in life you were taught the use of arrows as direction indicators. You learned to take your direction from an arrow. So now you do respond to an arrow in the way you were taught.

The beauty of the example of the arrow is that what is true of it is also true of a sentence of language. Someone says to you, 'Turn to the right'. The words *in themselves* do not mean anything. But you grew up in a community where you were introduced to the peculiar institution of giving and obeying orders. You learned what an order is, and what obeying an order is. Just as you learned the use of signposts. Your acquired mastery of these practices enables you to respond with understanding, without the mediation of an inner mental act.

Of course it could happen that a person turned right when the order to turn right was given, but nevertheless did not understand the order. For this to be intelligible, however, we must suppose some special circumstances: perhaps the order was given in a foreign tongue and he turned right only in imitation of others. And it can happen that someone understands an order but does not carry it out: for example, he does not acknowledge the authority of the person who gave the order; or he thinks that the order was given by mistake; or he is being rebellious; and so on. Explanations are needed for these failures. If someone asked, 'Why should there be any connection at all between understanding the order "Turn right", and *turning right?*'—an answer would be: If there was *no* connection then it would not *be* the order to turn right!

We sometimes say, 'I must understand the order *before* I can carry it out'. This may make it appear that understanding an order must always *intervene* between hearing it and executing it. But this isn't so. One case in which the above remark would be appropriate would be where the order required a number of steps, the sequence of which I had to arrange in my mind before proceeding to act. Another case would be that the order was given in a code which I must first decipher. Still another case would be when the order is unexpected, and I have to first ascertain whether it was seriously meant. Thus the remark, 'I must understand it before I can carry it out', has an appropriateness that is limited to special circumstances. It provides no justification for the assumption that a mental phenomenon of understanding must always come between receiving an order and executing it.

Not all thinking takes place in language; but much of it does. What worries us philosophically is the feeling that the language *cannot be enough.* You utter some words; I utter some words. Surely there must be more to a conversation than just *that!* Something must be added to the words, namely *meaning.* But how does meaning get into the words?

One answer we have considered is that the meaning of an expression is some existing thing, event, or state of affairs. For example, the meaning of the expression 'a storm' is the occurrence of a storm. But this won't do: for I might have said, 'There is a storm outside', or 'I expect a storm', when there was no storm. Those sentences had sense, even though there was no storm to serve as the meaning of the expression 'a storm'.

The next answer is to postulate some 'mental representation' of a storm as being the meaning of the expression 'a storm'. But this won't do either. A mental representation of a storm is not what I expect when I expect a storm.

The attempt to find the meaning of an uttered expression in something coexisting with the utterance cannot succeed.

Where then is the locus of meaning? In Wittgenstein's conception there is a clear answer. The locus of linguistic meaning is the *grammar* of the language. In his *Philosophical Grammar*[5] he says:

> Grammar is not accountable to any reality. Grammatical rules determine meaning (constitute it) and so they are not themselves answerable to any meaning and to that extent are arbitrary. (P. 184)

Wittgenstein goes on to give two illustrations of this point. He says:

> There cannot be any question whether these rules or other ones are the correct ones for the word 'not' (that is, whether they accord with its meaning). For without these rules the word has as yet no meaning; and if we change the rules, then it has another meaning (or none), and in that case we can just as well change the word too. (*PG*, p. 184)

> Why don't I call the rules of cooking arbitrary, and why am I inclined to call the rules of grammar arbitrary? Because I think of the concept of 'cooking' as defined by the purpose of cooking, but not of the concept of 'language' as defined by the purpose of language. If you do not cook according to the correct rules you cook badly; but if you follow other rules than those of chess you are playing a different game; and if you follow other grammatical rules than the customary ones, you are not saying something wrong, but you are speaking of something else. (*PG*, pp. 184–85)

Wittgenstein's remark that 'Grammar is not accountable to any reality', is a striking thought. It implies, for example, that the meaning of the word 'joy' did not arise from the observation of the phenomenon of

---

5. Wittgenstein, *Philosophical Grammar*, ed. Rush Rhees, trans. Anthony Kenny (Oxford: Blackwell, 1974). Hereafter cited as *PG*.

joy. Instead, the word you use to describe what you observe does not refer to *joy*, unless it has the grammar of the word 'joy'. One use of language is to describe reality; but the language has to have meaning *already* in order for you to use it that way.

The conception that the meaning of an expression is constituted by the grammar of the expression can be confusing and misleading. Wittgenstein is not using the word 'grammar' to mean the kind of grammar that we learn in school. In his sense of the word, 'grammar' comprises far more than syntax or sentence construction. In describing the grammar of an expression you would be saying something about the part that the expression plays in *the life* of the people who use it.

The grammar of the word 'promise', for example, pertains not just to the forms of words in which promises are made, but also to the various circumstances that are relevant to whether a promise has actually been *given*. It pertains to the part that a promise plays in creating expectations; to what kinds of circumstances are called 'breaking' a promise; to what counts as a 'reason' for breaking a promise; to how a promise differs from a forecast; to what part *trust* plays in the practice of making and accepting promises; to whether this practice could exist if promises were never kept. To describe the grammar of the word 'promise' would be to describe a particular pattern of human behavior, a pattern that is a blend of words and actions. It is to describe, in Wittgenstein's happy phrase, 'a form of life'. Once we understand Wittgenstein's use of the word 'grammar', the conception that the grammar of a word constitutes the *meaning* of the word is not so surprising.

To master the use of a word is to master a lot of grammar. But that doesn't mean that you are able, on demand, to give an *account* of that grammar—any more than you can give an account of how you balance on a bicycle, or tie your shoelaces. Someone employs a word in a way that strikes you as wrong, or odd, or funny—but that may be all you can say about it. Suppose someone says that the music of the *St. Matthew Passion* is 'delightful'. You might reply, 'I wouldn't use that word'. But to the question 'Why not?', you may not be able to answer. Or you might say, 'That music is *glorious*!'. If you added, 'What is "glorious" is not "delightful" ', that would be a 'grammatical' statement; it would be a comment on the relationship between these two concepts.

Let us return to the problem of the object of thought. When we think in language the object of thought is *given* by the language we use. I say of someone, 'I expect he is coming'. We have already noted a temptation to believe that the words 'he is coming' have a different sense in this expression of expectation than in the assertion 'He is coming'. We have also noted Wittgenstein's observation that this cannot be right, because then his coming would not fulfill my expectation (*PI* 444). Wittgenstein adds these remarks:

> But one could now ask: How does it look when he comes?—The door ·
> opens, someone walks in, and so on.—How does it look if I expect
> him to come?—I walk up and down in the room, look at the clock
> now and then, and so on.—But the one occurrence does not have the
> slightest similarity to the other! So how can one use the same words
> in describing them?—But perhaps I say as I walk up and down: 'I ex-
> pect him to come'.—Now there is a similarity at hand. But of what
> kind? (*PI* 444)

These superb remarks bring out the source of the feeling that there is *no* similarity between the description of the expectation and the description of his coming: but they also bring to light the actual similarity. The similarity between the two lies in the language! The linguistic expression of expectation contains the words 'he is coming'. These words specify what is expected. So of course his coming fulfills that expectation. This is settled solely by the grammar of the linguistic expression of expectation—nothing else has anything to do with it.

In an immediately following remark Wittgenstein says: 'It is in language that expectation and fulfillment make contact' (*PI* 445). This is one of those remarks that are so full of significance that it seems impossible to unpack all of it. Here is contained the solution of how it is possible for you to think of Napoleon *himself*, even though he no longer exists! You achieve this simply by using the name 'Napoleon' in a sentence. Nothing else is required—neither that Napoleon should have some sort of shadowy existence, nor that you should have some mental representation of him. The language does the whole job!

The same holds for the other difficulties about the objects of thought. When a desire is expressed in language, the language itself *says* what would satisfy that desire: a feeling of satisfaction or contentment does not come into it. If you are given an order, the language of the order *determines* what carrying out the order would be. When you express a memory in language, the language *specifies* the object of memory: no difficulty arises because of the present nonexistence of the past event; nor is a memory-image required, nor a 'feeling of pastness'—as Russell believed.

When we speak truthfully and without deceiving ourselves, the objects of our thought are what we *say* they are. There is no gap between our language and the objects of our thought, a gap that needs to be bridged by surrogates or mental intermediaries. We can think of 'the very object *itself*', whether it exists or doesn't exist, so long as our language contains a name or description for it.

14

Disentangling Moore's Paradox

In the two volumes of *Remarks on the Philosophy of Psychology*[1] and the first volume of *Last Writings on the Philosophy of Psychology*,[2] Wittgenstein wrote approximately 130 remarks on the verb 'to believe'. This concentration on a single verb was chiefly provoked by what Wittgenstein called 'Moore's Paradox'. What is Moore's paradox?

G. E. Moore noticed that such a sentence as 'I went to the pictures last Tuesday, but I don't believe that I did' would be an absurd thing for anyone, yourself for instance, to *say*. Moore remarked that this

> is a perfectly absurd thing to say, although *what* is asserted is something which is perfectly possible logically: it is perfectly possible that you did go to the pictures and yet you do not believe that you did.[3]

In a later essay Moore referred again to this 'absurdity'. Taking the example of someone's saying 'I believe he has gone out, but he has not', Moore's view continued to be that this is an absurd thing to *say*, but that

1. Ludwig Wittgenstein, *Remarks on the Philosophy of Psychology*, 2 vols.; vol. 1, ed. G. E. M. Anscombe and G. H. von Wright, trans. G. E. M. Anscombe; vol. 2, ed. G. H. von Wright and Heikki Nyman, trans. C. G. Luckhardt and M. A. E. Aue (Oxford: Blackwell, 1980). Hereafter cited as *RPP*, followed by volume and remark number.
2. Wittgenstein, *Last Writings on the Philosophy of Psychology*, vol. 1, ed. G. H. von Wright and Heikki Nyman, trans. C. G. Luckhardt and M. A. E. Aue (Oxford: Blackwell, 1982). Hereafter cited as *LW*, followed by remark number.
3. G. E. Moore, 'A Reply to My Critics', in *The Philosophy of G. E. Moore*, ed. P. A. Schilpp (Evanston: Northwestern University Press, 1942), p. 543.

what is said is 'logically possible'. As he put it, 'This, though absurd, is not self-contradictory; for it may quite well be true'.[4]

The central idea in Moore's view of the paradox is that such a sentence as 'It is raining and I don't believe it is raining' is an *intelligible* sentence. A number of philosophers have taken the same position. Like Moore, they have thought that the sentence itself is intelligible; it makes sense; we understand it; it expresses a logical possibility; it could even be true. What is 'absurd', or 'strange', or 'logically odd', is to *say* it.

I think this position is plainly wrong. If I asked someone what the weather is outside, he might reply 'It's raining', or 'I believe it's raining', or 'I believe it's not raining'. I would understand these replies. But if he said, 'It's raining and I don't believe it is', then I would not understand his sentence. I would think that I had misheard him. If he insisted on repeating the same words, and if he seemed to be serious, I would be stunned. Certainly I could not take his sentence as a report about the weather; nor as information about anything. I might react to it as to a piece of deliberate nonsense, a grammatical joke.

Why should a philosopher think that this combination of words is an intelligible sentence? There are a number of considerations that I shall take up one at a time.

'*It isn't self-contradictory*'. Moore was obviously influenced by the idea that a sentence of the form '*p*, and I don't believe *p*', is not self-contradictory. It is true that it doesn't *look* self-contradictory. But perhaps this appearance is deceptive. Before we can be sure that such a sentence is not self-contradictory, we must reflect on the ordinary meaning of the expressions 'I believe *p*' and 'I don't believe *p*'. I will return to this point.

The past tense. The sentences that figure in the paradox are sentences in which 'believe' occurs in the first person present tense. Examples are 'It's raining and I don't believe it is', and 'I believe it's raining and it isn't raining'. The corresponding *past* tense does make sense: e.g., 'I believed it was raining and its wasn't raining'. The fact that the past tense makes sense inclines one to think that the present tense *must* make sense.

One could reply that there is no justification for this '*must*'. But far more illuminating is Wittgenstein's observation about the way in which

4. Moore, 'Russell's "Theory of Descriptions"', in *The Philosophy of Bertrand Russell*, ed. P. A. Schilpp (Evanston: Northwestern University Press, 1944), p. 204.

the present tense, 'I believe *p*', is actually used. What he says is: ' "I believe *p*" means roughly the same as "*p*" ' (*RPP*, I, 472). He goes on to say: ' "I believe it's going to rain" means something like "It's going to rain", but "I believed then it was going to rain" doesn't mean anything like "It rained then" ' (*RPP*, I, 473). Wittgenstein asks the following question:

> What does it mean to say that 'I believe p' says roughly the same as 'p'? We react in roughly the same way when someone says the first and when he says the second; if I said the first, and someone didn't understand the words 'I believe', I would repeat the sentence in the second form, and so on. As I would also explain the words 'I wish you would go away' by the words 'Go away!'. (*RPP*, I, 477)

Wittgenstein adds the following important explanation of why 'I believe *p*' can have approximately the same meaning as '*p*'. He points out a significant logical difference between the first person and the third person of 'believe':

> That he believes such-and-such, we gather from observation of his person, but he does not make the statement 'I believe . . .' on the basis of self-observation. And *that* is why 'I believe p' can be equivalent to the assertion of 'p'. (*RPP*, I, 504)

I will return to this remark later. Right now I will say that Wittgenstein's statement that 'I believe *p*' means roughly the same as '*p*' is an accurate observation of the use of 'I believe'. Most of the confusion about Moore's paradox is due to a failure to notice this fact. On the surface it seems that '*p*' and 'I believe *p*' have entirely different 'content'. But if we go beneath the surface and remind ourselves of the way we actually use the expression 'I believe *p*' in daily speech, we see that what it commonly amounts to is a *tentative* or *hesitant* assertion of '*p*'.

Suppose I am indoors preparing to go out. I wonder whether I should take an umbrella; so I ask a person near the window to look out to see if it's raining. It is dark outside and hard to see through the window glass. The person says, 'I believe it's raining'. I would take this as a cautious assertion that it's raining, and would fetch my umbrella. My reaction would be roughly the same as it would be if the person had simply said, 'It's raining'.

Wittgenstein later puts this point in a slightly different way:

> Consider this: the words 'I believe it is raining' and 'It may be raining' (*Es dürfte regnen*) can say *the same*: inasmuch as in certain contexts it makes no difference which of the two sentences we use. . . . That is; in order to say that perhaps it is raining we do *not* need the concept 'believe', although we can use it for that purpose. (*RPP*, I, 821)

Suppose there were a characteristic tone of voice in which we said things of which we were not entirely certain, 'I believe . . .' is used to play the role of such a tone of voice. We have other linguistic devices that do the same. For example, 'It may be raining', or 'Perhaps it is raining'. Of course these sentences are also used in other ways. But they can be used to make the cautious assertion that it's raining. 'I believe it's raining' is typically used to do the same thing. As Wittgenstein says, 'I believe' does not *have* to be brought in to do that job. But it *can* be, and often is, used for that purpose.

A statement of the form 'I believe *p*', is not always a hesitant assertion of '*p*'. There are contexts in which it is an *emphatic* assertion of '*p*'. Suppose that in a certain town there have been rumors that the mayor is engaged in fraudulent practices. A supporter of the mayor, speaking before an audience, declares 'No one here believes that the mayor of our city is dishonest'. Someone shouts from the audience: '*I* believe he is dishonest!' In that context this would be a forceful assertion that the mayor is dishonest, not a hesitant one.

The fact that 'I believe *p*' is commonly an assertion of '*p*' destroys what might be called 'the argument from the past tense'. This argument assumes that 'I believe *p*' and 'I believed *p*' differ *only in tense*. This is an incorrect assumption. 'I believe p' is normally used to assert '*p*', sometimes hesitantly, sometimes emphatically. But the past tense, 'I believed *p*', is never an assertion of '*p*'. Moore's paradox exists only in the present tense.

The supposition. When Moore declared that a sentence of the form 'p, and I don't believe *p*', or 'I believe *p*, and p is not true', expresses 'a logical possibility' and 'may quite well be true', could he have confused an *assertion* with a *supposition*? For the corresponding supposition *does* make sense. There is no absurdity involved in saying, 'Let us suppose that I believe it's raining, and in fact it isn't raining'. What this supposition proposes *is* 'logically possible'. In this connection Wittgenstein makes the following remark: 'Moore's Paradox may be expressed like *this*: "I believe p" says roughly the same as "p"; but "Suppose I believe p . . ." does not say roughly the same as "Suppose p . . ." ' (*RPP*, I, 478). In saying that Moore's paradox 'may be expressed' in this way, Wittgenstein does not, of course, mean that Moore expressed it in this way. What Wittgenstein might mean by this curious remark is that if it were not for this logical difference between 'I believe *p*' and 'Suppose I believe *p*', then the sentences that Moore spotted would *not* be nonsensical.

Another thing that Wittgenstein's remark may suggest is that this difference between the assertion and the corresponding supposition could be called 'paradoxical', not because there is anything logically dubious about it, but because it is *surprising*: it goes against our expectations. For in other cases the relation between an assertion and the corresponding supposition is that what is asserted and what is supposed is *the same*. The assertion 'The ship sails at dawn', is the assertion of what is supposed by 'Suppose the ship sails at dawn'. The assertion says neither more nor less than what is supposed in the supposition. But this is not so in the case of 'I believe'. This is why Wittgenstein says: 'So it looks as if the assertion "I believe . . ." were not the assertion of what the supposition "I believe" supposes!' (*RPP*, I, 493). To suppose 'I believe it's raining' is *not* to suppose 'It's raining'. But to assert 'I believe it's raining' *is* to assert 'It's raining'. The assertion asserts something that is not supposed by the supposition. The assertion does not exactly *match* the supposition; it brings in another element.

But would it be right to say that 'I believe it's raining' is *not* the assertion that corresponds to the supposition 'Suppose I believe it's raining'? Surely not. What *other* assertion would be the corresponding one? There is no answer. We must simply *accept* this peculiar feature of the logical grammar of 'I believe'.

In this connection Wittgenstein makes a penetrating remark:

> With the words 'Suppose I believe that' you already presuppose the whole grammar of the word 'believe'. You are not supposing something that, so to speak, is given to you unambiguously through a picture, so that you can tack on to this supposition something other than the ordinary assertion. *You would not know at all* what you were supposing here, if you were not already familiar with the use of 'believe'. (*RPP*, II, 416)

If you substituted some assertion other than 'I believe p' as the assertion that 'corresponds' to 'Suppose I believe p', then you would not understand what you were supposing.

We have seen already that the *past tense* of 'believe' presents the same 'paradox' as does the *supposition*. The present tense, 'I believe p', *is* an assertion of 'p'; the past tense, 'I believed p', is *not* an assertion of 'p'. So it *looks* as if 'I believed it was raining' is not the 'correct' past tense of 'I believe it is raining'. But is there a 'more correct' match? Certainly not. We can apply here the same point that Wittgenstein made about the *supposition*. The assertion 'I believed' presupposes the whole grammar of 'believe', including that of the first person present. Otherwise you would not know what you were asserting in saying 'I believed'.

Is 'I believe p' a description of a mental state? We come now to the main source of perplexity about the absurd formulation, 'p, and I don't believe it', or 'I believe p, and p is not true'. On the one hand these conjunctions strike us as nonsensical. On the other hand, it seems that they should *not* be nonsensical; for the two parts of such a conjunction appear to be dealing with separate subject matters; they appear to be logically independent of one another. Their conjunction in a single sentence should not produce any logical conflict. As regards the conjunction 'I believe it's raining, and it isn't raining', one wants to say that the first part is about a mental state, while the second part is about the weather. So why shouldn't I be able to put together, without absurdity or inconsistency, a report of a mental state of mine and a report of the weather?

Let us agree that when I say 'It isn't raining', I am speaking about the weather. The problem lies in the assumption that when I say 'I believe it's raining', I am reporting or describing a mental state of mine.

We have already seen that 'I believe it's raining' is a cautious assertion of 'It's raining'. Now someone might agree with *that*, but hold that 'I believe it's raining' *also* reports or describes a mental state or attitude of the speaker. Wittgenstein imagines someone putting this view as follows: 'At bottom, with these words I describe my own mental state—but here this description is indirectly an assertion of the state of affairs that is believed' (*RPP*, I, 481). At first sight this appears to be a very plausible view. It amounts to saying that the statement 'I believe it's raining', does two jobs at once. It is *directly* a report or description of a mental state, and *indirectly* an assertion about the weather. This view would provide an explanation of why the whole conjunction is absurd: for the 'indirect' assertion of 'It's raining', carried by the first member of the conjunction, 'I believe it's raining', contradicts the explicit assertion by the second member of the conjunction, 'It isn't raining'. The interpretation is attractive, for it attributes the absurdity to a logical contradiction, yet it also preserves the inclination to think that 'I believe *p*' describes or reports a mental state.

But a pressing question arises. *Why* should what is primarily, or 'directly', a description or report of a mental state, be at the same time an 'indirect' assertion about the weather? What connection is there between a description of a mental state and a description of the weather? Why should 'I believe it's raining', construed as a description of a mental state, be an indirect assertion of 'It's raining'—rather than an indirect assertion of 'Today is Tuesday', or of 'Turkey wants to join the Common Market', or of anything whatever?

I think it is this problem that leads Wittgenstein to suggest that the interpretation in question is treating the sentence 'I believe it's raining' as if it were a *photograph*. Commenting on the idea that 'I believe it's raining' is an 'indirect' assertion of 'It's raining', he says: 'As in certain circumstances I describe a photograph, in order to describe what it is a photograph of' (*RPP*, I, 481). But if one does this one is assuming that the photograph is *reliable!* Wittgenstein turns this point into a profound criticism of the view at issue. He says:

> But if this analogy holds good, then I should have to be able to say further, that this photograph (the impression on my mind) is trustworthy. So I should have to be able to say: 'I believe that it's raining, and my belief is trustworthy, so I trust it'. As if my belief were a kind of sense-impression. (*RPP*, I, 482)

We are sometimes aware of having illusory sense-impressions. It looks as if the railroad platform is moving, but we know it is only our train that is moving. So often we trust our sense-impressions, but sometimes not. Now I can trust or distrust another person's belief. But can I do this with *my own* belief? Can I firmly hold a belief, but at the same time distrust it? Wittgenstein delivers this smashing remark: 'One can mistrust one's own senses, but not one's own belief' (*LW*, I, 419). I think that Wittgenstein has completely destroyed the conception that 'I believe p' is, first of all, a description or report of a mental state and, second, an assertion of '*p*'. For why does this mental state refer to '*p*' in particular? How does it pick out '*p*' from all of the things that might be asserted?

Presumably, because this mental state is or contains a 'picture' or a 'representation' of '*p*'. If I asserted '*p*' I would be assuming that my mental state (my belief) is a *reliable* picture, a trustworthy representation. This in turn implies that I can think of a *present* belief of mine as being reliable or unreliable—which is nonsensical. Wittgenstein has undermined the notion that the sentence 'I believe *p*' is 'primarily' or 'directly' a description of a mental state.

The chief source of our confusion about a sentence such as 'I believe it's raining, and it isn't raining' is our inclination to think that the first part is an assertion about what is *within* me, while the second part is an assertion about what is *outside* me. It *seems* there can be no conflict here; yet we feel that the whole sentence is absurd. Wittgenstein fixes his attention on this image of the contrast between something *within* me and something *outside* me. He says:

> 'It is raining and I believe it is raining'. Turning to the weather I say that it is raining: then, turning to myself, I say that I believe it.—But what do I do when I turn to myself, what do I observe? Suppose I say: 'It's raining, and I believe it will soon stop'—do I turn to myself at the second part of the statement?—Of course, if I want to find out whether *he* believes that, then I must turn to him, observe him. And if I wanted to find out by observation what I believe, I should have to observe my *actions*, just as in the other case I have to observe his.
>
> Now why don't I observe them? Don't they interest me? Apparently *not*. I hardly ever ask another person, who has been observing me, whether he has the impression that I believe such and such; that is, in order in this way to make inferences to my future actions. (*RPP*, I, 715)

From the actions and utterances of other persons I continually make inferences about their beliefs and likely future actions. But I don't do this in my own case. Why not? Wittgenstein says:

> How is it that I cannot gather that I believe it's going to rain from my own statement 'It's going to rain'? Can I then draw no interesting conclusions from the fact that I said this? If someone else says it, I conclude perhaps that he will take an umbrella with him. Why not in my own case?
>
> Of course there is here the temptation to say: In my own case I don't *need* to draw this conclusion from my words, because I can draw it from my mental state, from my belief itself. (*RPP*, I, 704)

The temptation to give this 'explanation' is nearly irresistible. One wants to say: 'I *know* what I believe; I don't have to infer it from my actions or my words'. This attempt at explanation can be criticized in various ways. One thing Wittgenstein does here is to scrutinize the meaning of the words, 'I know what I believe'. He begins with a sample statement of the 'explanation':

> 'Why should I draw conclusions about my behaviour from my own words, when in any case I know what I believe?' And what is the expression of my knowing what I believe? Isn't it expressed in this: that I do not infer my behaviour from my words? That is the fact. (*RPP*, I, 744)

This brief criticism exposes the emptiness of the proposed explanation. And the criticism applies equally to the idea that I don't have to infer *what I believe* from my actions or words, since I *know* what I believe without inferring it from anything. The point can be put like this: the only *meaning* that the words 'I *know* what I believe' will bear in this context is just that I do *not* infer what I believe from my words and actions. So the proffered explanation is circular.

That a person can determine by observation what others believe, but rarely, if ever, by self-observation what he himself believes, is something that applies not only to belief but to many psychological concepts. Wittgenstein's insight into this feature of the grammar of those concepts is one of his great contributions to the understanding of what it is to be a human being.

I want to try now to give an account of the part that this difference between the first person and the third person of 'believe' plays in the disentangling of Moore's paradox. I will return to a remark of Wittgenstein's that I quoted previously:

> That he believes such-and-such, we gather from observation of his person, but he does not make the statement 'I believe . . .' on the basis of self-observation. And *that* is why 'I believe p' can be equivalent to the assertion of 'p'. (*RPP*, I, 504)

This compressed reasoning can be expanded as follows: Since the statement 'I believe it's raining' is not based on self-observation, the only observation it is likely to be based on is an observation of the weather. So it can be roughly equivalent to the statement 'It's raining', when this is based on an observation of the weather.

Let us return to the problematic sentence, 'I believe it's raining, and it isn't raining'. Moore thought that '*what* is said' makes sense, expresses a logical possibility, could be true. The 'absurdity' lies only in *saying* it. It is as if one could *think* it, but not *say* it.

Wittgenstein's reflection on the way in which the expression 'I believe *p*' is commonly used leads to an entirely different view of the paradox. 'I believe *p*' is a cautious or hesitant assertion of '*p*'. The statement 'I believe it's raining, and it isn't raining', would be both an assertion and a denial of 'It's raining'. It would have the normal incoherence of a self-contradictory sentence. Each part of the sentence cancels the other part. The outcome is nonsense. Moore was wrong in claiming that '*what* is asserted is something which is perfectly possible logically'. For nothing is being 'asserted'; in a clear sense, nothing is being *said*.

Moore insisted that the sentence is not self-contradictory. But this was because Moore did not perceive those surprising features of the logical grammar of 'believe' which Wittgenstein brought to light.

I want to consider further the problem of whether a belief is a 'mental state'. Some philosophers have assumed that this is so. David Armstrong, for example, says that 'Belief is a dispositional state of mind which endures for a greater or lesser length of time', and that 'there must be some difference in A's state of mind if he believes *p* from his state of mind if he does not believe *p*'.[5] I find this a puzzling assertion. Armstrong is speaking in the most general terms. He is not saying just that *some* beliefs are mental states (or 'states of mind'), but that *all* of them are. And when Armstrong says that there must be some difference in a person's mental state if he believes *p* from his mental state if he doesn't, Armstrong is speaking with complete generality. Apparently he is holding that to believe *p* (regardless of what *p* is) *is itself* a mental state. And this would appear to imply the view that every statement of the form 'I believe *p*' describes or expresses a mental state.

I do agree that sometimes when people say things of that form they are describing or disclosing mental states. If a friend said to me, 'I believe I am going mad', that would tell me something about his mental

---

5. D. M. Armstrong, *A Materialist Theory of the Mind* (London: Routledge and Kegan Paul, 1968), p. 214.

state. Or if he said, 'I believe that all the people I see in the streets are spying on me'.

There can be a different kind of case in which a statement of the form 'I believe *p*' expresses, not a 'mental state', but an *attitude* toward a person. Suppose a man is accused of intending to avoid payment of a debt. A friend of his says in his defense, 'I believe he will pay it'. I am supposing that he does not say this on the basis of any special information, but instead that he is declaring his faith in the integrity of his friend. As I am imagining the situation, this would not be a cautious or hesitant assertion, but a firm statement of trust. His statement, 'I believe he will pay the debt' does two jobs here: it asserts 'He will pay the debt', and it expresses an attitude toward the accused person.

Whether a statement of the form 'I believe *p*' describes or expresses a mental state, or mental disposition, or an attitude, depends on the subject matter and the particular circumstances. *Sometimes* sentences of that form are used in that way. What is wrong is the assumption that this is *always* so: that the words 'I believe *p*', *by their very meaning*, describe or disclose or express some mental state or disposition or attitude. This is an example of *thinking without looking*! Wittgenstein's treatment of Moore's paradox should teach us better.

When a farmer studies the sky and then says, 'I believe it will snow this afternoon', his remark is tantamount to the cautious assertion, 'It will snow this afternoon'. In saying 'I believe it will snow this afternoon', he need not be ascribing to himself, or expressing, any mental state, disposition, or attitude. He need not even be saying that he is in a hesitant frame of mind about whether it will snow. As Wittgenstein points out, 'A hesitant assertion is not an assertion of hesitancy' (*LW*, I, 522).

Although I have been emphasizing the fact that there is a common use of sentences of the form 'I believe such and such', in which the speaker is not talking about himself, is not describing some attitude of his, but is talking about the such and such—yet it is true that in certain situations someone who says 'I believe such and such' *is* talking about himself. I do not wish to give the impression that Moore's paradox arises *only* when the speaker is talking about the such and such, and not when he is talking about himself.

Let me give an example. Suppose that a committee of a trade union has been debating the question of whether the members of the union should go on strike. The advantages and disadvantages of a strike have been thoroughly discussed. There seems to be no point in continuing the debate, even though there still is disagreement. The chairman then says: 'It would be fruitless to hear again the reasons for or against a strike. What I want to hear from each of you is whether you personally believe there should be a strike'. He puts to each member the question, 'Do you believe there should be a strike?' When a member replies, 'I do believe there should be a strike', it seems right to say that here he is talking about, or for, *himself*—that the primary thing he is doing is expressing his own attitude on the issue. Yet it would be a logical absurdity for him to say, 'I do believe there should be a strike, but there shouldn't be one'.

The important question, therefore, is not whether when one says 'I believe *p*' he is talking about himself, but rather *how* he is talking about himself, when that is what he is doing. Wittgenstein has reminded us that usually I say of someone, 'He believes *p*', on the basis of observing *him*, but that usually I do not say 'I believe *p*' on the basis of observing myself. 'He believes *p* but not-*p*' is not an absurd form of words. Moore's paradox exists only in the *first person* of the present tense. But it does not exist even there, when (as sometimes happens) the statement 'I believe *p*' does arise from self-observation and recollection. If I remember certain things I have said and done in the recent past, or certain ways I have reacted, and if solely on the basis of these recollections I exclaim, 'It appears that I believe *p*', or 'I seem to believe *p*', or 'So I believe *p*'—then there would be no absurdity in adding, 'but not-*p*'. It would not be absurd, for there I would be speaking of myself *as if* I was another person!

Thus, at the most fundamental level, Moore's paradox arises from the fact that there is an essential difference between the normal use of the first person singular present tense of 'believe' and the use of the third person form. The grammar of the word 'believe' reflects a striking feature of human life, namely, the fact that there is an attentive observation which we direct on other people, and not on ourselves.

NORMAN MALCOLM

Memorial Address by G. H. von Wright

Norman Malcolm's death came as a shock to his friends.[1] Only a few of us knew of his illness until a few weeks before he died. He did not wish it to be known and he did not let it disturb his daily routine more than necessary. He fought it with characteristic strength and optimism to the very end.

Norman was one of my closest friends, and the story of our friendship is integral to the story of his and also of my life.

I first met Norman at Cambridge in Wittgenstein's class in the Lent Term 1939. He had come there from Harvard to study with G. E. Moore who had agreed to supervise his work on a doctoral dissertation. I had come from Helsinki to do postgraduate work with C. D. Broad. Norman knew of Wittgenstein's presence from silly rumors but knew little or nothing about his philosophy; I knew something about Wittgenstein's philosophy but had no idea that the man was at Cambridge. For both of us meeting Wittgenstein became the decisive event in our intellectual development. We have both described in print our first dramatic encounter with this overpowering personality.

At that time, Norman and I had not yet become close friends. I cannot remember that we had had any discussion then. But I vividly recall his strong midwestern accent when he spoke up in the class. I must con-

1. On November 21, 1990, a Service of Thanksgiving for the life of Norman Malcolm was held in the Chapel of King's College, London. Personal addresses were given by G. H. von Wright and Peter Winch.

fess that in the beginning it put me off a little. Later I came to appreciate its charm. But I was always struck by the contrast between the somewhat rustic sound of Norman's voice and the highly cultured and
elegant English of his writings.

Then came the war and we returned from Cambridge to the countries from which we had come. Norman completed his postgraduate
studies at Harvard. At that time he had neither a job nor money. C. I.
Lewis, the philosopher, invited him to stay in his home so that he could
finish his dissertation—a generosity which Norman always remembered with warm feeling. Soon after, he got his first academic appoint-
ment as instructor at another distinguished American university,
Princeton. When the United States had joined the war, he resigned the
instructorship and enlisted in the U.S. navy. He first served on a patrol
vessel in the Caribbean and was later transferred to a destroyer-escort
in the Atlantic. 'I know you'll make a good soldier', Wittgenstein wrote
him—and knowing the courage and composure which Norman
showed later in life when facing adversity or conflict I am certain that
Wittgenstein was right. On one of the passages across the Atlantic, in-
cidentally, he had occasion to pay a short visit to Cambridge and see
Wittgenstein.

In the academic year 1946–47 we both returned to Cambridge and
met again in Wittgenstein's class. It was then that we got to know each
other well and became friends. We had discussions together. 'You are
one of the very few people I have met whose conversation has been
profitable to me' he wrote in the first letter I got from him after we had
returned from Cambridge to our respective home-countries. Thus
started a correspondence which lasted for more than forty years. In the
course of it we exchanged some 330 letters, among them many long
ones. Half or so of Norman's are written in his clear, beautiful, and en-
ergetic handwriting, so pleasing also to the eye.

When we started to write to each other Norman had already found a
permanent academic place for himself in the Sage School of Philosophy
at Cornell University. After serving thirty years on the Cornell faculty he
retired and moved to London. I think it is true to say that his years of re-
tirement were the happiest in his whole life. He liked London, the me-
tropolis, with its art treasures, concerts, theaters, and bookshops. He
enjoyed the bustling life in Hampstead Village and his morning runs on
the Heath. The nearness to the Continent made possible travel and long
holidays in Italy, Spain, and the South of France. Never before had he

had so many chances for a rich and varied cultural life as during his last thirteen years—and he amply availed himself of the opportunities.

Norman had the good fortune of being guided on his way to philosophy by teachers who were not only excellent representatives of their profession, but also set examples of intellectual honesty and rigor, moral integrity, and complete devotion to their calling. In Norman's case they were three. Wittgenstein, of course, ranked supreme among them. But also the other two made a lasting impact on the formation of Norman's intellectual character.

In Lincoln, Nebraska, where Norman went to college, his teacher in philosophy had been Oets Bouwsma. I know little about his philosophy, but when later I got to know him personally, I was impressed by his honest and straightforward manners and seriousness—qualities which were congenial to Norman and probably helped him develop his own endowments. Through Bouwsma Norman was introduced to the writings of G. E. Moore. It was not, however, the Moore of *Principia Ethica* or of *Ethics* which Norman got to admire so much as Moore as an author of essays on the basic problems in the theory of knowledge and in what nowadays is called the philosophy of mind. Norman's own mature work falls almost entirely in these same areas of philosophy. Another early interest of his, also of Moorean inspiration, was the philosophy of logic. Norman's first published papers testify to it. In his later writings, however, he seldom deals with logical topics, and the study of formal logic remained alien to Norman.

At Cambridge, both before and after the war, Norman had weekly discussions with Moore and was a regular attendant at Moore's 'at homes'. He got very fond of Moore as a person, and also his admiration for Moore as a philosopher did not diminish when he had come under the spell of Wittgenstein's very different way of thinking. In a memorial essay, which was in origin a paper given during Norman's yearlong stay in Finland in the early 1960s and actually first published in Finnish translation, Norman says: 'The qualities that contributed to Moore's philosophical eminence—were—complete modesty and simplicity, saving him from the dangers of jargon and pomposity; thorough absorption in philosophy, which he found endlessly exciting; strong mental powers; and a pure integrity that accounted for his solidity and his passion for clarity'. These very words could also do as a self-characterization. Of Norman's three masters, Moore was the one, I would say, whose intellectual character was most in tune with his own. Both from the point of view of choice of problems and style of writing Norman's work belongs in the tradition, nowadays somewhat out of fashion, of George Edward Moore.

Attending Wittgenstein's lectures had laid the foundation of Norman's and my friendship. Our impressions and recollections of Wittgenstein cemented also our personal relations when we met again in the 1950s—first at Oxford where Norman spent a sabbatical year and later in the United States when I was on my first *séjour* at Cornell. It was in the course of our conversations that the idea matured that we should record in writing our impressions of that remarkable man, who had been known personally only to a relatively small circle of friends and pupils but had already long been a legend abroad. The legend, moreover, was infected by false rumors and distortions of fact. Norman's *Memoir* and my 'Biographical Sketch', though written independently, thus had the character of a 'joint venture' and I think it appropriate that the two writings continue to be published together.

Norman's *Memoir of Wittgenstein* is, in my opinion, a classic of biographical literature. It struck me at once how 'true to life' it was. It pictured exactly the Wittgenstein whom I too had known: his magnetizing spiritual charm, his unquenchable thirst for honesty and truth, but also his caprice and impatience, which could make him fearful even to his friends. The complexities of a character like Wittgenstein's can perhaps best be captured in impressionistic glimpses from conversations and meetings rather than in attempts to draw a full-scale and fact-loaded portrait. A comparison which always struck me is between Malcolm's *Memoir of Wittgenstein* and Grillparzer's sketches collected under the heading of *Erinnerungen an Beethoven*.

The *Memoir* testifies to Norman's excellence as a writer. So does his entire literary output. Perhaps I am not a fully competent judge, not being myself a native speaker of English. Let me nevertheless say for what it is worth that I know no other contemporary writer of philosophic prose who equals Norman in clarity, directness, and strength of expression. His style is refreshingly free of the constrained witticism and glib smoothness characteristic of philosophical journalism and would-be cleverness. There is no trace of vanity in it. It gets its uniquely personal stamp from its complete and unselfish devotion to the cause.

For full thirty years, from 1947 to 1978 Norman taught philosophy at Cornell. During his long and distinguished career as a teacher he was a major force in raising the Cornell philosophy department from relative insignificance to one of the top schools—both undergraduate and graduate—in his country. But even more important than the excellence thus attained for Cornell were the repercussions his teaching had on the climate of philosophic thinking in the entire Anglo-American world. For several decades the new way of thinking nourished and at times dominated creative philosophy of the West.

Discussion even more than teaching, I should say, was the intellectual atmosphere in which Norman felt most at home. I witnessed this at innumerable meetings of the Cornell Philosophy Club, but also in the regular dialogues we had together whenever we met otherwise than casually. This happened, for example, during the academic year which Norman spent with his family in Finland in the early 1960s. Norman was a superb discussion partner. He did not spare his opponent. His attack on positions that seemed to him wrong was merciless. He had a wonderful talent for inventing good examples both in support of his own point and for exposing the weakness of his adversary's. Discussion with Norman might end with a frustrating feeling that one had not oneself been able to defend one's point against his with sufficient clarity or force. But for that same reason the discussions were a constant urge to reconsider one's opinion, to dig deeper, and perhaps eventually find for oneself a more solid ground to stand firm on. A fine specimen of Norman's discussion techniques is preserved for posterity in his dialogues with David Armstrong, *Consciousness and Causality* in a volume of the series Great Debates in Philosophy.

When Norman left Cornell and took up his new abode in London, he had already amply earned his *otium post tot labores* as academic teacher. But moving to England at the age of sixty-seven did not mean the end of his teaching career. For thirteen more years, to the very end of his life, he gave graduate seminars in the university which is now commemorating him. He was appointed to a Visiting Professorship at King's and, shortly before he died, made a Fellow of the College. This token of recognition was not, however, intended to mark the end of his teaching there. The end was set only by his fatal illness.

I shall quote here the judgment passed on his London lectures— 'renowned for their lucidity, depth and intellectual honesty'—in a perceptive obituary in *The Times*. 'His impact at King's', it is said there, 'was twofold. He was a shining example as a teacher, and his high standards of philosophical clarity, his contempt for pretentiousness and his striving for truth and understanding affected all who worked with him'. I am sure there are many here present who can testify to the truth of these words.

This is not the place to recount or to evaluate Norman's own contributions to philosophy. But a few remarks on their general character should be made.

Norman was not a conspicuously many-sided philosopher. He did not explore the regions of what is sometimes called practical philosophy, i.e., ethics and social and political philosophy. Nor were pure and applied logic much to his taste. Moreover, he was by temperament not a scholar who takes great interest in the hermeneutic task of interpreting past thinking or tracing sources and influences. Yet his observations on problems in medieval and classic European thought, particularly Descartes, are often helpful guides also to pure historical understanding. And his last published book with the well-chosen title *Nothing Is Hidden* is, besides being a weighty addition to ongoing debate, one of the best contributions to the scholarly grasp of the work both of the early and of the later Wittgenstein.

From a thematic point of view the bulk of Norman's writing, including that of a quasi-historical nature, forms a singularly accomplished and solid whole. As already noted, its area is the philosophy of mind, comprising both the epistemological aspects relating to our cognitive faculties and the metaphysical ones centering round the mind-body relationship. This combination of diversity within a unity gives to Norman's work its distinctive excellence.

In his writings on the philosophy of mind Norman can be said to be waging a two-front war: against introspective mentalism on the one hand and against various forms of a naturalist theory of the mind on the other. On both fronts he drew support from and also defended views of Wittgenstein. But the battlefield itself was essentially post-Wittgensteinian. Adversaries were partly revivers of Cartesian dualism from the 1960s onward and partly, soon even mainly, defenders of a variety of materialist theories of the mind. In conversation with me, Norman often expressed astonishment and even disappointment at the fact that many things were coming back again which, after the breakthrough of the later Wittgensteinian ideas in the 1950s and early 1960s, had seemed to us for ever superseded and cleared away from the table of serious philosophical debate. The reaction grew in strength. A new discipline emerged, known as cognitive science, which indulges in speculation and theorizing of a kind utterly opposed to the commonsense 'nothing is hidden' approach which Norman forcefully championed against what seemed to him a new tribe of philosophic savages. I don't think that he ever felt like being on the defensive in the sense that he had been much impressed by the arguments of his adversaries or forced to reconsider his own basic convictions. But he certainly felt with increasing strength in his later years that he was fighting against a mainstream of contemporary thinking imbued with the scientistic spirit of the time. I do not think the fact depressed him. This would have been contrary to the way in which he faced challenges generally. It rather stimulated his fighting spirits and provoked him to make new efforts in the defense of what he thought of as clear and sound thinking.

The fearless determination to fight for the truth, the unwillingness to yield to compromise, and the complete devotion to the cause which characterize Norman's work also reflect his character as a man. He had nothing of the smoothness which makes many people conceal their opinions for the sake of avoiding confrontation. His honesty and outspokenness gave to his manners an edged bluntness which some may have found, on occasion, offensive. He could also be impatient with others and show lack of forbearing understanding and tolerance of people whom he thought could not live up to his own standards, intellectually or morally.

But what was rough with Norman lay, so to speak, in the skin, not in the heart. He was the most affectionate and faithful of friends, and the sweetness which laid at the bottom of his heart could shine forth also from his predominantly serious face. I remember his firm handshake— in particular from some unforgettable moments of meeting again and departing for a long time. Norman's seriousness, moreover, did by no means exclude a jocose sense of humor which could burst out in roaring laughter at some comical episode or queer feature of human character. His acquaintance with the *comédie humaine* also stemmed from an exceptionally wide and perceptive reading, particularly in his later years, of fiction and historical narrative.

Shortly before he died, Norman completed a manuscript which is a comment on a word by Wittgenstein. It goes: 'I am not a religious man but I cannot help seeing every problem from a religious point of view'.[2]

Seeing things from a religious point of view is not the same as having a religion. But for some of us it is the nearest we can come to it. Nor-

2. Norman Malcolm, *Wittgenstein: A Religious Point of View?*, edited with a response by Peter Winch (Ithaca: Cornell University Press, 1994).

man had a deep need to come to grips with this and in the manuscript he tries to capture certain analogies between a philosophic outlook as he understood it and a religious view of the world.

The religious point of view can be one of *wondering* at the existence of the world, or one of *awe* and *gratitude* at the marvels of life; but it can also be a feeling of *failure* to comply with divine commands or of *lack* of love for one's neighbor. Norman was alive to all these components but the strongest, I believe, was a feeling of falling short of his own severe measure.

'Belief in God', Norman once wrote, 'is not an all or none thing—it can wax or wane'. But belief in God in any degree requires, he continues, 'some religious action, some commitment, or if not, at least a bad conscience'.

How far Norman advanced on the way to belief in God is more than I can judge. When first I came to know him he had not yet started his pilgrimage. Complete repose for his restless heart he did not find. But if salvation is reward for unceasing striving, Norman fully deserved it.

Index